The History of the Frisians

Crafted by Skriuwer

Copyright © 2024 by Skriuwer.

All rights reserved. No part of this book may be used or reproduced in any form whatsoever without written permission except in the case of brief quotations in critical articles or reviews.

At **Skriuwer**, we're more than just a team—we're a global community of people who love books. In Frisian, "Skriuwer" means "writer," and that's at the heart of what we do: creating and sharing books with readers worldwide. Wherever you are in the world, **Skriuwer** is here to inspire learning.

Frisian is one of the oldest languages in Europe, closely related to English and Dutch, and is spoken by about **500,000 people** in the province of **Friesland** (Fryslân), located in the northern Netherlands. It's the second official language of the Netherlands, but like many minority languages, Frisian faces the challenge of survival in a modern, globalized world.

We're using the money we earn to promote the Frisian language.

For more information, contact : **kontakt@skriuwer.com** (www.skriuwer.com)

TABLE OF CONTENTS

CHAPTER ONE: EARLY ROOTS AND PREHISTORIC TIMES

- Earliest settlements in coastal marshes
- Adaptation to flooding through terpen
- Archaeological evidence of social organization

CHAPTER TWO: FRISIANS AND THEIR EARLY NEIGHBORS

- Expansion of trade and cultural exchanges
- Formation of tribal structures and social hierarchies
- Iron Age adaptations and early linguistic developments

CHAPTER THREE: THE ROMAN ERA AND FRISIAN ENCOUNTERS

- Initial contacts with Rome and tribute relationships
- Military conflicts and short-lived revolts
- Influence of Roman trade and governance on coastal communities

CHAPTER FOUR: THE MIGRATION PERIOD AND THE RISE OF FRISIAN IDENTITY

- Post-Roman power vacuums and tribal consolidation
- Shifts in settlement patterns and linguistic continuity
- Formation of early political structures

CHAPTER FIVE: THE EMERGENCE OF THE FRISIAN KINGDOM

- Key rulers like Aldgisl and Redbad
- Conflict with the Frankish realm and neighboring powers
- Growth of maritime trade and local governance

CHAPTER SIX: RELIGIOUS INFLUENCE AND THE IMPACT OF CHRISTIAN MISSIONS

- *Arrival of missionaries (Willibrord, Boniface)*
- *Confrontations between pagan customs and Christian doctrine*
- *Gradual establishment of church structures and parishes*

CHAPTER SEVEN: SHIFTS IN POWER AND EARLY MEDIEVAL CHALLENGES

- *Integration into Carolingian rule and local responses*
- *Impact of Frankish governance on Frisian freedoms*
- *Continuing role of communal assemblies and water management*

CHAPTER EIGHT: THE VIKING THREAT AND FRISIAN ADAPTATIONS

- *Raids and coastal fortifications*
- *Alliances, ransoms, and resilience of local communities*
- *Long-term effects on trade and settlement patterns*

CHAPTER NINE: INDEPENDENCE, FRISIAN FREEDOM, AND REGIONAL CONFLICTS

- *Reassertion of local autonomy and the notion of "Frisian freedom"*
- *Emergence of chieftain lineages and towns*
- *Tensions with neighboring lords (Holland, Utrecht) and feudal claims*

CHAPTER TEN: SOCIAL AND ECONOMIC STRUCTURES OF MEDIEVAL FRISIA

- *Rural life, class distinctions, and trade guilds*
- *Communal water management and dike building*
- *Evolution of local law codes and assemblies*

CHAPTER ELEVEN: TRADE NETWORKS AND CITY GROWTH

- Expansion of maritime commerce within the North Sea and Baltic
- Urbanization, market rights, and guild formation
- Conflicts between towns and rural districts over tolls and jurisdiction

CHAPTER TWELVE: EXPANSION OF LOCAL POWERS AND EXTERNAL PRESSURES

- Rise of powerful chieftains (Vetkopers vs. Schieringers)
- Influence of Holland, Utrecht, and German princes
- Intensifying factional disputes shaping local alliances

CHAPTER THIRTEEN: THE LATE MIDDLE AGES AND INTERNAL RIVALRIES

- Vetkoper–Schieringer feud and its consequences
- Draw of Burgundian rule amid fractious local politics
- Economic toll of factionalism on trade and agriculture

CHAPTER FOURTEEN: INFLUENCE OF FOREIGN RULERS AND SHIFTING ALLIANCES

- Burgundian and Habsburg encroachment
- Collaboration or resistance among local chieftains and towns
- Gradual loss of medieval independence

CHAPTER FIFTEEN: ECONOMIC CHANGES AND CULTURAL EXPRESSIONS

- Integration into the Habsburg Netherlands
- Reformation currents and their early impact
- Economic shifts tied to trade regulations and agricultural consolidation

CHAPTER SIXTEEN: POLITICAL RESTRUCTURING AND RELIGIOUS TURMOIL

- Dutch Revolt and Frisia's alignment with the emerging Republic
- Spread of Calvinism, suppression of Catholic public worship
- Stadtholder dynamics and the shaping of provincial autonomy

CHAPTER SEVENTEEN: THE SEVENTEENTH CENTURY

- Participation in the Dutch Golden Age's commercial networks
- Agrarian stability and rising social stratification
- Persistent communal ethos in water boards and local assemblies

CHAPTER EIGHTEEN: THE EIGHTEENTH CENTURY

- Stagnation in the late Dutch Republic and Patriot movements
- Regent oligarchies vs. calls for liberal changes
- Water management successes amid slowed maritime dominance

CHAPTER NINETEEN: THE NINETEENTH CENTURY

- Napoleonic rule, Kingdom of the Netherlands, and constitutional reforms
- Agricultural modernization and early industrial ventures
- Frisian language revival and evolving dual identity

CHAPTER TWENTY: REFLECTIONS ON HISTORICAL LEGACY

- Summation of communal freedom traditions and water management
- Enduring maritime and agricultural legacies
- Cultural renaissance, language movements, and the path toward modern Frisia

CHAPTER 1: EARLY ROOTS AND PREHISTORIC TIMES

1. Introduction to Early Frisia

Frisia, as we call it today, spans coastal regions that border the North Sea. This stretch of land lies primarily in what we now know as the northern Netherlands and northwestern Germany. Before it was clearly defined, these areas were inhabited by groups of people who lived off the land and sea in prehistoric times. Historians and archaeologists often use the name "Frisians" for those who came to inhabit these regions, though the people who actually lived there in the earliest times did not call themselves by that name. The name "Frisian" emerges more concretely in later historical sources, but many of the foundations of Frisian society can be traced back to prehistoric groups in these coastal zones.

The land in which the earliest Frisians settled was a patchwork of wetlands, marshes, and peatlands. The North Sea coast could be both bountiful and dangerous. Flooding was frequent, and storms could reshape the coastline dramatically. Over generations, the people in this region developed a close relationship with this unpredictable environment. They learned to raise small mounds, called "terpen" (in later Frisian or Dutch usage) or "wierden" in some parts, to keep their dwellings safe from high tides and floodwaters. Although the word for these mounds in prehistoric times might have been different, the concept itself—creating elevated living spaces—goes back thousands of years.

2. The Physical Landscape and Its Influence

The physical environment of prehistoric Frisia was not just the coastal strip but included barrier islands, tidal flats, and estuaries of rivers like the Ems, Weser, and the Rhine-Meuse delta farther south. Due to shifting sea levels and land reclamation in later periods, it is sometimes challenging to outline exactly where the prehistoric communities lived. However, archaeological finds—such as pottery shards, simple wooden structures, and traces of farming—indicate a mix of fishing, hunting, and small-scale agriculture.

Because the region was prone to flooding, communities had to innovate in how they organized their living spaces. They built elevated areas where they could keep livestock and store harvests. Over time, these elevated areas grew larger, as people added more soil and refuse to raise them higher. This created artificial hills that were safer from storm surges. Sometimes entire villages formed on these mounds, making them permanent features of the landscape.

The coastline, with its wetlands and shallow seas, provided abundant marine resources. People collected shellfish, fished local waters, and sometimes hunted seals. Inland, the peatlands and forests offered game, though these areas were more difficult to traverse. Thus, the first people who would eventually be known (in a broad sense) as Frisians were well adapted to a life of both agriculture and seafaring, shaped by a environment that demanded resilience.

3. Prehistoric Settlements and Archaeological Evidence

Archaeologists typically divide European prehistory into several main periods: the Stone Age (including Paleolithic, Mesolithic, and Neolithic), the Bronze Age, and the Iron Age. In what became Frisia, evidence of human activity stretches back thousands of years into the Mesolithic period. Mesolithic communities were small, with people living nomadic or semi-nomadic lives, hunting and gathering resources from the land.

As these communities transitioned to the Neolithic period, they began to adopt agriculture. The discovery of cereal grains and domesticated animal bones in archaeological sites along the coastal regions indicates that they raised crops and kept cattle, sheep, and goats. The shift from a hunter-gatherer society to a more settled agricultural one laid the foundation for more permanent structures. Over time, these communities developed new ways of life, including specialized tools for farming, fishing, and managing livestock.

One important aspect of prehistoric life was the burial customs. Burial mounds or other forms of interment can offer clues about social hierarchies and spiritual beliefs. In the northern Netherlands and parts of Germany, archaeologists have found burial sites that suggest a degree of organizational structure, indicating these prehistoric communities were not just small, scattered bands but had some social cohesion. This would have been crucial in a place regularly affected by flooding and storms.

4. Cultural Exchanges and External Influences

Though often depicted as isolated, the people in prehistoric Frisia did not live in complete seclusion. Trade and cultural exchange occurred along the coast of the North Sea. Goods such as amber, furs, and perhaps salt from the marshlands might have been exchanged with inland communities. Over centuries, contact with regions to the south and east allowed new ideas and technologies to spread. For instance, metalworking techniques introduced into northern Europe would have gradually found their way into the coastal communities. This exchange laid early groundwork for the seafaring and trading skills that later Frisians would be famous for.

Early trade routes were not highways but rather rivers, estuaries, and the sea. Simple boats could travel along these waterways, linking people across distances. The evidence of imported items, such as certain types of pottery or metal objects found in coastal archaeological sites, shows that even in prehistoric times, the region was connected to broader European developments. These connections set the stage for future Frisian engagement with expansive trade networks that would become more prominent in the later Iron Age and especially in the medieval period.

5. Social Structure in Prehistoric Coastal Groups

The social structure of these early coastal groups is difficult to reconstruct. Written records are non-existent for prehistoric times. But from burial remains, settlement patterns, and artifacts, one can infer a society of small villages, possibly with some loose forms of leadership. Leaders might have been those who controlled certain resources (like cattle or farmland) or those who had spiritual authority. Over time, as settlements grew more permanent, certain families might have accumulated more wealth (in the form of livestock or trade goods).

Given the harsh environment, communal cooperation was likely vital. Building and maintaining dikes or mounds to protect settlements from flooding would have required a coordinated effort. This need for cooperation could have given rise to local assembly structures or councils of elders. These rudimentary forms of governance may have foreshadowed later traditions of Frisian independence and collective decision-making that became notable in medieval times.

6. Early Language and Identity

It is important to emphasize that these prehistoric communities did not refer to themselves as "Frisians" as we do now. The term "Frisian" emerges later in historical writings. However, the people living in these coastal areas likely spoke early Germanic dialects, evolving over centuries into the Frisian language group. Language is a central aspect of identity, but it does not remain static. The prehistoric speech forms would be largely unrecognizable to speakers of later Old Frisian.

Still, these early dialects formed a root from which the Frisian language eventually grew. Shared linguistic features might have distinguished them from other groups in central Europe. The real shaping of a distinct Frisian identity took place much later, but the seeds of it—through language, customs, and adaptation to the coastal environment—can be traced back to these prehistoric times.

7. Technological Developments

From the Stone Age through the Iron Age, new technologies spread across Europe. Flint and stone tools were eventually replaced or supplemented by bronze, and then iron, as these metals became available. Each shift had significant impacts on farming, warfare, and trade. The presence of iron tools by the later prehistoric period improved agricultural productivity and might have boosted population growth in coastal settlements. Stronger tools meant people could farm more effectively, cut wood faster, and manage larger herds.

While some metal was locally produced, much of it was obtained through trade. This again underscores the connections prehistoric coastal dwellers had with other regions. The presence of well-crafted items such as bronze ornaments suggests that certain families or groups had the means to acquire luxury or prestigious goods, pointing to a society more complex than once assumed.

8. Environmental Challenges and Adaptations

Living in coastal marshlands meant constant risk. Storm surges could wash away an entire year's work or even destroy villages. The building of artificial dwelling mounds was an ingenious solution to these challenges. Over time, these mounds became higher and more elaborate. Archaeological layers in these mounds reveal how communities grew, how diets changed, and how trade evolved.

Another adaptation was the development of drainage techniques and the creation of small dikes to protect farmlands. While large-scale dike systems are more a feature of medieval and later periods, the earliest forms of water management can be traced to prehistoric communities. This demonstrates that the people in these areas had a thorough understanding of their environment and a communal willingness to undertake large projects for shared benefit.

9. The Transition to the Bronze Age

The Bronze Age (roughly 2000–800 BCE in Northern Europe) saw increased social stratification. While coastal communities might not have been as hierarchical as those in more resource-rich inland areas, some distinctions likely grew among the population. Bronze tools, weapons, and ornaments were markers of status, and controlling the resources or trade routes that brought these items in could confer power.

Cultural practices, such as burying important individuals in elaborate barrows or introducing new styles of pottery, show external influences. Sites along the Wadden Sea coast reveal items from distant regions, indicating that people living in what we now call Frisia were participants in a network of exchanges spanning parts of North and Central Europe. The coastline provided easier travel by boat than overland in many cases, further linking these communities to broader Bronze Age developments.

10. Religion and Rituals in Prehistoric Frisia

While specific details about prehistoric Frisian religion are sparse, general patterns in Northern Europe suggest that people revered natural forces: the sun, the sea, fertility deities, and spirits of the land. Certain artifacts—like bent swords or broken jewelry found in wetlands—might indicate ritual offerings to water spirits. The sea was central to their existence, both as a source of life and a constant threat. Thus, it is logical that beliefs and rituals would honor or appease sea-related deities or spirits.

Inland wetlands and bogs, with their unique and mysterious qualities, were also sites of votive offerings in many parts of Northern Europe. Occasionally, well-preserved artifacts or even human remains are found in these bogs, indicating possible ritual sacrifices. The specifics for the prehistoric coastal groups that would later become the Frisians vary, but it is reasonable to assume they shared many of these pan-European ritual practices.

11. Regional Variations within Prehistoric Frisia

It is important to note that prehistoric Frisia was not a single, monolithic area. The region stretched across what is today multiple provinces in the Netherlands (such as Friesland and Groningen) and parts of northwestern Germany (including East Frisia and North Frisia). Each area had its own local environment and possibly unique cultural traits. Archaeological research shows differences in pottery styles, building techniques, and burial practices from one locale to another.

Yet there were also overarching similarities in how these communities adapted to the marshy environment and how they built their artificial dwelling mounds. Over time, as interaction increased, these cultural differences might have diminished, leading to a more uniform coastal identity. This trend toward a shared coastal culture set the foundation for what would, in the historical period, be identified as "Frisian" lands.

12. The End of Prehistory and the Dawn of Written Records

Prehistory in this region lasted until the appearance of written sources, which began sporadically with Roman accounts. By the time the Romans and other literate peoples took notice of the North Sea coast, the cultural identity we can retroactively label "Frisian" was starting to solidify. This does not mean the people suddenly adopted a single identity overnight; rather, external observers began to group them under one name based on shared linguistic and cultural traits. It is a reminder that historical identity is partly a matter of how outsiders perceive a region.

For the people themselves, the transition from prehistory to history did not feel abrupt. They continued in their agrarian and seafaring ways. However, this period would soon become marked by significant interactions with powerful neighbors. The centuries to follow would define the name "Frisian" more clearly, as references to them appear in Roman sources. But it all began with these prehistoric societies that learned to live with water, shape the land, and trade with distant communities.

13. Continuities from Prehistory

When looking at later Frisian society, one can observe continuities that stretch back into prehistory. The enduring importance of water management is a prime example. The communal spirit that might have developed out of necessity to manage dikes, mounds, and drainage systems became a hallmark of Frisian culture in the medieval period. The language base formed during these times, evolving through the centuries, contributed to a distinct linguistic identity. Additionally, the trade networks that began in a rudimentary form in prehistory laid the groundwork for more extensive Frisian trade connections in later eras.

14. Summary

Prehistoric Frisia was marked by settlement in a challenging coastal environment, adaptation to flooding, and participation in broader trade networks. Archaeological evidence reveals a society that combined farming, fishing, and hunting. They built artificial dwelling mounds for flood protection and likely organized communal efforts to manage water. The earliest forms of a Frisian identity were shaped here, long before the name itself was widely used. These prehistoric foundations are crucial to understanding the later development of a people who would become known for their maritime skills, unique language, and strong sense of communal rights.

This chapter has taken a closer look at the earliest chapters of Frisian history—before the name "Frisian" even entered the historical record. The next chapter will move forward to examine the Bronze Age to Iron Age transition in more detail, exploring how these developments further shaped the people of the coastal lowlands.

CHAPTER 2: FRISIANS AND THEIR EARLY NEIGHBORS

1. Bronze Age-Iron Age Transition

The Bronze Age and Iron Age were significant periods of change in Northern Europe. For those living in the region that would eventually be called Frisia, these centuries saw advancements in technology, shifts in trade routes, and gradual changes in social structures. Bronze tools gave way to iron implements, which were more durable and easier to produce once iron ore sources were established. This transition was not instantaneous; it varied from one community to another and depended on access to resources or trade networks.

During this time, the coastal communities deepened their connections with the broader world. Sea routes facilitated trade, bringing in not only metals but also ideas from cultures far to the south and east. We see, for example, influences from Central European styles of metalwork or designs reminiscent of the Hallstatt or La Tène cultures (though these are more commonly associated with Celtic groups further inland). The transition also marks a period in which the earliest written accounts of Northern European coastal peoples start to appear, though these accounts were often from outsiders.

2. Expanding Trade Networks

In the Bronze Age, long-distance trade became more organized. Ambitious traders and travelers navigated rivers and coastal waters, exchanging goods such as bronze ingots, tin, gold ornaments, and exotic materials like amber from the Baltic region. Frisia's coastal location made it a crossroads for such routes. Estuaries of the Rhine, Ems, and Weser linked inland Europe with the North Sea. This strategic position helped the coastal groups gain access to diverse resources and maintain economic ties with neighboring populations.

One of the key goods in Northern Europe was amber, often called "the gold of the north." Though much amber came from the Baltic Sea area, some trade routes passed through or near Frisia. This helped local populations acquire prestige goods in exchange for staples like salt, fish, hides, or grain. Bronze items, especially swords and decorative pieces, could also serve as indicators of status, potentially boosting the influence of local chieftains or leading families.

3. Technological and Societal Shifts

The shift from bronze to iron around 800–500 BCE in Northern Europe led to widespread societal changes. Iron tools made farming more efficient. Stronger plows could turn heavier soils, and iron weapons increased the defensive capabilities of communities, although warfare likely remained small-scale among neighboring groups. Owning iron weapons might have given some leaders a military edge, allowing them to expand their influence or protect trade routes.

Social structures evolved as well. Hierarchies could become more pronounced because access to iron ore sources or control of trade routes meant power. Local leaders or elites who managed or had connections to the production of iron goods could wield more authority. They could also reward loyal followers by gifting them iron tools or weapons. This system of reciprocity helped cement alliances in a world where formal state structures did not yet exist.

4. Early Contacts with Germanic and Celtic Groups

The area that would become Frisia was not culturally or linguistically isolated. The tribes living in these coastal regions shared some cultural and linguistic ties with other Germanic groups, but they also experienced Celtic influences. The boundary between Celtic and Germanic zones in the Iron Age was fluid, shaped by migration, trade, and occasionally conflict.

To the south, Celtic groups dominated much of Central Europe during the late Bronze Age and early Iron Age. They spread artistic styles (like the La Tène art) and influenced trade patterns. To the east and north, various Germanic-speaking peoples were also forming. The coastal groups we associate with the Frisian lands participated in this dynamic environment, interacting with both Celtic and Germanic neighbors. Artifacts found in the region sometimes reflect a blend of influences, demonstrating that the local populace was open to adopting and adapting new styles.

5. Formation of Larger Tribal Entities

By the later Iron Age, tribal identities started to become more defined. Although details remain scarce, we know from later sources that communities along the North Sea coast were recognized as distinct groups. These might have been the loose forerunners of the "Frisii," "Chauci," or other tribes that Roman authors would later mention. These larger tribal entities were not necessarily unified under a single king but could have been confederations of smaller groups. Unity and identity might have been driven by factors like linguistic similarities, common religious practices, or shared economic interests.

A tribal structure could vary widely. Some were controlled by prominent families or clans, while others functioned with assemblies of warriors or elders who made decisions collectively. The environment also played a role in limiting or encouraging the formation of large polities. Coastal marshes, tidal islands, and scattered farmland often made centralized governance challenging. Instead, communities might have been relatively independent, yet still part of a broader cultural-linguistic grouping.

6. Role of Warfare and Raiding

During the Iron Age, competition for resources could lead to skirmishes and raids. There is no evidence of large-scale, prolonged warfare akin to what might be found in the Mediterranean world. Rather, conflicts would have occurred between neighboring tribes or among factions within a region. Control over trade routes, fertile farmland, or sources of iron ore might have been key motivations.

Iron weaponry, superior to bronze, had a dramatic impact on how warfare was conducted. Swords, spears, and axes made of iron were cheaper to produce and more durable. However, the nature of settlement patterns (small villages, scattered farmsteads) and the absence of large, organized states meant that warfare was likely a mix of opportunistic raids and localized battles. This environment could encourage alliances for mutual protection, especially in the face of more formidable, distant threats.

7. Religious and Spiritual Developments

In the Bronze Age and Iron Age, religion in Northern Europe was deeply tied to nature and the cycle of seasons. Rituals often involved offerings to gods or spirits thought to influence fertility, weather, and prosperity. Coastal communities would have paid particular homage to deities associated with the sea or storms. Ceremonial deposits of weapons, jewelry, or tools in wetlands or bogs were common, symbolizing a sacrifice to supernatural forces in exchange for favor or protection.

As tribal identities formed, so did communal religious practices. Sacred groves, springs, or other natural sites could serve as communal centers where rites and festivals took place. The worship of ancestor spirits might have also been significant, with genealogical ties forming part of a tribe's sense of identity. The eventual arrival of the Romans and their pantheon would later add a new layer of religious complexity.

8. Settlements and Housing

Longhouse-type structures were common in Iron Age Northern Europe, serving as both homes for extended families and shelters for livestock. Coastal variations might have included building these structures on raised ground to protect from floods. Archaeological digs in parts of the coastal Netherlands and northern Germany have uncovered the remains of wooden post buildings with thatched roofs, large enough to house multiple generations of a family, as well as small numbers of animals during harsh weather.

Communities remained relatively small, clustered around safe areas on higher ground or on man-made mounds (terpen). Each cluster might be economically self-sufficient to a degree, with farmland and grazing areas surrounding them. Over time, some settlements grew into more prominent market or craft centers, but large urban centers were not typical of the Bronze Age or early Iron Age in this region.

9. Burial Customs and Social Stratification

Burial practices in the Bronze and Iron Ages varied. Some communities buried their dead in barrows, while others used flat graves or cremation. Grave goods could include items that signified the status or role of the deceased—a warrior might be buried with his weapons, while a wealthier individual might be interred with fine jewelry or imported goods. The presence of imported items, such as certain types of metal artifacts or pottery, suggested that the individual had access to far-reaching trade connections.

Variations in grave goods point to differences in social status. An elite warrior might be interred with multiple weapons and ornaments, while common farmers or fishers might have simpler burials. These practices reveal the gradual emergence of social strata in coastal communities, setting the stage for the kind of hierarchical relationships that would become more pronounced when these societies encountered the political and military power of Rome.

10. External Perceptions and the First Mentions of "Frisians"

By the late Iron Age (roughly the first century BCE), Roman expansion brought them into contact with Germanic tribes in northern Gaul and across the Rhine. Although early Roman writings might not have detailed the coastal groups extensively, references begin to appear, naming people like the Frisii (Frisians) and the Chauci. These names are among the first written records of peoples who lived in the region we are discussing.

It is crucial to note that Roman authors often had limited knowledge of distant groups. They tended to lump various coastal communities under a few broad labels. Still, these mentions are significant because they confirm that, by the time Rome had reached the Rhine frontier, certain tribal identities, including that of the Frisii, had become recognizable to outsiders. This external labeling would shape future understandings of who the Frisians were.

11. Cultural Unity and Diversity

The concept of a unified Frisian people in the late Iron Age should not be taken too literally. While the Romans might have used a single term, the people living along the coast likely maintained a degree of local diversity. Dialects varied from one estuary to another, and cultural practices might differ slightly depending on environment and outside influences. What united them in the eyes of the Romans was a shared location (the coastal region north of the Rhine) and certain cultural-linguistic similarities that distinguished them from tribes farther inland.

This interplay between unity and diversity is a recurring theme in Frisian history. Even in medieval times, Frisian "freedom" and local independence became key parts of their identity. Tracing it back to the Iron Age, one can see how scattered communities might have cooperated or even recognized common ties, but they also maintained a sense of local autonomy.

12. Coastal Environment and Changes Over Time

Throughout the Bronze and Iron Ages, the coastline continued to shift. Rising sea levels or major storm surges could carve new inlets or destroy existing settlements. This forced inhabitants to remain vigilant and adaptable. Some areas might have been abandoned for safer ground. Others found ways to build higher mounds or develop rudimentary drainage systems. Over centuries, these experiences honed the skills that later medieval Frisians would employ to manage dikes and polders.

The environment also influenced diet. Fish, shellfish, and marine mammals supplemented the grains and meats of farmed livestock. Salt extraction from coastal marshes became an important economic activity in the Iron Age, as salt was crucial for preserving food. Control of salt production could be a source of power, and it served as an important trade commodity, allowing coastal communities to barter with inland tribes.

13. The Edge of the Roman Sphere

As Rome expanded, the region near the Rhine River became a frontier zone. While some Germanic tribes along the Rhine engaged in trade or alliances with the Romans, the coastal communities stood somewhat apart. The Romans referred to them, but direct control and systematic occupation of Frisia would only come later, in certain periods. Still, Roman influence trickled in through trade. Roman coins have been found in coastal settlements, signaling that commerce and cultural exchange were not unusual.

This edge-of-empire status would shape future developments. When the Romans eventually attempted to assert authority in the north, the tribes' responses ranged from cooperation to resistance. The story of these early interactions sets the stage for the following centuries, where Frisia's relationship with Rome—first as trading partners, then as subjects, and later as occasional rebels—would be a defining element of their history.

14. Early Political Structures and Assembly Traditions

Though we lack detailed records of how these Iron Age communities organized themselves politically, it is likely that they had assemblies or councils where free men could voice opinions and make communal decisions. This idea stems from a common Germanic tradition noted by Roman writers like Tacitus. Tacitus described assemblies where warriors would gather and leaders would be chosen or affirmed. The seeds of later Frisian assemblies might lie in these early practices.

Local chieftains, or heads of influential families, might have presided over such gatherings. While they might not have had absolute power, they had enough influence to coordinate community projects or alliances. Over time, these assemblies could expand their authority when larger coalitions formed against an external threat. This political culture, founded on collective decision-making among freemen, would become characteristic of medieval Frisia, which was famously resistant to feudal overlords.

15. Daily Life and Economy

Life for the average coastal inhabitant revolved around farming, fishing, and raising livestock. Men and women had distinct but sometimes overlapping roles. Men might clear fields, fish, and take part in conflicts or raids. Women often managed household tasks, wove cloth, and helped with farm labor. Children were introduced early to tasks like tending animals or collecting shellfish, contributing to the household economy as soon as they could.

Tools included iron or bronze sickles for harvesting, wooden plows with iron tips for tilling, and woven nets or traps for fishing. Pottery styles evolved over time, with some forms being local adaptations and others influenced by contact with external cultures. Simple clothing was made from wool or linen, dyed with natural pigments. While not a luxurious existence, it was sustainable, with communities often producing most of what they needed locally.

16. Clan and Family Structures

Extended families, or clans, likely formed the core unit of social organization. Land and property might be passed down through these families. Loyalty and kinship ties were essential for survival, especially in times of hardship or conflict. Marriages were often arranged to strengthen alliances or secure access to resources. Over generations, certain families could become more prominent, leading to the emergence of local elites.

Yet, for many families, life remained relatively modest. The demands of living in a flood-prone environment necessitated collective work, which sometimes leveled out extreme disparities in wealth. A chieftain or wealthy farmer might own more cattle or have a sturdier dwelling, but he still depended on the cooperation of the community to maintain mounds, dikes, or drainage channels.

17. Artisan Skills and Cultural Expressions

Although overshadowed by larger civilizations like the Romans or the Celts, Iron Age coastal communities had their own artistic and artisanal achievements. Local craftsmen worked in wood, bone, and metal. They produced functional items—like farming tools and fishing hooks—and decorative pieces—like brooches or arm rings. Some motifs in metalwork reflect a blend of local traditions and broader European styles. This suggests that artisans were influenced by traveling craftsmen or the exchange of ideas through trade.

Cultural expressions could also take the form of music, oral poetry, or storytelling, though these forms leave little trace in the archaeological record. Such oral traditions would carry down the collective memory of the people, preserving tales of ancestors, heroes, or significant events. In a preliterate society, these stories played a key role in shaping identity and passing down knowledge.

18. Significance of the Bronze to Iron Age Epoch for Frisia

The Bronze to Iron Age epoch established patterns that would be recognizable in future Frisian history:

- **Adaptation to a challenging environment**: The constant struggle against tides and floods demanded communal effort.
- **Trading and maritime connections**: Even before the medieval Frisian seafaring reputation, these coastal communities participated in long-distance trade.
- **Formation of tribal identities**: Larger tribal groupings emerged, which Rome later labeled as "Frisii," among others.
- **Social hierarchies**: Increased metal use and trade networks fostered more defined social structures, setting the groundwork for local leadership.
- **Oral traditions and collective memory**: Without written records, cultural identity and history were preserved through storytelling and communal gatherings.

19. Transition into the Roman Contact Period

As the Iron Age progressed, interactions with the Roman Empire intensified. Rome's hunger for expansion and resources led them to push northward, eventually encountering the tribes along the Rhine and the North Sea coast. This pivotal period would bring the Frisii directly under Roman observation, marking the move from prehistory into a proto-historical phase. Tribes might have seen both opportunity (through trade and alliances) and threat (through military conquest).

Some groups chose to cooperate, hoping to gain Roman favor or secure trading privileges. Others resisted, fighting to maintain autonomy. The early phase of this encounter laid the groundwork for future centuries of friction, accommodation, and occasional rebellion. The coastline, once on the periphery of Europe, would become a stage for geopolitical struggles that shaped local identities more sharply.

20. Conclusion

In Chapter Two, we explored the continued development of coastal communities through the Bronze and Iron Ages. These centuries were filled with gradual but significant transformations. From technological advances in metalworking to the formation of tribal networks, we see how the seeds of Frisian culture took root. Trade connections, adaptation to a difficult environment, and the emergence of distinct community identities all played major roles in shaping the people who lived there.

Although we do not have direct records from these coastal populations themselves, archaeology and references in external sources begin to highlight the presence of a people who would become known to Rome as Frisii. The next chapters will delve into the Roman period in detail, examining how the presence of Rome influenced Frisian society and paved the way for the early medieval identity that would flourish after the empire's decline.

CHAPTER 3: THE ROMAN ERA AND FRISIAN ENCOUNTERS

1. Introduction to the Roman Frontier

By the first century BCE, the expanding Roman Republic (soon to become the Roman Empire) had pressed northward into regions of Europe previously unknown to most Mediterranean peoples. The frontier along the Rhine River became an important boundary, separating the empire's provinces from the various Germanic-speaking tribes beyond. Among those tribes were the Frisii—one of the earliest groups in the coastal lowlands that the Romans began to recognize as distinct. While we cannot be certain that all people in the area identified themselves as Frisii, Roman sources use this name, making it the first time the coastal population appears in written historical records.

The Romans did not arrive in the Frisian coastal region with immediate plans to conquer every patch of land. Instead, they were interested in securing the Rhine frontier, controlling trade, and dealing with tribes who posed a threat or who could become allies. Over time, Roman legions and administrators learned about the coastal marshes, the unpredictable tides, and the people who lived by fishing, farming, and salt extraction. These earliest encounters set the stage for a complicated relationship: sometimes peaceful and cooperative, sometimes marred by uprisings and conflict.

For the Frisii themselves, Rome's arrival meant entry into a broader world of political alliances, trade opportunities, and cultural exchanges. At first, contact may have seemed beneficial. Roman goods—ranging from coins to luxury items—flowed into tribal territories. However, Roman demands, such as tribute and loyalty, could cause friction. As we trace the steps of the Roman era in Frisia, we see how local leaders balanced the advantages of contact with a powerful empire against the desire to remain autonomous. The result was a long period of shifting alliances, short-lived truces, and occasional conflict that shaped Frisian society in lasting ways.

2. The Frisii in Roman Sources

The Frisii first appear in Roman writings around the time of Julius Caesar and later more explicitly in accounts by Roman historians such as Tacitus. Caesar himself never campaigned deep into Frisian territories, focusing instead on the tribes closer to the Rhine in Gaul. However, his campaigns indirectly brought Roman attention to the northern coast. Early references describe the Frisii as a Germanic people occupying lands "beyond the Rhine," and some sources highlight their skill in navigating marshy coastlands.

Tacitus, writing in the late first or early second century CE, noted that the Frisii were divided into Greater Frisii and Lesser Frisii, possibly reflecting separate branches or a difference in power among local chieftains. In his *Germania*, Tacitus described various Germanic customs and societies, though not all of these observations specifically target the Frisii. Still, his writings give us hints about how Romans perceived these northern tribes: as strong, hardy, and capable of independent action. Roman authors often wrote from a viewpoint that mixed ethnographic curiosity with political motive, so their accounts are partial snapshots rather than complete pictures.

These early documents demonstrate that, by the dawn of the first century CE, "Frisii" was a recognizable name in Roman political and military circles. Traders, administrators, and commanders would have been aware of the Frisii's location and resources. This attention might have grown after the coastal tribes began providing, or refusing to provide, certain tributes—like cattle hides or salt—to Roman officials. When Roman governors sought ways to bolster the economy of frontier provinces, they turned to local populations for taxes or goods, which, in turn, influenced how the Frisii responded to Roman demands.

---

3. Drusus's Campaigns in the North

One of the earliest Roman figures to push beyond the Rhine and encounter northern tribes was Nero Claudius Drusus, a Roman general active during the reign of Emperor Augustus at the end of the first century BCE and early first century CE. Drusus led multiple campaigns across the Rhine, aiming to subdue or at least neutralize Germanic tribes that might threaten Roman Gaul. He constructed forts along the river and moved northward toward the coastal regions.

During these expeditions, Drusus likely came into contact with the Frisii. While his main efforts targeted tribes like the Cherusci or the Chauci, the presence of a Roman military force so close to Frisian lands would have introduced new dynamics. Some Frisian leaders may have sought alliances with Drusus, hoping to use Roman support to gain an edge over local rivals. Others might have viewed the Romans with suspicion, worrying about the possibility of forced subjugation.

Drusus also explored maritime routes in the North Sea. Roman sources mention fleets navigating the coastal waters, investigating potential ports and the layout of the tide-influenced shoreline. This would have given Roman strategists important intelligence on the region's geography. For the Frisii, the sight of Roman galleys off their coasts must have been both awe-inspiring and intimidating. These campaigns did not immediately force all coastal tribes under Roman rule, but they set in motion decades of closer Roman scrutiny—and eventual attempts at tighter control.

---

4. Early Alliances and the Frisian Tribute Relationship

The Roman Empire preferred to manage frontier regions through client relationships when possible. This meant that if a tribe was willing to negotiate terms—often involving tribute or auxiliary troops—Rome might allow them some internal autonomy rather than imposing direct garrisons. In the case of the Frisii, an early arrangement was reached where they supplied tribute, possibly in the form of cattle hides or other valuable goods, in exchange for peace and official recognition.

Cattle hide tribute was particularly noted by Roman authors because certain tribes in northern Europe, including the Frisii, were renowned for producing high-quality hides. These could be used by the Roman military for tents, armor straps, and other purposes. In return, the Frisii would have received Roman coins and possibly trade privileges. Roman merchants traveling from the south might pay visits to Frisian markets, offering wine, pottery, and Roman metalwork in exchange for local products. This arrangement, while beneficial to some Frisian chieftains, likely caused tension among those who disliked external demands placed on their resources.

Tribute relationships always carried a risk. If local communities felt overburdened by demands or saw no real benefit, they might rebel. Likewise, if Roman governors felt that the tribute was insufficient or if the tribe was uncooperative, they might respond with military force. In these early decades of Roman-Frisian interaction, the arrangement held, but it was fragile. Over time, the friction between Roman authority and Frisian independence grew more pronounced, setting the stage for future confrontations.

5. The Teutoburg Forest Event and Its Impact

In 9 CE, one of the most famous events in Roman-Germanic history occurred: the Battle of Teutoburg Forest. Under the leadership of the Cheruscan chieftain Arminius, several Germanic tribes ambushed and destroyed three Roman legions commanded by Publius Quinctilius Varus. This catastrophic defeat halted Roman expansion east of the Rhine. While the Frisii were not the central players in that battle, its outcome deeply affected them and all tribes near the Rhine frontier.

After Teutoburg, the Roman Empire reassessed its ambitions beyond the Rhine. Emperor Augustus reportedly remarked, "Varus, give me back my legions!" indicating the shock and significance of the defeat. The empire pulled back from attempting direct conquest of vast Germanic territories. Instead, they focused on consolidating and fortifying the Rhine line. This shift meant that the Frisii, and other northern groups, found themselves on a border that the empire now regarded with caution.

Roman military presence along the Rhine increased, as did Roman interest in ensuring that local tribes near the frontier would not join any large-scale Germanic uprising. For the Frisii, this resulted in tighter scrutiny of their tribute obligations. Rome wanted to prevent them from becoming an ally to more hostile groups. Some Frisian chieftains tried to maintain amicable ties, seeing an advantage in the stable trade environment that Rome could provide. Others might have resented growing Roman demands. The tension between these factions within Frisian society would eventually lead to open conflict.

6. Frisian Society Under Roman Influence

Despite their distance from the main Roman provinces, Frisian communities felt the empire's influence in subtle and direct ways. Roman coins, pottery, and small luxury items began to circulate more widely. Archaeological sites in the northern Netherlands and coastal Germany reveal the presence of Roman goods in settlements that can be associated with Frisian inhabitants. This does not mean the Frisii became "Romanized" in the same way that some tribes closer to the Roman limes did. The coastal marshes and the relative autonomy of their communities allowed them to preserve much of their own customs. Still, the infiltration of Roman items indicated a certain level of economic integration.

Social structures might also have felt the Roman touch. Local elites who cooperated with Rome could amass wealth and status. They might display Roman-made accessories—such as brooches or glassware—to assert prestige. The local warrior class potentially gained from trading or negotiating with Roman officials. Meanwhile, average farmers and fishers continued their daily routines, tending livestock or casting nets, possibly seeing little direct benefit from Roman association apart from occasional trade. However, if Roman tribute demands increased, these commoners would be the ones shouldering the burden of producing more cattle hides or other resources.

Religion is another aspect of life that might have experienced mild Roman influence. Some Frisii stationed as auxiliaries in Roman armies or traveling to Roman settlements might have encountered Roman deities or religious customs. They could bring back stories and small tokens of foreign gods. Nonetheless, the spiritual beliefs of the Frisii almost certainly remained anchored in local Germanic traditions—worship of nature, ancestors, and regional deities. Roman religious influence would remain minimal compared to what would happen centuries later with the spread of Christianity, but some early cross-pollination of ideas may have begun.

---

7. Economic Exchanges With Rome

Economically, contact with Rome opened up new possibilities for the Frisii. Roman merchants had an appetite for northern goods such as furs, amber, salted fish, and high-quality hides. Additionally, salt itself was a valuable commodity that could be produced in the coastal areas by evaporating seawater or processing salt marsh plants. In return, local elites welcomed items from the Roman world: metal tools, weapons, coins, and perhaps wines or olive oil. Even if these items were not everyday needs, they served as markers of status and connected the Frisii to far-reaching networks.

The presence of Roman currency in Frisian territory reveals that some form of monetary exchange took place, at least among local elites or in larger trade gatherings. This facilitated more complex economic interactions than mere barter. Over time, Frisian merchants or middlemen could profit by bridging the gap between inland Germanic tribes and Roman markets. They might bring goods from the interior to coastal points, where Roman or Gallic traders could pick them up and transport them south. In turn, products from the Mediterranean could filter northward.

However, such economic benefits did not come without costs. The tribute system was a form of enforced economic extraction. If a Roman governor decided the Frisii were not providing enough hides or other goods, he could send soldiers to demand compliance. This possibility always loomed in the background, tempering whatever economic gains some Frisians enjoyed. Meanwhile, the dependence on Roman coins and goods could create vulnerabilities: if Rome decided to cut off trade or if warfare disrupted supply lines, local elites might find themselves in trouble.

---

8. The Frisian Revolt of 28 CE

Tensions that had been building between the Frisii and Rome eventually boiled over. According to Tacitus, in the year 28 CE, the Frisii revolted against excessive tribute demands. The Roman governor in the region had insisted on a certain quota of cattle hides, specifically those of exceptionally large size, to fulfill army requirements. Over time, these demands became punishing, with Roman tax collectors seizing livestock or even forcibly taking children as pledges for unpaid tribute. Such harsh measures ignited anger among Frisian communities.

The revolt began when local Frisian chieftains, fed up with Roman exploitation, rallied warriors to attack Roman officials and forts. Tacitus mentions that the Frisii laid siege to a Roman fort (possibly near the coast), overwhelming its garrison. This local uprising alarmed Roman authorities, who realized they had underestimated the resilience and fighting capability of the coastal tribes. In the aftermath, the Frisii effectively rid themselves of immediate Roman oversight, forcing Roman legions to pull back to the south of the Rhine for a period.

Although the revolt is less famous than the Teutoburg disaster, it was significant for the Frisii. It demonstrated their willingness to unite against an external threat, and it temporarily liberated them from oppressive tribute. Rome did not immediately respond with a major invasion to re-subjugate them, possibly because the empire was preoccupied with other frontiers or internal matters. As a result, the Frisii gained a measure of independence that would shape their relationship with Rome for decades. The memory of that successful stand likely fueled a sense of pride and self-sufficiency among Frisian warriors.

---

9. Mid-1st Century Tensions

Following the revolt of 28 CE, there was a period of uneasy coexistence. Some Roman sources imply that the empire had learned not to push too harshly on the Frisii's tribute obligations. Others suggest that, for a time, the Frisii were left largely to their own devices, as long as they did not threaten the Roman provinces. Traders still moved across the region. Diplomatic missions from local chieftains to Roman settlements may have continued. But a lingering mistrust likely remained on both sides.

During the mid-first century CE, the Roman Empire was expanding and consolidating in many directions—Britannia, the Danube, and areas of the Near East. The northern Rhine frontier, while important, was one frontier among many. Roman governors in the region often had to weigh the risk of confronting tribes like the Frisii against the resources needed. If the Frisii were not actively raiding Roman territories, it might have seemed more strategic to maintain a cautious peace rather than risk a costly campaign in difficult coastal terrain.

Meanwhile, the Frisii had other concerns. They shared boundaries with tribes such as the Chauci (to the east) and various small Germanic groups inland. Political alliances or conflicts among these tribes could shift, and local leaders needed to navigate these changes. The memory of the revolt's success still resonated, and the Frisii guarded their autonomy. At the same time, some local chieftains did not want to completely sever ties with Rome, since trade brought wealth and Roman goods bolstered their own prestige. This tension between desiring freedom from Roman demands and benefiting from Roman commerce became a defining aspect of Frisian politics in the first century CE.

10. Shifting Tribal Alliances

In the broader Germanic world of the first century CE, alliances were constantly in flux. Tribes might forge pacts for mutual defense or to gain trade advantages. In times of crisis—such as famine or threat from a larger power—these alliances could splinter. For the Frisii, living along the coastal marshes and tidal flats, forging alliances with neighboring tribes might have been one way to counterbalance Roman influence. Alternatively, they might align with Rome against rival groups who threatened their lands.

These shifting alliances were not purely military. Marriages between elite families from different tribes could cement friendships. Trade partnerships, too, could foster cooperation, as certain tribes excelled in particular goods or crafts. Because the Frisii were known for their cattle and possibly salt production, they might trade these with inland tribes in exchange for iron ores or other resources not abundant on the coast.

Roman watchers, based in forts along the Rhine or in the provincial capital of Germania Inferior, kept an eye on these developments. They hoped to prevent a repeat of large-scale Germanic uprisings and were willing to offer incentives—like gifts or recognition of chieftains as "friends of Rome"—to tribes that cooperated. However, the Frisii had shown their willingness to resist Roman demands, making them a wildcard in the region's political game. This unpredictability shaped how Roman commanders approached negotiations or potential conflicts with them.

11. The Batavian Revolt and Frisian Involvement

In the late first century CE, the Roman world underwent a turbulent period known as the Year of the Four Emperors (69 CE). Chaos in Rome often echoed in the provinces, and this was the context for the famous Batavian Revolt. The Batavi were another Germanic tribe living near the Rhine, initially loyal auxiliaries to Rome. Their leader, Gaius Julius Civilis, took advantage of Roman instability to stage a rebellion. This revolt attracted various tribes from the region, all with grievances against Roman rule or ambitions for regional power.

The role of the Frisii in the Batavian Revolt is not fully clear from surviving sources. Some accounts hint that Frisian warriors may have joined, at least in part, hoping to gain further autonomy or plunder. Others suggest the Frisii were cautious, having recently struggled with Rome themselves, and chose not to commit entirely. It is plausible that Frisian factions took different sides: one group might have allied with the Batavi, while another group remained neutral or even aligned with Rome to hedge bets.

The outcome of the Batavian Revolt was ultimately a Roman victory. Civilis negotiated a peace, but Roman reprisals and the general havoc of war left their mark on the region. For the Frisii, the revolt reinforced a lesson: even when Rome was temporarily weakened, the empire still had vast resources to muster. Aligning with a rebellion might gain short-term benefits but could also invite retribution. Meanwhile, the fact that some Frisians could join or at least influence regional upheavals showed that they were not insignificant players. Their presence on the North Sea coast gave them strategic value, and their willingness to fight for their autonomy was well-known to Roman officials.

12. Roman Fortifications in Frisian Territory

During the late first and second centuries CE, the Roman military built and maintained a series of forts and watchtowers along the Rhine and some coastal areas. While the primary defensive line was the Rhine limes, smaller outposts or temporary fortifications might have existed within Frisian lands, especially if Roman governors sought to oversee trade routes or keep tabs on tribal movements. These forts were not massive legionary bases like those deeper inside Roman territory; they were more often small castella housing auxiliary units.

The exact locations and extents of these fortifications have been pieced together through archaeological findings such as remnants of Roman pottery, coin hoards, and building foundations. In some places, the marshy soil preserved wooden structures or palisades that give insight into Roman construction techniques adapted for wet environments. The presence of these outposts meant that at times Roman soldiers were living near or among Frisian villages, which could foster trade but also lead to friction or cultural exchange.

For Frisian leaders, the presence of a small Roman garrison might be a mixed blessing. It offered potential protection against raids by rival tribes, but it also served as a reminder of Rome's power. Roman officers stationed at these forts acted as intermediaries for diplomacy, tax collection, or punitive expeditions. Over time, some Frisians might see the Roman presence as a chance for profit—selling supplies or negotiating favorable terms—while others bristled at the loss of full autonomy. This push and pull defined the second century CE in Frisian-Roman relations.

13. Cultural and Religious Interactions

One of the lesser-discussed aspects of Roman-Frisian contact is the cultural and religious dimension. Though the Frisii maintained their Germanic beliefs, small-scale interaction with Roman religious practices likely occurred. A Frisian auxiliary serving in the Roman army in Gaul might see temples dedicated to Jupiter, Mars, or local Celtic-Roman hybrid deities. He might bring back stories or small tokens to his home village.

Additionally, trade centers or forts along the Rhine occasionally became melting pots of different cultures: Gauls, Romans, Germans, and even traveling merchants from the Mediterranean. In such places, a Frisian might encounter new customs in dress, language, or spiritual rites. This kind of cultural blending was more subdued in the coastal marshes themselves, which remained somewhat remote. Still, for those Frisii who traveled or served in Roman units, exposure to the broader empire was a formative experience.

While we have no strong evidence that the Frisii adopted Roman gods in large numbers, it was not unheard of for Germanic tribes to identify a local deity with a Roman counterpart. For instance, a local thunder god might be equated to Jupiter or an equivalent. Over centuries, some level of syncretism could develop, though it seems minimal before the spread of Christianity in later eras. Overall, Roman religious influence in Frisia remained marginal compared to the more pressing concerns of tribute, trade, and military affairs.

14. Decline of Roman Authority in the Region

As we move into the third century CE, the Roman Empire began to experience larger internal and external stresses. Civil wars, crises of succession, and incursions by new confederations of Germanic tribes (like the Alamanni and later the Franks) weakened Rome's control over distant frontiers. The province of Germania Inferior, which included territories near the Rhine delta, faced increasing pressure from these external threats.

In Frisia, the gradual decline of Roman attention meant fewer resources allocated to controlling or influencing the local population. Forts might have been abandoned or minimally staffed. Trade routes still existed, but the frequency and safety of Roman merchant caravans might have dropped. As a result, Frisian communities found more freedom to manage their own affairs without direct Roman oversight.

Yet, this loosening of Roman authority also meant that Frisia had to contend with other groups pushing into coastal lands. Saxons and other Germanic peoples from the east began migrating or raiding along the North Sea coast. If Rome no longer garrisoned outposts to repel these newcomers, the Frisii had to defend themselves. Some of these interactions could lead to alliances or merges between the Frisii and neighboring tribes, reshaping the coastal demographic landscape. The late Roman era thus becomes a time of flux, with Frisia caught between a fading empire and the arrival of new powers.

15. Evolving Political Structures Among the Frisii

From the time of the first Roman contact to the empire's gradual withdrawal, Frisian leadership structures also evolved. Earlier chapters described how pre-Roman Frisia likely consisted of scattered communities with local chieftains or councils. During the height of Roman interaction, some chieftains gained prestige—and possibly more centralized power—through dealings with Rome. After the empire's influence began to wane, these new power centers did not simply vanish. Instead, they adapted, filling the vacuum left by Rome's retreat.

This adaptation could include forming larger alliances among Frisian communities. Previously, each local group might have answered to its own chieftain. Now, under external pressures, they might unite under a more prominent leader who could organize defense efforts or negotiate with outside forces. These developments laid foundational elements for the later, more cohesive Frisian polities that would emerge in the early medieval period.

Archaeological evidence suggests that some settlements grew during this time, hinting at a modest concentration of wealth or population. But we do not see large urban centers or heavily fortified towns like in the Romanized areas further south. Instead, the traditional pattern of terp (artificial mound) villages continued, reflecting the ongoing struggle with the sea. Leaders who could coordinate both water management and defense might naturally gain greater authority, shaping the direction of Frisia's political evolution.

---

16. The Frisii in the Late Roman Era

During the late third and fourth centuries CE, references to the Frisii in Roman texts become sporadic. Some Roman military records refer to Frisian individuals serving as auxiliaries. Others mention raids along the coast, sometimes attributed to Saxons, Franks, or other confederations. The Frisii may have been caught between these larger tribal coalitions. They could have joined alliances for protection or found themselves absorbed into bigger groupings.

It is also possible that some portion of the Frisii migrated or dispersed. Coastal flooding events might have forced relocations. Political upheavals or fear of raids could have driven some to seek new lands. Meanwhile, pockets of Frisian communities that stayed in the traditional homeland might have become more insular, relying on local networks and minimal contact with the crumbling Roman administrative framework.

By the late fourth century, the Western Roman Empire was in steep decline. Emperor after emperor struggled to maintain control. The focus of the central authorities turned to defending core provinces—Italy, Gaul, Hispania—leaving the northern frontier increasingly vulnerable. For the Frisii, this meant the Roman presence that once demanded tribute was more or less gone. Freed from direct oversight, they had to navigate a new world in which migrating Saxons, Angles, Jutes, and others would reshape the coastal regions forever.

17. The Emergence of Saxon Pressure

While the Frisii had dealt with Roman demands for centuries, they now faced the rise of the Saxons. Originating further east, Saxon groups began pushing westward, possibly driven by population pressures or the desire for new lands. They also took part in raiding across the North Sea, targeting the coasts of Britannia. Some Saxons may have settled in Frisian territories, especially in areas not heavily defended or those left open after Roman withdrawal.

For the Frisii, this was a challenging development. Their population might have been smaller than the Saxon migrant groups, or at least not as mobile. Maintaining control over their lands required unity and strategic alliances. Some Frisii might have integrated with Saxon newcomers through intermarriage or mutual defense pacts. Others might have resisted. Over generations, a cultural blending could occur, with Saxon language and customs influencing Frisian ones, or vice versa.

Despite these pressures, the Frisian cultural core did not vanish. Many people continued to speak a Germanic dialect that would evolve into Old Frisian. They maintained distinctive legal and social practices, sometimes shaped by their older experiences with Rome. As the empire receded, new tribal and regional powers vied for dominance, and the Frisii were an integral part of that shifting mosaic.

CHAPTER 4: THE MIGRATION PERIOD AND THE RISE OF FRISIAN IDENTITY

1. The Collapse of Roman Power in the North

By the early fifth century CE, the Western Roman Empire was in a state of ongoing crisis. Political fragmentation, economic troubles, and repeated incursions by various Germanic groups weakened central authority. In 410 CE, Rome famously withdrew its legions from Britannia, signaling that the empire would no longer defend its distant provinces. While the Roman army had already scaled back its presence around the Rhine and in northern territories, this period marks a clear endpoint for Roman control in much of northwestern Europe.

For the Frisii, the final departure of Roman forces and administrators meant that any lingering tribute demands or direct oversight disappeared. This sudden vacuum, however, did not produce immediate stability. Neighboring groups—Saxons, Angles, Jutes, and Franks—were also on the move, looking for new places to settle or raid. The disappearance of the Roman frontier system meant that the old lines of defense were gone. Fortified posts were abandoned, trade networks shifted or broke down, and local populations found themselves without the external framework that had, for better or worse, structured their relations for centuries.

In Frisia, the end of Roman power created both freedom and danger. Freedom, because local leaders no longer had to submit tribute or fear Roman retribution. Danger, because larger tribal confederations or bands of raiders could arrive with little warning, seeking resources or new farmland. The ability of the Frisii to respond effectively to these challenges would shape their evolution in this new, post-Roman world.

2. The Concept of the Migration Period

Historians often label the fifth and sixth centuries CE as the Migration Period (or the Völkerwanderung in German), characterized by large-scale movements of peoples throughout Europe. The collapse of Roman authority allowed tribes and confederations—Goths, Vandals, Burgundians, Lombards, Saxons, Angles, and others—to move into former Roman provinces. Some of these groups aimed to settle; others were more interested in plunder. Over time, they established new kingdoms and polities across the continent.

In the coastal regions of the North Sea, the Migration Period is best known for the departure of Angles, Saxons, and Jutes to Britain, laying the foundations of what would become Anglo-Saxon England. But the Frisian lands were also affected. While some Frisians may have joined these migratory waves to Britain or settled in other parts of Europe, many remained in their ancestral marshes and terpen. They had to deal with the dynamic of smaller migrating groups passing through or seeking land. On the other hand, the relative remoteness of the Frisian coast could serve as a shield if groups found the marshy environment unappealing or difficult to conquer.

The significance of the Migration Period for Frisian history lies in how it reshaped the balance of power in northwestern Europe. As new kingdoms formed to the south and east, the Frisii adapted by developing their own distinct identity. Freed from the overshadowing presence of Rome, they could build alliances or resist pressures in ways that would establish the foundations of what later became known as the Frisian "kingdom" or region.

---

3. Germanic Migrations

Long before the fall of Rome, Germanic groups from the interior of Europe had been moving westward. Some fled from the Huns, who erupted onto the European scene from the Eurasian steppes. Others simply migrated in search of better farmland or to escape internal power struggles. The Saxons were one such group: they expanded from their original heartlands (likely in what is now northern Germany) toward both the North Sea coast and the interior.

The Saxon expansion exerted pressure on the Frisii. Some Saxons might have settled in parts of the Frisian coastal zone, blending with local populations. In other cases, they simply passed through or launched raids. The net result was a mix of conflict, trade, and intermarriage. Over time, boundaries between "Saxon" and "Frisian" in certain areas could become blurred, at least culturally and linguistically. The essential difference might remain the local identity tied to the coastal environment—dwelling mounds, dike construction, and tidal farming practices that were less familiar to inland Saxons.

Despite these pressures, Frisian communities in many locations held on to their distinct traditions. The watery terrain could act as a defensive advantage, limiting how effectively outside forces could project power. Some researchers even theorize that the continuing need for communal cooperation against floods strengthened local social bonds, making the Frisii resilient in the face of external challenges. The idea of a "free" Frisian community, resistant to subjugation, might have its roots in this era, when large-scale migrations threatened to overwhelm smaller populations—yet the Frisii persisted.

---

4. Saxon, Angle, and Jute Movements

While Saxon migration had a direct impact on Frisia, Angles and Jutes mostly looked across the sea to Britain. Still, these groups traveled via or near Frisian territories, possibly stopping to trade or replenish supplies. Some might have lingered temporarily, forming small enclaves along the coast. Others simply passed by sea, leaving little mark. The overall effect of these migrations was a fluid, shifting demographic landscape throughout the North Sea region.

Frisian ports—though not ports in the modern sense—became staging points for those heading to Britain. Local chieftains might have allowed traveling groups to trade for food or ships, especially if they could gain something in return. Conversely, they might block passage if they feared a hostile takeover. In this way, Frisian leaders gained a kind of strategic role, controlling or facilitating access to routes across the water. This role foreshadows the later medieval period, when Frisian merchants and sailors became prominent in the North Sea trade network.

A side effect of this maritime traffic was the cross-pollination of cultural practices. Though the Angles and Jutes mostly established themselves in eastern Britain, some cultural or technological ideas could flow back to the Frisian coast. Boat-building techniques, navigational knowledge, or even certain social customs could migrate along with traveling peoples. This interplay further shaped the evolving identity of the Frisian communities, keeping them connected to the broader North Sea world.

5. The Frisians' Shifting Territories

As various Germanic groups migrated, the geographical boundaries of what one might call "Frisia" also shifted. The classic idea of Frisian territory is a coastal stretch from what is now the northern Netherlands to the coast of modern Germany and perhaps extending into parts of the Danish peninsula. During the Migration Period, some inland areas once inhabited by Frisii may have been lost to encroaching Saxons or Franks. Conversely, some coastal stretches might have seen an influx of people identifying as Frisii, seeking safety from the turmoil further inland.

Also, climatic and environmental changes could alter the viability of certain coastal zones. Floods, storms, or changes in sea level might render some areas temporarily uninhabitable. People often moved to higher ground, building new terpen or reinforcing older ones. This continuous reshaping of settlement patterns was a defining characteristic of Frisian life. Unlike tribes that roamed widely, the Frisii largely adhered to the same littoral zone, learning to adapt rather than uproot entirely.

By the end of the Migration Period, the concept of Frisia as a continuous coastal region was more solid than ever, despite boundary fluctuations. Even if the exact lines on the map were not yet drawn, outsiders increasingly recognized that a distinct community occupied those marshes. As we shall see, the seeds of a future Frisian kingdom or realm took root during this time, planted by leaders who capitalized on local unity in the face of external threats.

6. Formation of Small Kingdoms

Throughout Europe, the vacuum left by Rome's decline allowed local warlords or chieftains to enlarge their domains, sometimes calling themselves kings. In Gaul, for instance, the Franks emerged as a major power under leaders like Clovis. In Britain, small Anglo-Saxon kingdoms took shape. Along the coast that would become Frisia, a similar process may have occurred, although it is less documented.

Archaeological evidence suggests the emergence of hierarchical centers. Some settlements grew larger than others, possibly functioning as the seat of a local ruler. Grave goods in certain burial sites indicate that a new stratum of elite individuals existed, adorned with high-quality weapons or jewelry. Though we do not have a detailed list of Frisian kings from this period, references in later centuries mention earlier dynasties or lines of chieftains. Such lineages, real or partly legendary, provided continuity and legitimacy.

It is crucial to emphasize that these early Frisian "kingdoms" would not resemble the highly structured, bureaucratic states we see later in medieval Europe. Power was personal, resting on a leader's ability to command loyalty, distribute spoils, and defend territory. That said, these small polities laid the groundwork for more cohesive rule. Over time, as they consolidated, they could stand up to—or negotiate with—larger entities like the Franks.

---

7. Influence of Hunnic and Eastern Movements

Though the Huns were mostly active in Central and Eastern Europe, their westward push set off chain reactions among Germanic tribes. Groups displaced by the Huns sometimes migrated into Roman territories. Those groups, in turn, put pressure on tribes closer to the Rhine and North Sea. In this grand domino effect, the Frisii ended up facing new neighbors or receiving refugees who had been forced out of their original lands.

This process underscores how events far away could ripple into the Frisian world. The chain of migrations that began with the Huns reshaped the entire map of Europe. For coastal societies like the Frisii, the outcome was unpredictable. On one hand, a flooded population of refugees could strain local resources. On the other, new arrivals could bring skills, forging alliances that strengthened local communities. Over generations, these shifts contributed to a mixture of cultural elements in Frisia, adding layers to an identity already shaped by centuries of adaptation.

---

8. Cultural Blending and Language Evolution

In the centuries following Rome's withdrawal, the Frisian language began to diverge more clearly from other West Germanic tongues. Latin had some influence—largely through trade or the short-lived presence of Roman fortifications—but the main influences came from neighboring Germanic dialects. Saxon, Frankish, and other tongues interacted with local Frisian speech, shaping vocabulary and grammar in small, incremental ways.

The coastal environment also played a role in unifying Frisian dialects. People who built terpen, managed dikes, and fished the tidal flats shared specific terminology for these activities. Common challenges—like flooding—brought communities together, encouraging mutual aid and exchange of knowledge. This process reinforced a shared coastal culture and with it, linguistic continuity.

Material culture changed as well. Archaeologists note that pottery styles, clothing fastenings (like brooches), and weapon types show a mixture of local development and external influences. Such blending is typical of Migration Period societies, where new forms emerge from contact with diverse groups. Over time, the Frisian cultural identity crystallized around a distinct language and set of social customs, setting the stage for later medieval references to a "Frisian people" with shared laws and traditions.

---

9. Emergence of the Early Frisian Elite

During the Migration Period, leaders who could protect settlements from raiders or coordinate communal projects gained prestige. These elites might have controlled trade routes, collecting tolls or taxes from merchants. Some might have brokered deals with Saxon or Frankish groups, providing safe passage or supplies in exchange for neutrality. Such strategic power translated into wealth, often displayed through precious metal items or lavish burials.

Grave finds in what is now the province of Friesland (in the Netherlands) and other coastal areas sometimes reveal richly furnished tombs from this era. High-quality swords, gold or silver ornaments, and imported goods appear alongside the deceased. These burials suggest that the individuals interred held positions of authority—warlords, clan heads, or petty kings. Their ability to amass luxury items indicates extensive trade networks that might stretch from the British Isles to the Rhineland or even beyond.

While we lack direct written accounts of these early Frisian elites, we can infer that they played a crucial role in forging unity. They might have resolved disputes between villages, organized defensive measures against raiders, and managed large communal projects to counter flood threats. Over generations, certain lineages gained renown, forming the backbone of what would later evolve into the recognized rulers of Frisia.

---

10. Conversion or Continued Paganism

Across continental Europe, the decline of Rome did not automatically bring about rapid Christianization. In fact, among the Germanic peoples, the spread of Christianity varied significantly. The Franks, for instance, adopted Christianity more quickly, influenced by the Roman Gaulish Church and the conversion of their King Clovis around 500 CE. In contrast, the Frisii remained mostly pagan well into the early Middle Ages. They continued worshiping nature deities, ancestral spirits, and practicing rites tied to the sea and seasons.

This religious difference sometimes placed the Frisii at odds with their Christian neighbors, especially as the Franks became more fervent in spreading the new faith. However, in the Migration Period itself, formal missionary efforts in Frisia were still minimal. Christian bishops and priests tended to focus on regions closer to their established centers. Only later, in the seventh and eighth centuries, did major Christian missions target the Frisian lands with more intensity. In this era of fluid migrations, religion was just one part of a broader cultural mosaic.

Nevertheless, pockets of Christian influence could form if individuals traveled to a Christian territory or if a local leader married a Christian spouse. Isolated cases might exist of Christian burials or small wooden chapels near the coast. But these were exceptions rather than the rule. Pagan rituals—like offerings in bogs, veneration of sacred groves, and celebrations of seasonal festivals—remained the dominant religious expression among most Frisian communities.

11. The Impact of Trade Disruption

When Rome collapsed in the west, the extensive trade networks that had once spanned the empire inevitably suffered. Though some commercial routes persisted, the scale and security of trade declined. Pirates or raiders could threaten shipping lanes, and the breakdown of Roman roads made overland transport riskier. For the Frisii, who had partly relied on trade for obtaining luxury items or specialized goods, this disruption posed challenges.

However, local and regional trade never ceased entirely. The coastal location of Frisia gave it an advantage: seaborne routes could remain viable even if inland roads decayed. Small ships continued to ferry goods along the North Sea coast, linking communities in what is now the Netherlands, Germany, Denmark, and England. In this environment, Frisian merchants or sailors might have found new opportunities, building relationships that replaced former Roman markets. Over time, this maritime skill set would become a hallmark of Frisian identity in later centuries.

Still, the immediate post-Roman environment was uncertain. A local leader might secure a monopoly on a particular route, only to lose it if a stronger power emerged. Goods like salt or fish remained staples. Cattle and hides continued as important exports. The changing political map forced adaptability. This sense of resilience through shifting economic tides would characterize the Frisian approach to commerce for generations.

12. Shaping of a Distinct Frisian Identity

As the Migration Period progressed, external threats and the diminishing memory of Rome fostered a stronger internal sense of who the Frisii were. They might not have called themselves "Frisians" in the exact way modern historians do, but tribal affiliation and local customs clearly defined a community distinct from Saxons, Franks, or Danes. Factors that contributed to this distinct identity included:

- **Coastal Adaptation**: Mastery of dike building, terp construction, and tidal agriculture.
- **Shared Language**: A Germanic dialect evolving along its own path, reinforced by communal activities and relative isolation.
- **Common Threats**: Repeated external pressures created solidarity among scattered villages, leading to collective defense efforts.
- **Cultural Continuity**: Pagan religious practices, burial customs, and local legal traditions that remained consistent even as neighbors changed.

By the time we approach the seventh century, references in outside sources, such as Frankish chronicles, begin to describe areas of coastal land as "Frisian," reflecting the recognized presence of a unified people. While still fragmented into various sub-groups or petty domains, these communities had enough in common that outsiders grouped them together under one name.

---

13. Early Mentions of Frisian Laws or Customs

Although the earliest written Frisian law codes date to the medieval period (several centuries later), some historians believe that basic legal traditions or customs existed much earlier. Oral law, passed down by tribal elders, governed disputes over land, inheritance, and personal injuries. The same communal assemblies that might have decided war or peace with neighboring groups likely also enforced local rules.

The sense of "Frisian freedom," which later became a famous concept, possibly has roots in these Migration Period assemblies. People who lived in the harsh coastal environment had to cooperate for survival; this communal approach encouraged an ethos that placed local decision-making above subservience to distant lords. While we cannot claim a direct line from early assemblies to the sophisticated legal texts of the High Middle Ages, the continuity of such practices suggests that the Frisii placed high value on collective judgment and local autonomy.

14. Coastal Resilience and Settlement Patterns

Throughout the Migration Period, the building and maintenance of terpen (dwelling mounds) remained central to Frisian life. Archeological layers in these mounds often reveal continuous habitation over centuries, with each generation adding layers of soil, refuse, and peat to raise the settlement further against rising waters or storm surges. This practice exemplifies Frisian resilience: instead of abandoning flooded lands, they adapted them.

New technology for water management might have emerged as well. Simple drainage ditches, small dikes, and communal efforts to keep farmland workable show that the Frisii consistently refined their relationship with the sea. Over time, these skills became an essential part of Frisian identity. They also contributed to societal structures because collaborative labor was needed. Those who could organize large-scale water management projects often became recognized community leaders.

In some areas, communities expanded outward once older mounds became large enough or once new dikes created safer farmland. Settlement patterns thus evolved in a patchwork, influenced by environmental challenges and population growth. Yet the sense of shared struggle against the sea never disappeared, uniting Frisian groups who might otherwise have been politically separate.

---

15. The Threat of Rival Tribes

Amid these environmental challenges, the Frisii also faced threats from neighbors who might raid or conquer. The Franks, growing in power to the south, presented a significant concern. By the mid-sixth century, the Merovingian dynasty ruled much of Gaul and parts of western Germany. They expanded northward, sometimes clashing with Saxons and other groups. Eventually, they turned their eyes to Frisia as well, both for strategic reasons (gaining access to the coast) and economic incentives (taxation, trade, resources).

As we shall see in upcoming chapters, the tension between the rising Frankish kingdom and the Frisian coastal peoples would shape the destiny of Frisia for centuries. Initially, the Frisians might have avoided direct confrontation by maintaining autonomy or forging short-term deals. Yet, the Merovingians would not always remain content to let their northern neighbors operate independently. Conflicts or negotiations with the Franks would become a recurrent theme in the centuries ahead.

Other threats included shifting alliances among Saxons or Danes. A powerful Saxon warlord might covet Frisian trade routes. Danish raiders could appear along the coast, testing the defenses of Frisian settlements. In this environment of unpredictable hostility, forging a broader Frisian unity made strategic sense—an advantage that, in time, might pave the way for recognized Frisian leadership figures, possibly kings or dukes who could coordinate large-scale defense.

16. Alliances with the Merovingians?

While the Franks could be a threat, they could also become allies—if the circumstances were right. The Merovingians sometimes preferred diplomacy over outright conquest, especially if a friendly Frisian chieftain would allow Frankish merchants safe passage to the North Sea or share in valuable trade. Such alliances might include marriage pacts, the exchange of gifts, or agreements to fight common enemies.

From the Frisian perspective, a Merovingian alliance could provide protection against other aggressors. However, it came with risks. Merovingian kings often demanded tribute or submission from their allies, eventually absorbing them into the Frankish realm. The Frisians had a deep tradition of independence, so the prospect of becoming subordinates to a distant king was likely unappealing. This tension—seeing the Franks as both potential partners and likely overlords—would define much of Frisian diplomatic strategy in the sixth and seventh centuries.

Despite the potential for alliances, large-scale Frankish interference in Frisia appears sporadic at first. The Merovingians were more focused on internal power struggles and expansion into regions with richer farmland or established Roman towns. The coastal marshes, while strategically important for trade, were not always their top priority. This "window" gave the Frisii time to consolidate and evolve their leadership structures further before the major confrontations of the seventh and eighth centuries.

17. The Precursor to the Frisian Kingdom

By the late sixth and early seventh centuries, sources begin to hint at the existence of a recognized Frisian realm or series of realms under a more unified rule. Though these sources are fragmentary, references in Frankish chronicles and later legends mention rulers with Frisian backgrounds or alliances. This period represents the transition from scattered Migration Period communities toward a more cohesive political entity often referred to as the "Frisian kingdom."

Archaeological records show increasing prosperity in certain coastal centers. More significant fortifications or hall-like structures suggest a higher level of social organization. Craft production, especially metalworking, hints at specialized workshops that catered to an elite class. Meanwhile, stable maritime trade routes across the North Sea and into the Baltic may have fueled economic growth. All these factors made the idea of a unified Frisian leadership more plausible.

Though we lack the exact names and genealogies of these early Frisian leaders (they emerge more clearly in the seventh century, as we will see with figures like King Aldgisl and King Redbad), we can posit that the seeds of their power were sown in the Migration Period. The interplay of tradition, environment, external pressures, and the desire for collective defense led to a sense of communal identity. By forging pacts among local chieftains, certain strong figures could rise as overlords or "kings," at least in name, representing a larger swath of the Frisian coast.

CHAPTER 5: THE EMERGENCE OF THE FRISIAN KINGDOM

1. Introduction to the "Kingdom" Concept

By the dawn of the 7th century, the people we call "Frisians" had survived the collapse of Roman power, navigated the upheavals of the Migration Period, and developed a stronger sense of shared identity along the North Sea coast. In previous chapters, we traced how scattered communities unified in response to external threats and challenging environments. Now, we see the rise of more prominent leadership figures—individuals sometimes referred to as "kings" in historical sources, even though their realms differed greatly from the centralized kingdoms found elsewhere in Europe.

During this time, references appear in Frankish chronicles and other early medieval writings to leaders who governed substantial stretches of Frisian territory. While these leaders likely did not exercise absolute authority over every village or coastal settlement, they were recognized enough by outside powers—such as the Frankish Merovingians—for historians to speak of a "Frisian kingdom." This kingdom was not always tightly centralized; nonetheless, it marked a milestone. For the first time, outsiders recognized that a strong figure (or figures) represented and led the coastal lowlands collectively.

In this chapter, we explore how this kingdom emerged. We look at the political environment of the 7th and early 8th centuries, when major leaders such as Aldgisl and Redbad interacted with neighboring powers. We examine how economy, maritime trade, internal social structures, and the challenges from the expanding Frankish realm shaped Frisian fortunes. By focusing on local rulers, alliances, and conflicts, we see how Frisia carved out a place among Europe's early medieval polities. Although the term "kingdom" might have nuances—some might call it a loose confederation—it was a turning point for the Frisians in forging a more unified identity.

2. The Historical Context: Frisia Amid Larger Powers

2.1 The Merovingian Franks

To the south, the Merovingian dynasty controlled large parts of what is now France, Belgium, and western Germany. Since the early 6th century, Merovingian rulers like Clovis and his successors had expanded their domains, sometimes fighting rival Germanic groups or entering alliances when it suited them. By the 7th century, different branches of the Merovingian family sometimes warred among themselves, splitting the Frankish realm into segments like Neustria, Austrasia, and Burgundy. These internal rivalries could divert attention away from Frisia, allowing Frisian rulers to maintain independence—at least temporarily.

Nevertheless, the Franks saw coastal access as strategically valuable. Ports or river mouths along Frisian territory could open up trade across the North Sea and beyond. Gaining partial control over these routes promised wealth and influence. While some Merovingian kings were content with friendly ties or mild tribute, others aimed for outright submission. The result was a century-long tug-of-war, with periods of conflict followed by intervals of relative peace.

2.2 Neighboring Tribes and the North Sea

From the east, Saxon groups continued to evolve, and to the north, Danes consolidated their own power. Across the sea, in Britain, Anglo-Saxon kingdoms were forming—Northumbria, Mercia, East Anglia, and others—and these kingdoms sometimes had contact with the coastal mainland. Frisia's geographical position placed it at a crossroads of maritime trade, linking the British Isles with the Rhine estuary and beyond. As maritime commerce grew, Frisian ports became hubs of exchange for goods like cloth, salt, metals, and slaves.

This unique position also meant risk. Any power wanting to dominate North Sea trade might set sights on Frisian coastal towns. Frisian rulers had to balance alliances with both Frankish and Anglo-Saxon entities. Skilled seafaring and established trading traditions gave the Frisians leverage: their ships were well suited to shallow waters and tidal flats, making them essential for local transport. Frisians, in turn, needed to ensure that neither the Franks nor the Saxons (or others) seized total control of these maritime routes.

2.3 Internal Unity vs. Local Autonomy

The concept of a Frisian kingdom might suggest tight unity, but Frisia was still a patchwork of local communities, each with its own leaders. Though an overarching "king" might negotiate with foreign powers, local chieftains kept a good deal of autonomy. If a king demanded too much from distant coastal villages, those communities could simply opt out or align with a competing leader. The physical environment—marshes, waterways, and scattered terpen—further encouraged decentralization.

Thus, any Frisian king needed both diplomatic and military skill to hold the realm together. He also needed to maintain the loyalty of local elites who oversaw day-to-day life in each region. In turn, these elites might look to the king for protection against foreign raids or for help in settling disputes. Balancing these mutual interests, a king might come to embody a broader Frisian identity. But that identity remained flexible; the concept of "one Frisia" was still in flux.

---

3. King Aldgisl: An Early Ruler of Frisia

3.1 Aldgisl Enters the Historical Record

One of the earliest named Frisian kings (or leaders) mentioned in written sources is Aldgisl, who appears in the mid to late 7th century. Frankish chronicles and later hagiographical works reference him in passing, describing interactions with Frankish envoys and church figures. By piecing these references together, historians conclude that Aldgisl ruled a substantial portion of Frisia, probably including areas around the central or western coast near the Rhine mouths.

The details of Aldgisl's life are sparse, but one episode often recounted is his reception of the exiled bishop Wilfrid of York (an Anglo-Saxon churchman from Northumbria) around the late 7th century. According to some accounts, Wilfrid found refuge at Aldgisl's court after conflicts forced him away from his homeland. This suggests Aldgisl was open to diplomacy with Christian figures—though it does not necessarily prove that Aldgisl himself was Christian.

3.2 Relations with the Merovingians

During Aldgisl's reign, the Merovingians were politically divided. Their internal struggles allowed Frisia some breathing room. Aldgisl may have used this opportunity to strengthen trade connections and enhance his own power. By hosting exiled figures or traveling missionaries, he showed that Frisian rulers had enough influence to offer safe haven, thereby boosting Frisia's profile in the North Sea world.

However, tension with the Franks never fully disappeared. Some sources indicate that Aldgisl engaged in minor conflicts or skirmishes with Frankish nobles near the Rhine. At times, the Merovingian leaders might have demanded tribute or attempted to impose a count or official to oversee Frisian trade. Aldgisl's willingness to resist such measures—while maintaining open trade—underscores the delicate balancing act he performed.

3.3 Economic Growth and Maritime Trade

Under Aldgisl, Frisian ports likely grew more active. Coastal settlements, including possible trade centers such as Dorestad (near the Rhine delta), became bustling points of exchange. Merchants from Anglo-Saxon England, the Frankish interior, and even Scandinavia might have visited, trading textiles, metal goods, amber, salted fish, and slaves. The Frisian kingdom—if we call it that—profited from its role as a broker, collecting tolls or taxes on goods passing through.

Such prosperity required a measure of security. Aldgisl would have to ensure that pirate raids or local banditry did not disrupt commerce. The presence of stable leadership in the region—someone recognized by foreign traders as "king"—helped guarantee that business could be conducted predictably. In turn, revenues from trade fortified Aldgisl's position, allowing him to reward loyal chieftains or maintain a retinue of warriors who could defend trade routes.

3.4 Cultural Snapshot of Aldgisl's Time

Culturally, the 7th century remained steeped in pagan customs among most Frisians. Rituals honoring ancestors and nature spirits continued, though Christian influences trickled in through visiting priests or traveling merchants. Frisian elites sometimes wore elaborate brooches or swords with decorative inlays, blending local artistic motifs with styles gleaned from Frankish or Anglo-Saxon craftsmanship. Funeral practices varied—some elites were buried with grave goods, while in other areas cremation still prevailed.

Aldgisl's open attitude toward guests like Wilfrid might have introduced Frisian courtiers to Christian ideas. Yet there is no evidence that Aldgisl himself embraced the faith. Instead, he seemed to occupy a middle ground, welcoming foreigners who could benefit him politically or economically, without forcing any broad religious shift on his people. This stance foreshadows the complex interplay between pagan customs and Christian missionaries that would intensify in the decades to come.

---

4. King Redbad: Power, Expansion, and Conflict

4.1 Ascendancy After Aldgisl

Following Aldgisl's reign, the next prominent Frisian king to appear in historical sources is Redbad (sometimes spelled Radbod), who gained power likely in the late 7th century. Redbad is one of the most famous Frisian rulers, remembered for his strong resistance against Frankish encroachment and for his role in shaping Frisian identity during a critical period.

Information about Redbad comes from Frankish annals, missionary writings, and later legends. He is often depicted as a staunch pagan who fiercely opposed Christian missionaries—though the situation was likely more nuanced. His relationship with Christianity was bound up in his broader struggle against Frankish aggression, since the Merovingian kings promoted Christian expansion as part of their realm's influence. For Redbad, rejecting Christianity could be as much about rejecting Frankish dominance as preserving native beliefs.

4.2 Territorial Ambitions and Warfare

Redbad's reign coincided with a resurgence of Frankish power—particularly under the Austrasian mayor of the palace, Pepin of Herstal, and Pepin's successors. While the Merovingian kings still held nominal authority, real power was shifting to the Carolingian "mayors," who sought to unify and expand the Frankish realm. This put Frisia in the crosshairs of a renewed expansionist policy.

Accounts describe multiple clashes between Redbad's forces and Frankish armies. One important conflict reportedly occurred around 689 at the Battle of Dorestad, near the vital trade center by the Rhine delta. Sources say Redbad was defeated, forcing him to retreat northward and temporarily lose control of southern portions of Frisian territory. This was a significant blow, as Dorestad was economically crucial. However, Redbad regrouped. Later references show he continued to wield influence, even staging counterattacks. Some chroniclers mention renewed hostilities into the early 8th century, with Redbad regaining or at least contesting lost ground.

4.3 Diplomacy and Marriage Alliances

Redbad's conflict with the Franks did not mean war was constant. Periodic truces or negotiations occurred, potentially sealed by marriage alliances. Details are scant, but some sources hint that Redbad or members of his family might have married into Frankish aristocracy to secure a temporary peace. Conversely, the Franks may have offered tribute or recognized partial Frisian autonomy in exchange for Redbad's pledge not to raid Frankish lands.

In dealing with other neighbors—such as Saxons or Danes—Redbad may have sought alliances that would strengthen Frisia's position. The same maritime trade networks that Aldgisl fostered remained vital, so maintaining good relations with Anglo-Saxon kingdoms in England could also be helpful. Records of direct contact with English rulers are not abundant, but given that English missionaries (such as Willibrord) traveled through Frisia, it is reasonable to think Redbad had some diplomatic ties to those regions as well—though the dynamic was often complicated by the religious question.

4.4 Redbad's Stance on Christianity

Much of Redbad's legacy in later tradition revolves around his reputed refusal to convert to Christianity. There is a famous (though possibly apocryphal) anecdote in which Redbad stands in a baptismal font, prepared to be baptized by a missionary—only to ask if he would see his ancestors (who were pagan) in heaven. When told no, he stepped out of the font, saying he would rather join his pagan forefathers. While the literal truth of this story is debated, it symbolizes Redbad's reputation as the champion of old Frisian religion against Frankish-backed Christianity.

Historians suggest that Redbad's "anti-Christian" stance was as much political as religious. Conversion to Christianity often went hand in hand with acknowledging Frankish overlordship, since the Merovingians (and soon the Carolingians) promoted the faith. For Redbad, allowing large-scale Christian mission in Frisia might have opened the door to Frankish political influence. By clinging to pagan rites, he affirmed independence. Yet, we also see occasional negotiations between Redbad and Christian bishops like Willibrord, showing that total hostility was not always the case. Redbad might have permitted some missionary work in areas under his control, especially if it served a diplomatic purpose or helped with trade contacts to Christian realms.

4.5 Redbad's Later Campaigns and Death

Around 714, Pepin of Herstal died, causing a power struggle among the Franks. Redbad took advantage of the turmoil to reassert Frisian strength. Some chronicles state that he reconquered lost territory, pushing Frankish influence back beyond the Rhine. This final period of his reign seemed to showcase a Frisian resurgence, though it was not destined to last long after his death.

Redbad died around 719, leaving a power vacuum that the Franks quickly aimed to fill. The Carolingian mayors of the palace, notably Charles Martel, sought to reimpose Frankish dominance over Frisia. Without Redbad's leadership, the Frisians struggled to resist. The defeat at subsequent battles (like the Battle of the Boarn in 734) would seal much of southern Frisia under Frankish control. Still, Redbad's legacy as a strong Frisian king who fiercely resisted outside rule became legendary, influencing the way Frisians remembered their past and their freedoms.

---

5. Society Under the Frisian Kings

5.1 Economic Foundations

Throughout Aldgisl's and Redbad's reigns, trade was the lifeblood of Frisia's economy. The region's strategic position at the mouth of the Rhine, combined with numerous smaller rivers and inlets, created natural hubs for commerce. Archaeological digs at places like Dorestad and other coastal settlements show evidence of bustling markets where merchants could exchange goods with people from far-flung regions.

Key exports included salted fish, textiles (some produced locally), hides, and perhaps slaves captured in raids or bought from inland tribes. Imports ranged from precious metals and wine (from the Frankish or Rhineland regions) to luxury items like glassware or fine weapons. As trade grew, so did the wealth of Frisian elites, who could charge tolls or taxes on goods passing through. This wealth financed the building of defenses and supported the retinues of the kings, giving them leverage in negotiations with rivals.

5.2 Rural Life and Terpen Communities

Away from the busy trading centers, most Frisians lived in small, tight-knit communities. They farmed crops like barley, rye, and wheat where the land allowed, while raising cattle, sheep, and pigs. Fishing and gathering shellfish supplemented diets. Many families lived on terpen (artificial dwelling mounds) to protect themselves from floods, continuing a tradition that stretched back centuries.

Local governance often revolved around assemblies of free men, guided by local chieftains or elders. Even with a recognized king in power, these assemblies had strong influence, especially regarding land disputes, communal flood defenses, or local justice. This culture of local autonomy would persist far beyond the 8th century, shaping later narratives of Frisian "freedom" from feudal overlords.

5.3 Military Organization and Warrior Culture

Under leaders like Aldgisl and Redbad, Frisian warriors defended coastal territories against Frankish invasions and other threats. Weaponry typically included spears, swords, and shields. Helmets and mail armor were less common but might be found among wealthier warriors. Boat warfare played a role too, given Frisia's extensive waterways. Being able to mobilize ships quickly gave the Frisians an advantage in marshy or tidal regions, allowing them to strike or retreat with speed.

Warriors often came from noble or freeman backgrounds. Bonds of loyalty between a king and his war band were cemented through gifts—like fine weapons or jewelry. In return, warriors pledged to fight for the king's cause. Success in battle could enhance a warrior's personal reputation and social standing. Defeats, however, might cause disunity, as local chieftains might withdraw their support if a king failed to protect them or secure victory.

5.4 Art, Craftsmanship, and Cultural Expressions

Frisian artifacts from the 7th and 8th centuries reveal a blend of influences: local Germanic motifs, Frankish and Anglo-Saxon elements, and occasional Roman-Byzantine echoes channeled through trade. Metalworkers produced brooches, belt fittings, and weapon decorations featuring intricate patterns—often geometric designs or animal figures. Glass beads, some locally made and some imported, adorned necklaces. Even simpler communities possessed pottery that fused traditional forms with styles seen across the North Sea world.

Poetic or oral traditions likely flourished, although no direct texts survive from this era. The epic tales of heroes, clan ancestry, and battles would have been recited at gatherings, transmitting values and historical memory. These stories helped consolidate a collective identity, particularly during tense conflicts with the Franks. Ceremonial events—seasonal festivals, rites honoring gods or ancestors—reinforced social bonds and underscored the distinctiveness of Frisian cultural life.

---

6. Relations with the Anglo-Saxon World

6.1 Trade and Cultural Exchange

Frisia had deep connections with Anglo-Saxon England in the 7th and 8th centuries, well before the Norman Conquest of 1066. These connections mostly revolved around trade. Anglo-Saxon kingdoms like Northumbria, Kent, and Mercia had surplus goods—especially woolen textiles and metal goods—that found eager buyers on the continent. Meanwhile, Frisians provided salted fish, hides, and passage across the channels. The routes across the North Sea grew well-traveled, and Frisian merchants became familiar figures in English ports.

This exchange was not just economic. Missionaries, scholars, and travelers crossed the water. Some Anglo-Saxon religious figures came to Frisia, either to evangelize or to pass through en route to missionary efforts deeper in the continent. While Christianization efforts would intensify in the 8th century (as we will see in Chapter Six), the seeds were planted earlier by individual priests or monks moving through Frisian lands, sometimes welcomed by local elites like Aldgisl—if it served political or trade interests.

6.2 Diplomatic Ties and Language Affinities

Anglo-Saxon and Old Frisian languages shared close similarities, both belonging to the North Sea Germanic group. Many everyday words, especially related to seafaring or farming, sounded alike, fostering easier communication than with some other Germanic dialects. This linguistic affinity might have encouraged mutual understanding. Diplomatic ties, though less frequent than with the Franks, could be smoother when envoys could converse without requiring extensive translation.

There are hints that some Anglo-Saxon nobles or exiles might have sought refuge in Frisia under Redbad—similar to how Wilfrid found refuge under Aldgisl. Such cases illustrate that the Frisian court, though not as lavish as a major Frankish palace, was still seen as a viable safe haven. By protecting exiles, Frisian kings gained allies who might repay the favor later. These alliances were part of the broader tapestry of North Sea politics.

6.3 Missionary Ventures from England

Missionaries from England, such as Willibrord, would become major figures in the Christianization of Frisia. While the main thrust of these missions belongs to the 8th-century narrative, it is worth noting that the seeds were sown in Aldgisl's and Redbad's time. The interplay between Anglo-Saxon clergy and Frisian rulers would prove crucial, especially when Frankish military power started pushing religious conversion as well. This mix of religious, political, and cultural factors shaped how Frisians viewed the English realm—both as a source of potential alliances and as a conduit for a religion associated with Frankish power.

---

7. Shifting Boundaries and the Frankish Threat

7.1 The Growing Might of the Carolingians

As mentioned, the Merovingian kings lost real power to the Carolingian mayors of the palace—like Pepin of Herstal, Charles Martel, and later Pepin the Short. These figures transformed the Frankish realm into a more disciplined, expansionist power. Charles Martel's military reforms, including the increased use of cavalry, strengthened the Frankish army. After Redbad's death, Martel focused on bringing

Frisia firmly under Frankish sway, culminating in battles that subdued much of southern Frisia.

By the mid-8th century, the Carolingians had overshadowed the Merovingians entirely. For the Frisians, this meant facing a more unified and determined foe. The Frankish ambition was not just to collect tribute but to fully integrate Frisia into a Christian Frankish kingdom. Subsequent Frisian leaders—none as famous as Redbad—struggled to resist. Eventually, large parts of Frisia came under Frankish control, setting the stage for deeper political and religious changes.

7.2 The Loss of Southern Frisia

Key battles, such as the Battle of the Boarn (in 734), signaled the end of robust Frisian independence in regions south of the major estuaries. Frankish chroniclers claim a decisive victory over Frisian forces, leading to occupation of important coastal trade centers. While some northern districts might have retained a degree of autonomy for a while longer—owing to distance and challenging terrain—the more prosperous southern zones, including Dorestad, fell under direct Frankish oversight.

Frankish administrators, sometimes known as counts, established themselves in these newly conquered territories. They oversaw taxation, upheld Frankish law (or a hybrid system), and supported the efforts of Christian missionaries. Yet, pockets of resistance likely lingered, especially among local elites who had benefited from the independence of earlier Frisian kings. In time, however, the expanding Frankish system exerted strong pressure, chipping away at any residual local defiance.

7.3 Local Autonomy Beyond Frankish Reach

Not all of Frisia succumbed at once. Northernmost areas—parts of what we now call Friesland in the Netherlands, plus portions of East Frisia and beyond—remained outside direct Frankish administration for several more decades. Geography played a role: the wetlands, tidal flats, and barrier islands made it more challenging for Frankish forces to project power. Local communities might pay lip service to Frankish overlords without hosting permanent Frankish garrisons.

In these zones, the memory of figures like Redbad stayed strong, fueling a sense of cultural pride and self-rule. Assemblies maintained local customary law, and families continued old burial rites or pagan traditions away from the watchful eye of Frankish clerics. Yet, over time, missionary efforts pushed north, and each generation saw more assimilation into the growing Carolingian world. By the early 9th century, the entire Frisian coast, in one form or another, had experienced Frankish influence. But in the 7th and 8th centuries, the period of emerging Frisian kings stands out as a significant chapter of relative self-determination.

8. The Lasting Legacy of the Early Frisian Kingdom

8.1 Symbol of Independence

Although the "Frisian kingdom" of Aldgisl and Redbad did not endure beyond the 8th century in a strict political sense, its influence persisted in Frisian collective memory. Later medieval texts, written when Frisia had a looser confederation of districts, pointed back to these kings as symbols of freedom and resistance to foreign domination. Redbad, especially, became a heroic figure in some accounts—a guardian of ancestral ways against an intrusive Frankish empire.

This sense of independence continued to shape Frisian identity into the High Middle Ages, when the region became known for its "Frisian Freedom" charters. While those freedoms were a product of later political developments, they drew on the idea that Frisians had once governed themselves under their own kings. The memory of a self-ruled Frisia, even if the actual kingdom had been modest and short-lived, served as an ideological cornerstone.

8.2 Cultural and Economic Foundations

The 7th and 8th centuries laid the groundwork for Frisia's long history of maritime commerce. Even under later Frankish or Germanic overlords, Frisian merchants and sailors retained a reputation for skill and adaptability. They had pioneered North Sea routes, establishing ties with England, Scandinavia, and the Rhine hinterlands. This tradition would endure and expand, particularly when new market centers rose in the medieval period.

Culturally, the era of the Frisian kingdom strengthened the distinctiveness of the Frisian language and customs. Although Frankish governance would gradually introduce elements of Latin Christian culture, local traditions proved resilient. Over time, these traditions adapted and absorbed Christian influences without losing their core identity. In this sense, the emergent kingdom provided a cohesive platform on which future Frisian society would build.

8.3 Transition into Frankish Rule and Beyond

After Redbad's death, most of Frisia was subsumed, to varying degrees, by the expanding Frankish realm. Frankish nobles appropriated some lands, and missionaries gained official backing to spread Christianity. In the next century, the Carolingian Empire under Charlemagne would reorganize much of Western Europe into new administrative units. Frisia, though part of that broader empire, retained unique local patterns of settlement, water management, and legal traditions.

As we move forward, the story of Frisia becomes intertwined with Frankish politics, Christian missions, and the broader medieval transformations. But the significance of the 7th and 8th centuries remains: this was when Frisia first coalesced under recognizable kings, engaged actively in North Sea trade, and confronted a powerful neighbor on almost equal footing. That memory, whether romanticized or historically precise, fueled a sense of Frisian identity for centuries to come.

CHAPTER 6: RELIGIOUS INFLUENCE AND THE IMPACT OF CHRISTIAN MISSIONS

1. Introduction: Faith and Power

Christian missionaries arrived in Frisian lands at a time when political and cultural currents were shifting. As outlined in Chapter Five, kings like Aldgisl and Redbad had to balance their own traditions against alliances with the Christian Franks. Religion in the early Middle Ages was never a purely spiritual matter—it was interwoven with power structures, diplomacy, and social order. For the Frisians, adopting or resisting Christianity could shape trade relations and alliances; for the Franks, sending missionaries was part of a broader strategy to extend influence.

In this chapter, we focus on the 7th and 8th centuries, when missionary efforts began in earnest. We explore the roles of key figures such as Willibrord and Boniface, how these individuals interacted with Frisian rulers, and the varied responses of local communities. We also examine the practical methods of mission—building churches, performing baptisms, and negotiating with local leaders. Lastly, we look at the broader transformation of Frisian society as Christian beliefs took root, altering legal codes, cultural practices, and ties to the outside world.

2. Pre-Christian Religious Traditions in Frisia

2.1 Pagan Roots

Before Christian missionaries arrived, Frisian spiritual life revolved around a pantheon of Germanic gods, ancestral spirits, and local deities tied to nature. Sacred groves, springs, and bogs played central roles in worship. Communal ceremonies might honor deities linked to fertility, the sea, or war. The specifics remain partly unknown due to the lack of written records, but archaeologists have found ritual deposits—like weapons and jewelry in wetlands—that echo broader Germanic pagan traditions.

Frisians also observed seasonal festivals, aligning with agricultural cycles and maritime rhythms. The community aspect was strong; religion was less about centralized priesthood and more about locally led rites, sometimes guided by a respected elder or seer. This decentralized structure made it hard for missionaries to target a single "high priest." They had to work community by community.

2.2 The Social Fabric of Paganism

Frisian paganism was tightly woven into daily life. People believed in protective spirits for homes, farmland, and seafaring. Offerings might be made for safe voyages or good harvests. Meanwhile, the memory of ancestors was key: the dead were often believed to remain spiritually present, influencing the living. When a powerful family's lineage was honored, it reinforced the family's standing in the community.

Such beliefs supported local hierarchies. A chieftain who claimed descent from a revered line or demonstrated favor from local deities could bolster his authority. In turn, the "public" religious rites associated with that leader could unify the settlement. This system gave a sense of belonging and continuity—something missionaries would eventually challenge by offering a universal faith that transcended local boundaries.

---

3. Early Contacts with Christianity (Before Widespread Missions)

3.1 Roman Echoes and Isolated Christian Traders

Though the Roman Empire never thoroughly Christianized Frisia, Roman traders and soldiers sometimes carried Christian beliefs northward. By the 5th century, a few scattered Christians might have lived or passed through the Frisian coast, but no organized mission took hold. Some Frisians serving as mercenaries in Roman or post-Roman armies could have encountered Christianity, returning home with only fragments of new beliefs.

In the 6th century, as Frankish Gaul became increasingly Christian, merchants and travelers from the south might have mentioned Christian ideas in Frisian markets. Still, these interactions were sporadic. Without consistent preaching, local families likely saw Christianity as a curiosity, tied to foreign powers, rather than a direct challenge to their own rituals.

3.2 Aldgisl and Wilfrid: A Glimpse of Tolerance

A pivotal moment arrived in the late 7th century, when King Aldgisl reportedly offered shelter to Bishop Wilfrid of York (as briefly noted in Chapter Five). Wilfrid had faced political problems in Northumbria and sought refuge across the sea. Aldgisl's willingness to host a Christian bishop hints at pragmatism rather than wholehearted acceptance of the new faith. Perhaps Aldgisl valued Wilfrid's connections to the English Church or saw an opportunity to gain favor with Anglo-Saxon allies.

During Wilfrid's stay, he might have engaged in low-key evangelism, though sources do not mention major conversions. Still, his presence signaled to other church leaders that Frisia was not closed off. If a pagan king could host a Christian bishop without conflict, there might be more room to plant the seeds of faith.

4. Willibrord: Apostle to the Frisians

4.1 Background and Arrival

The most famous early missionary to Frisia is Willibrord, an Anglo-Saxon from Northumbria (or possibly the kingdom of Lindsey) who became a leader of the mission to the Frisian people. He arrived around the late 7th century, first under the auspices of the Frankish leader Pepin of Herstal, who wanted to expand both Frankish political power and Christianity in the region. Willibrord's mission aligned with Pepin's goals, offering a spiritual justification for Frankish influence.

In 690, Willibrord traveled to Rome to receive papal support. Pope Sergius I consecrated him as archbishop for the Frisians (the see of "Archbishop of the Frisian people," sometimes identified with Utrecht). Armed with papal approval, Willibrord returned to Frisia, determined to establish a network of churches and convert local leaders. His approach combined diplomacy with devout zeal, often seeking the support of powerful chieftains or kings—if that meant acknowledging Frankish overlordship as well.

4.2 Conflicts with King Redbad

When Willibrord arrived, King Redbad was still the dominant Frisian ruler, and he was deeply suspicious of Frankish-driven Christianity. The two men clashed. Some stories recount how Redbad expelled Willibrord's group from certain territories and destroyed Christian sites. Willibrord's own letters (or those attributed to him in hagiographies) reference repeated setbacks. Yet, the mission persisted, especially in southern Frisia, where Frankish military victories ensured some measure of protection for Willibrord's activities.

In areas where the Franks had established control—like around Dorestad—Willibrord founded small churches and baptized local converts, often those who benefited from Frankish trade ties. He also tried to convert people in Redbad's domain, though with limited success. Redbad's opposition meant that pagan traditions continued to flourish, and missionaries had to tread carefully. The result was a patchwork of Christian enclaves in the south and pagan strongholds in regions more firmly under Redbad's grip.

4.3 Establishing Ecclesiastical Centers

Despite the challenges, Willibrord managed to set up lasting Christian institutions. One such center was in Utrecht, near the old Roman fortress of Traiectum. Protected by Frankish arms, Utrecht became a base for missionary work, with priests fanning out to preach in surrounding villages. Over time, the mission gained enough stability to build simple wooden churches, train local converts as clergy, and celebrate Christian festivals.

This structure was still fragile. If local support waned or if a pagan uprising occurred, Christian sites could be destroyed. Yet, each time they rebuilt, the missionaries reinforced their presence. By forging ties with aristocratic families who had something to gain from alliance with the Franks, Willibrord cultivated supporters. These families might convert partly out of genuine belief, partly out of political advantage. In return, Willibrord provided them with a link to the broader Christian world—a valuable network in an age of expanding trade and shifting power blocs.

4.4 Willibrord's Broader Influence

Willibrord's mission to the Frisians also extended beyond Frisia itself. He led outreach to neighboring peoples, sometimes accompanying Frankish expeditions. He is credited with playing a key role in the early Christianization of parts of present-day Holland, as well as missions into Denmark (briefly) at the request of Frankish rulers. His life became a model for later missionaries like Boniface, who admired Willibrord's perseverance in hostile lands.

In the early 8th century, Willibrord was an elder statesman of the missionary movement. Though Redbad's resistance thwarted a full Christian takeover of Frisia during Willibrord's prime, the region's southern territories had a growing Christian minority. When Redbad died, conditions for the mission improved. Willibrord lived long enough to see the Carolingians tighten their grip on Frisia, paving the way for more stable church structures. He died around 739, leaving behind a network of small Christian communities, many of which would remain focal points of ecclesiastical activity for centuries.

5. Boniface and the Deepening of Christian Influence

5.1 Boniface's Background and First Steps

Following in Willibrord's footsteps came Boniface (originally named Wynfrith), another Anglo-Saxon missionary determined to bring the gospel to Germanic peoples. Born in Wessex (southern England), Boniface had a strong clerical education and initially worked in his home region. Yearning to spread Christianity on the continent, he arrived in Frisia in the early 8th century, around 716, possibly while Redbad was still alive. At first, he assisted Willibrord but soon traveled elsewhere in Germanic lands (such as Hesse and Thuringia), coming back to Frisia only after Redbad's death.

5.2 Return to Frisia and Confrontation with Pagan Traditions

With Redbad gone, and the Frankish mayor Charles Martel (and later his sons) consolidating rule over much of Frisia, Boniface found a more favorable climate for missionary work. By the mid-720s, parts of southern and central Frisia were under Frankish governance, making it easier for Boniface to preach without fear of immediate expulsion. Pagan practices still flourished, however, especially in rural areas.

Boniface was known for direct actions against pagan symbols—stories recount him cutting down sacred trees in other Germanic regions to demonstrate the powerlessness of pagan gods. In Frisia, he may have employed similar tactics, though direct references are fewer. Even so, he urged new converts to abandon old rites, burn ritual objects, and accept Christian sacraments. Such moves provoked resistance from some locals who saw these acts as insults to ancestral deities. Yet under Frankish protection, Boniface could push forward, establishing churches and appointing priests across the territory.

5.3 Ecclesiastical Foundations and Synods

Boniface not only converted people but also organized church governance. A well-structured church hierarchy was vital for ensuring that conversions would endure after a missionary left. By working closely with Frankish officials, Boniface set up diocesan boundaries that overlapped with Frankish administrative units. Utrecht, started by Willibrord, became one such important bishopric. Boniface also influenced how newly converted communities handled Christian teachings, encouraging them to adopt standardized practices aligned with Rome.

Synods (church councils) were held to establish rules on doctrine and discipline. Boniface insisted on uniform liturgical practices, correct biblical teaching, and the proper ordination of priests. Although these details might sound minor, they were central to unifying the church in a region once dominated by diverse pagan beliefs. By shaping the clergy and ensuring their loyalty to the wider Christian hierarchy, Boniface made the church in Frisia more robust.

5.4 Martyrdom at Dokkum (754)

Tragically, Boniface's missionary career ended in violence. In 754, while traveling to northern Frisia (an area still resistant to Christianity), he and his companions were attacked near Dokkum. Sources differ on whether the killers were pagan Frisians outraged by his efforts or simply robbers seeking booty. Hagiographical accounts frame it as a martyrdom for the faith—Boniface trying to protect sacred texts and receiving a martyr's death at the hands of pagans. In any case, his death became legendary within Christian Europe, inspiring future generations of missionaries.

For Frisians, the memory of Boniface's death was complex. Some might have seen him as an intruder linked to the Frankish empire. Others, who had converted, viewed him as a heroic figure of the Church. Over time, local Christian communities honored him with chapels and stories, weaving him into the region's religious tapestry. His martyrdom also reinforced Frankish resolve to stamp out lingering paganism in Frisia, intensifying military and ecclesiastical pressure.

6. Strategies and Methods of Conversion

6.1 Building Churches and Monasteries

One of the most practical missionary strategies was establishing permanent structures where new converts could gather. Churches, often built of wood at first, acted as visible symbols of the Christian faith. Monasteries, though fewer in early Frisia, served as centers of learning, scribal activity, and agricultural innovation. Missionaries trained local men as priests or monks, who would then continue preaching in their native language.

Over time, some important church sites transitioned from wooden chapels to more robust stone buildings as resources allowed. These sites often stood near or even atop former pagan sacred places, a symbolic move to claim spiritual authority. While this practice angered some traditionalists, it eased the transition for many locals, who found it more natural to gather for worship where they had previously performed rituals.

6.2 Adapting Pagan Customs

Christian missionaries in Frisia recognized they could not uproot long-standing traditions overnight. Instead, they often adapted or reinterpreted certain elements of pagan culture. Festivals tied to seasonal cycles might be replaced or absorbed by Christian feasts. Ancient holy days were timed to coincide with saints' feasts. The veneration of local holy sites sometimes continued, but with a new Christian context—placing crosses or dedicating altars to saints.

Such adaptation was a pragmatic way to minimize friction. However, strict missionaries like Boniface criticized overindulgence in "pagan superstitions." They urged local Christians to abandon all old customs, but in practice, many communities kept vestiges that blended the new faith with local heritage. This process of syncretism is common in missionary histories worldwide and helps explain why Christianity in Frisia developed unique local flavors.

6.3 Fostering Elite Support

Converting high-status families was a key missionary tactic. If a local chieftain or noble agreed to be baptized, his household and dependents often followed. Christian missionaries might offer political alliances with the Franks to sweeten the deal. Acceptance of baptism thus carried potential rewards, from trade benefits to military backing. Still, some elites remained hesitant, fearing they would lose authority if they abandoned the old gods venerated by the community.

Those who did convert often gained new prestige—aligning themselves with the expanding Frankish realm and the powerful institution of the Church. They might receive gifts from Frankish leaders, such as land or relics, enhancing their status. Consequently, the spread of Christianity sometimes mirrored the spread of Frankish hegemony, blurring the lines between sincere religious conviction and political opportunism.

---

7. The Changing Face of Frisian Society

7.1 New Religious Hierarchies

As Christianity took hold, Frisian communities saw the rise of local priests, some of whom were of Frisian descent. These priests worked under bishops like Willibrord or his successors. Gradually, churchmen became mediators in disputes, guardians of moral codes, and organizers of festivals. Over the 8th century, the Church gained wealth through donations of land or treasure, accumulating a form of authority separate from traditional chieftains.

This new religious hierarchy interacted with the secular leadership that recognized Frankish overlords. Sometimes the lines overlapped, with a local count or noble also playing a role in church affairs. Other times, conflicts arose—especially if a bishop demanded behaviors that clashed with local customs. Yet, in the broad view, the presence of a structured church contributed to a more uniform set of moral and legal standards in regions that once had varied pagan practices.

7.2 Shift in Legal Practices

Christianization brought changes in Frisian law. While older Germanic legal customs continued (including wergild systems and local assemblies), new regulations emerged concerning marriage, inheritance, and oaths. The Church insisted on monogamous unions sanctioned by Christian rites, challenging polygamy or informal unions. Clerics also promoted the sanctity of church property and pressed for Sunday observance, limiting trade or labor on that day.

Over time, Frankish rulers codified these influences in law codes applied to Frisian territories. Some older laws remained, but the Christian moral framework now underpinned many regulations. For instance, while older laws might have permitted vengeance killings or trial by ordeal, the Church increasingly discouraged such practices, advocating penance or ecclesiastical oversight of disputes. The shift was gradual—full transformation would take centuries—but the seeds were planted in this early period of mission activity.

7.3 Cultural Integration and Resistance

As more Frisian communities converted, local artwork, jewelry, and burial customs evolved. Christian symbols—cross pendants, inscriptions of saints' names—began appearing alongside or replacing older pagan motifs. Graves with Christian markers might omit grave goods that had once been essential for the afterlife. Meanwhile, many families still chose to bury their dead in the old style, either openly rejecting Christian doctrines or blending them with longstanding traditions.

Open resistance flared occasionally, especially after Boniface's martyrdom. Some northern districts remained staunchly pagan, resisting the Church as a tool of Frankish control. But as the Carolingian state grew stronger under Pepin the Short and Charlemagne (late 8th and early 9th centuries), open rebellion became riskier. Gradually, pockets of pagan resistance diminished or went underground, overshadowed by the new Christian norms.

8. Missionaries and the Frankish State: A Two-Edged Sword

8.1 Christianization as a Political Tool

For the Carolingians, spreading Christianity was never purely about religion. It was also a means of extending political reach. By supporting missionaries, Frankish leaders legitimized their rule in the eyes of the Church, which in turn crowned and anointed Frankish kings. For Frisians, accepting baptism often implied loyalty to the Carolingian empire. This linkage caused many to view Christian missions with suspicion—were they simply preludes to foreign domination?

On the other hand, some Frisian elites found advantage in aligning with the Frankish state. Conversion could bring military alliances, trade privileges, and acceptance in the broader Christian community of Western Europe. These benefits were especially attractive for coastal leaders who depended on cross-channel commerce. They realized that remaining staunchly pagan might cut them off from profitable ties with neighboring Christian realms.

8.2 The Ebb and Flow of Resistance

Despite these incentives, resistance persisted. Even after Boniface's death, occasional uprisings targeted churches or Frankish outposts. Some local leaders invoked memories of Redbad, framing Christian infiltration as an attack on Frisian identity. Since the sea and marshes provided natural defenses, smaller communities could hold out, at least until a major Frankish campaign forced submission.

Yet, the overall trend by the late 8th century was toward accommodation. Steady Frankish military pressure, combined with economic interdependence, eroded large-scale pagan resistance. Many younger Frisians grew up in communities with at least nominal Christian presence, so the older religious ways lost traction over generations. By the dawn of the 9th century, open defiance of Christianity was increasingly rare, even if remnants of pagan customs lingered in local festivals or folk practices.

9. Outcomes and Long-Term Effects

9.1 Firm Establishment of the Church

By the end of the 8th century, Christianity had established a firm base in Frisia, particularly in the formerly wealthy trade centers along the southern coast and major river valleys. Monasteries, such as those built by Willibrord and his successors, became repositories of learning and cultural exchange. Bishops in Utrecht or other emerging dioceses served as spiritual and administrative leaders, connected to the Carolingian empire's broader ecclesiastical structure.

Though pockets of pagan tradition survived, the official stance of Frisian territories under Frankish control was now decidedly Christian. This shift had profound consequences for local governance, law, and social norms. Over the next centuries, the Church would further shape Frisian identity, integrating local culture into a wider Christian context. Some aspects of older customs would adapt into Christian practice (such as harvest festivals reinterpreted as saints' days), while others faded away.

9.2 Integration into the Carolingian World

As Frisia grew more Christian, it also became more integrated into the Carolingian empire politically. Frankish counts governed large tracts of Frisian land, collecting taxes and enforcing Carolingian decrees. This integration pulled Frisian nobles into the empire's feudal networks—though "feudalism" was still in a formative stage. Royal charters mention Frisian lands, acknowledging their unique water management challenges and maritime traditions.

For ordinary Frisians, these changes meant greater involvement in the empire's markets, as well as new obligations like tithes to the Church. The increased centralization might have been unpopular, especially when it conflicted with local assemblies that prized older traditions of self-rule. Nonetheless, the new order was a reality that the majority eventually accepted or found ways to navigate.

9.3 Enduring Local Traditions

Despite official Christianization and Frankish rule, many distinct Frisian practices persisted. Terpen-dwelling communities kept cooperating on flood defenses. Local dialects continued to develop into what we recognize as Old Frisian, preserving unique legal vocabulary. Even in Christian times, communal assemblies had strong voices, a tradition that contributed to later claims of "Frisian freedom." Pagan beliefs morphed into folklore or folk customs, sometimes quietly blended with saint veneration.

As a result, when one speaks of a fully "Christian" Frisia in the 9th century, it means official structures and public ceremonies conformed to Church norms, but everyday life still had a distinctive coastal flavor shaped by centuries of adaptation. The missionaries' success was real, but it coexisted with an enduring sense of local identity that did not vanish under the cross.

10. Conclusion

In the 7th and 8th centuries, Christian missionaries—most notably Willibrord and Boniface—brought a new faith into the Frisian lands. Their efforts took place in the wider context of Frankish expansion, making the Christian mission both a spiritual venture and a political tool. While powerful Frisian rulers like Redbad resisted, eventually the combination of missionary persistence and Carolingian pressure ensured that large parts of Frisia accepted the new religion.

This transformation altered Frisian society from the inside out, changing rituals, laws, and alliances. Church centers arose, elites benefited from connections to Frankish power, and younger generations grew up in an environment where Christianity was increasingly the norm. Yet, the process was never simple or one-sided. Resistance, syncretism, and local adaptations marked the path of conversion, leading to a distinctive blend of faith and cultural tradition.

The story of Christianization sets the stage for the next phase of Frisian history. In the wake of Boniface's martyrdom and the ongoing Carolingian integration, the 8th and 9th centuries would bring new pressures—both from within and beyond the empire. **Chapter Seven** will examine the **shifts in power and early medieval challenges** that arose as Frisia became more enmeshed in the Frankish realm, contended with Viking incursions, and faced social as well as economic transitions. Through it all, Frisia's coastal heritage and strong local identity continued to play a defining role.

CHAPTER 7: SHIFTS IN POWER AND EARLY MEDIEVAL CHALLENGES

1. Introduction: Frisia Under Changing Rule

In the previous chapters, we saw how Frisia evolved into a distinct coastal region, developed early kingship under figures like Aldgisl and Redbad, and then became increasingly drawn into the orbit of the Frankish realm. By the mid-8th century, the Carolingians were on the rise, gradually replacing the Merovingians as the dominant royal family in the Frankish kingdom. Their consolidation of power meant that Frisia, once fiercely independent under native kings, was now part of a larger imperial system. In this chapter, we explore the implications of that shift during the 8th and early 9th centuries.

The period saw dramatic changes in leadership, law, and society. With the disappearance of the Frisian "kingdom" in the south, the Carolingian dynasty and its officials set about reshaping local governance. Meanwhile, Christianity continued to expand, transforming cultural practices and social norms. Yet, despite this assimilation, many coastal communities preserved traditional structures that gave them a measure of local control. As we will see, new threats—and opportunities—emerged in this era, laying the groundwork for how Frisians would respond to challenges in the 9th century and beyond.

In examining these changes, we will look at the role of Carolingian administrators, the shifting status of local elites, the function of Church institutions, and the economic patterns that sustained Frisian trade networks. We will also see how local assemblies, traditions of dike building, and communal decision-making continued despite foreign oversight. This tension between central authority and local autonomy is a recurring theme throughout Frisian history, and it is particularly visible in the 8th and early 9th centuries.

2. Carolingian Consolidation and Frisia's Position

2.1 The Rise of the Carolingians

By the late 7th and early 8th centuries, the Carolingian family, initially holding the office of "mayor of the palace," had risen to real power in the Frankish kingdom. Pepin of Herstal, Charles Martel, and Pepin the Short each strengthened Carolingian authority by defeating rivals and expanding into peripheral regions. Their successes prepared the way for the most famous Carolingian ruler, Charlemagne (Charles the Great), crowned Emperor in 800.

Under Charles Martel and his successors, the Frisians faced a more direct push to become integrated into the Frankish realm. Repeated conflicts with the last independent Frisian king, Redbad, ended with the Franks taking over key southern Frisian areas. Following Redbad's death (c. 719), there was no single Frisian monarch capable of mounting united resistance across all coastal territories. This paved the way for the Carolingians to consolidate their hold, especially over the trade-rich regions near the Rhine delta.

2.2 Administrative Reach Into Frisian Lands

As the Carolingians expanded north, they established or reinforced existing centers of governance. Frankish counts and other officials took charge of regions that had once acknowledged their own local chieftains or kings. These counts—representing Carolingian royalty—were responsible for collecting taxes, enforcing royal decrees, and supporting the Church. Some were Frankish nobles, while others could be local elites who found it advantageous to work with the new regime.

Over time, these administrative appointees built small fortifications or utilized older Roman/early medieval sites near critical waterways, ensuring they could oversee trade routes. Notably, Dorestad, once a vibrant Frisian trade hub, became directly supervised by Frankish authorities who wanted to protect and tax commerce there. Such supervision was essential to the Carolingian economy: controlling the flow of goods brought revenue and influence.

2.3 Impact on Coastal Autonomy

The deeper the Carolingians penetrated into Frisia, the more local autonomy was eroded, at least in an official sense. Formerly independent chieftains and local assemblies faced new expectations—tribute or taxes for the Carolingian treasury, support for Frankish military campaigns, and adherence to Christian norms. Some local leaders adapted, gaining rank in the Carolingian system and preserving a portion of their power. Others resisted, either passively or through sporadic uprisings that ultimately were suppressed by Frankish armies.

Yet, geographical obstacles limited complete assimilation. The northernmost coastal and island communities were distant from central administrative centers, making it harder for Carolingian officials to impose strict oversight. These areas often continued to govern themselves through assemblies, acknowledging the Carolingians in name but retaining day-to-day freedom. Thus, Frisia in the 8th century was not a single unified zone under the Carolingians; it was a mosaic of regions, some tightly governed and others left semi-autonomous.

---

3. The Role of Charlemagne and His Policies

3.1 Frisia in the Carolingian Empire

When Charlemagne became sole ruler of the Franks in the late 8th century, he undertook grand campaigns to consolidate and expand the empire's borders—most famously against the Saxons to the east. While Frisia was not his primary battlefield, it had strategic importance: it offered key maritime connections and potential resources. Charlemagne reinforced the administrative framework his predecessors established, sending missi dominici—envoys of the king—to inspect local regions, including Frisian territories.

These royal envoys checked whether local officials adhered to Carolingian edicts, monitored compliance with Christian practice, and handled major legal disputes. They served as the "eyes and ears" of the emperor. In the process, they brought Frisia more firmly into Carolingian governance. Their presence gave Frisian communities a direct link to the imperial court—though local assemblies might have viewed them with caution, seeing them as instruments of central control.

3.2 Christianization and Education

Charlemagne also championed Church reform and education. His royal court attracted scholars like Alcuin of York, who promoted learning across the empire. The emperor encouraged the founding of monastic schools and scriptoria, where texts (often religious) were copied and studied. In Frisia, older missionary stations and newly established church centers benefited from this push: priests were better trained, and liturgical standards became more uniform.

While the main impetus was religious, there were political benefits. A well-organized clergy that reported ultimately to the emperor strengthened imperial unity. In Frisian areas, newly literate local priests could record property transactions, maintain records, and preach loyalty to the Carolingian order. Over time, the deeper spread of literacy—limited though it was—helped integrate Frisia more tightly into the cultural sphere of the empire.

3.3 The Economy Under Charlemagne

Under Charlemagne, markets and trade remained vital, and the emperor had a vested interest in ensuring stability in commerce. For Frisia, maritime trade had always been a mainstay, connecting the North Sea coast to England and the Rhineland. Charlemagne's rule, despite occasional warfare, ushered in a period of relative stability that could foster economic growth. Dorestad, although it would later decline, reached a peak of prosperity during the early Carolingian era.

Archaeological finds from sites in the central Dutch river area confirm an influx of foreign goods—pottery from the Rhine region, glassware from Francia, and textiles possibly from England—pointing to robust exchange. Frisian merchants, known for their seafaring expertise, maintained networks that reached across the North Sea and even into the Baltic. Royal oversight brought new taxes and tariffs, but also some protection against piracy. For local traders, the cost might have been worthwhile if it ensured safer routes and stable markets.

3.4 Legal Adjustments

Charlemagne's empire was known for attempting to codify local laws. He recognized that different peoples under his rule had distinct legal traditions. For Frisia, there existed a body of customary law—often transmitted orally—that the Carolingians sought to record and harmonize with Christian norms. This process did not erase Frisian legal practices overnight but gradually merged them with broader Frankish principles.

One significant shift was the diminishing role of purely pagan-based traditions. For instance, oaths might now be sworn on Christian relics rather than by invoking local gods or spirits. Blood feuds were discouraged, replaced by formal court procedures or wergild (monetary compensation) overseen by count and bishop. The transformation was slow, and older customs persisted in remote areas, but official documents from the 8th and 9th centuries show how Carolingian rule slowly molded Frisian jurisprudence to align with the imperial framework.

---

4. Local Governance and the Persistence of Assemblies

4.1 The Structure of Local Power

Even as Carolingian might loomed large, many Frisian communities retained local assemblies. These gatherings, composed of free men (and, in rarer cases, influential women), addressed disputes, allocated farmland, and organized communal flood defenses. Such assemblies had deep roots in Frisian tradition, dating back to prehistoric and early medieval times. Their continued function helped maintain a sense of local identity and autonomy.

When a Carolingian count or official demanded taxes, the assembly discussed how to meet those demands or whether to negotiate. Although open defiance was risky, assemblies could sometimes slow or alter the process of centralization by raising local concerns. Some records mention friction between Carolingian counts and local notables, illustrating how these assemblies acted as checks on external authority.

4.2 Communal Water Management

Frisia's coastal environment—defined by tidal flats, wetlands, and the ever-present threat of storm floods—required large-scale cooperation in water management. Terpen (artificial mounds) had been used for centuries, but as population grew and farmland expanded, Frisians increasingly relied on dikes and drainage systems.

Constructing and maintaining these defenses required communal labor, decided and organized at the local level.

While Carolingian officials recognized the importance of these structures (since flooding disrupted economic activity), they rarely micro-managed them. Thus, local assemblies kept the initiative, assigning labor obligations and resources for dike repairs. Over time, this collective water management culture reinforced communal bonds and a sense of shared responsibility. Even as they became part of the empire, Frisians took pride in their self-sufficient approach to holding back the sea.

4.3 Tensions Between Local Leaders and Frankish Counts

In areas closer to the Rhine, Frankish counts wielded more direct power, controlling markets and collecting tolls. Local chieftains might resent losing influence, especially if they had once governed trade routes or local jurisprudence. Some found ways to collaborate—receiving official titles or marrying into Frankish aristocracy—while others harbored grievances that could lead to localized unrest.

Documents from Charlemagne's reign reference legal conflicts in Frisian districts, where local leaders resisted or disputed Frankish tax claims. Although these are not full-scale rebellions like the Saxon Wars, they hint at an undercurrent of tension. Over the 8th and early 9th centuries, a pattern emerged in which local elites balanced cooperation with the empire against preserving some measure of authority. This dynamic set the stage for the evolving identity of Frisia under imperial rule: officially loyal, but often fiercely protective of traditional rights.

---

5. The Evolution of the Frisian Church

5.1 From Mission Stations to Parish Networks

Earlier chapters described how missionaries like Willibrord and Boniface laid the foundations of Christianity in Frisia. By the 8th century's middle decades, many southern and central Frisian areas had churches or chapels, served by priests who were often Frisians themselves. Over time, these scattered mission stations evolved into a more organized parish system. Bishops (especially the Bishop of

Utrecht) oversaw multiple parishes, and local priests performed baptisms, taught basic doctrine, and officiated at weddings.

In many villages, the church stood near or on a former pagan sacred site—helping the new faith take root in a place already significant to the community. Parish life revolved around the liturgical calendar, introducing feast days that replaced older seasonal festivals. While this transition was not always seamless, the presence of regular church services and clergy underscored the shift away from older beliefs toward a Christian worldview aligned with the Carolingian empire.

5.2 Monasteries and Cultural Influence

Although Frisia was not filled with large monastic complexes like some areas of Gaul or Germany, a few monasteries and convents sprang up. These institutions provided religious education, served as safe havens for pilgrims, and engaged in farming or craft production. Some were founded with royal charters, granting them land and privileges to ensure their sustainability. In this way, monasteries contributed to local economies, producing surplus goods and occasionally offering shelter to travelers or the poor.

They also became centers of writing and learning. Monks copied religious texts, sometimes adding local notes or annotations that give glimpses into Frisian society. While Latin was the primary language of the Church, Old Frisian words occasionally appear in documents dealing with landholdings or local customs. This small corpus of written materials, though limited, helps historians piece together how Christianity coexisted with local tradition.

5.3 Syncretic Practices and Residual Pagan Customs

Despite the Church's growth, many Frisians held onto customs with pagan origins, especially in remote or northern regions. Archaeological evidence suggests that grave goods sometimes appeared alongside Christian burials, indicating families still valued older beliefs. Folk celebrations might feature blessings over fields that blurred the line between Christian ritual and ancient fertility rites.

Clergy often tried to stamp out these remnants. Carolingian capitularies (royal decrees) show repeated efforts to ban pagan sacrifices, divination, or worship of trees and springs. Yet the persistence of such customs implies that local people found meaning in them. Over time, some of these practices were adapted or given Christian interpretations. Saints replaced old gods as protectors of farms or fishermen, and church festivals coincided with earlier agrarian feasts. As a result, Frisian Christianity in the 8th and 9th centuries was a patchwork of official doctrine and local tradition.

---

6. Economic Life in Early Medieval Frisia

6.1 Maritime Commerce and Coastal Hubs

Throughout the 8th century, Frisia remained a center of maritime exchange. Traders shipped goods along rivers like the Rhine, IJssel, and Meuse, linking inland regions to the North Sea. In turn, Frisian boats traveled to ports in England and Scandinavia. At its height, Dorestad was the most prominent emporium, bustling with merchants who handled furs, slaves, grain, wine, and luxury items such as glass and jewelry. This trade network supported a wealthy merchant class, which sometimes worked hand in hand with Frankish counts.

However, commerce faced challenges: storms could destroy ships, river siltation shifted trade routes, and occasional warfare disrupted markets. Rulers like Charlemagne tried to maintain safe conditions, since trade enriched the imperial treasury through tolls. Archeological layers in trading centers from this period often show imported pottery and coin hoards, indicating vibrant exchanges. The presence of Arabic coins (dirhams) in some Frisian finds hints that long-distance trade networks extended far beyond the immediate region.

6.2 Agricultural Patterns

Outside the trading towns, most Frisians were farmers, raising cereals, vegetables, and livestock. The coastal environment offered fertile soils—once drained and protected from floods—leading to decent yields. Communities often practiced mixed farming: some fields dedicated to grain, others for pasturage. Cattle remained an essential resource, not only as food but for hides, an export that had been historically important for Frisian communities (as mentioned in earlier chapters).

Under Carolingian influence, improvements in plow technology or field organization may have spread, although direct evidence in Frisia is sparse. Some historians theorize that larger landholdings formed around monasteries or noble families with ties to the imperial court. If so, local peasants would either rent land or owe labor to these estates. Yet, many smaller freeholders probably existed as well, preserving a measure of personal autonomy in a land where communal water management was still paramount.

6.3 Coinage and Markets

Carolingian rulers issued standardized coinage (often silver deniers), aiming to unify trade across the empire. Frisia, with its strong commercial tradition, became a zone where these coins circulated widely. Before Carolingian unification, older Merovingian and Frisian currency (including sceattas) had been used, but standard Carolingian deniers gradually dominated. This shift helped unify markets but also increased the empire's control over currency production and distribution.

Markets grew around churches or fortifications, hosting weekly fairs or seasonal trade gatherings. Even small villages might have occasional market days where farmers sold surplus produce. The presence of coins facilitated more complex transactions, gradually reducing the need for barter. While rural areas might still rely on exchange in kind (grain for fish, for instance), money-based trade was expanding, an indication of deeper economic integration under the Carolingian system.

7. Social Structures and Stratification

7.1 Nobles, Freemen, and Serfs

As Frisia adapted to Carolingian norms, social stratification became more apparent. Local elites who cooperated with Frankish counts solidified their status as nobles, holding lands under imperial grants. Freemen—small landholders and free peasants—continued to farm and participate in assemblies. Meanwhile, a portion of the population sank into serfdom or semi-servile status, especially on estates owned by the Church or powerful nobles.

Serfs were bound to the land, obligated to provide labor or produce to their lords. In the coastal environment, however, the communal nature of dike building sometimes blurred strict hierarchies. Even a powerful noble needed cooperation from serfs and freemen to maintain defenses. This dynamic may have prevented the development of an extreme feudal system in some Frisian zones, preserving elements of collective decision-making that were less common in other parts of the empire.

7.2 The Role of Women

Women's status varied according to class and local custom. Elite women—noble wives, widows, or abbesses—could hold land and wield substantial influence. Some became patrons of churches, donating property to monasteries in exchange for spiritual benefits. Carolingian law codes recognized women's rights in areas like inheritance and dower lands, though these rights remained subordinate to male guardianship in most cases.

In peasant communities, women contributed labor to farming, weaving, and household management. They might also participate in local religious festivities or assist in rudimentary healing practices passed down through families. Conversion to Christianity affected women's roles; for instance, church law discouraged pagan fertility rituals sometimes led by women. Still, the old traditions likely persisted in some households, especially where formal ecclesiastical oversight was minimal.

7.3 Slavery and the Slave Trade

Slavery existed in Frisia, though on a smaller scale than in large Mediterranean societies. Captives from wars or raids could be sold, and the North Sea trade included slaves among other commodities. Slaves might work on farms or in wealthy households, but the fluid nature of Frisian society allowed some slaves to gain freedom over time. Christian teaching also played a role: while the Church did not outright ban slavery, it promoted manumission (especially if it happened under a pious rationale).

Dorestad and other trading centers were known to handle slaves as part of broader commerce, connecting them to networks that reached the British Isles and beyond. The Carolingian state, eager to regulate this trade, might tax slave sales. Over the 9th century, however, changing political conditions and growing ecclesiastical pressure began to shift attitudes on slavery. Despite these shifts, the practice did not vanish overnight, remaining a reality in many coastal regions well into later medieval periods.

8. After Charlemagne: The Early 9th Century Landscape

8.1 Division of the Empire

Charlemagne's death in 814 marked the start of a more turbulent era. His son, Louis the Pious, inherited a vast empire that soon became riddled with internal conflicts, rebellions, and power struggles among the emperor's sons. For Frisia, these disputes sometimes meant abrupt changes in oversight. Counts loyal to one faction might fight counts loyal to another, disrupting local governance. Royal authority, once strongly centralized, began to wane, especially in outlying regions like Frisia.

Meanwhile, local elites exploited the weakening of imperial structures to reassert older autonomies. Some assemblies refused new tax demands if they suspected one Carolingian prince was at war with another. Bishops and monasteries might shift loyalties to whichever ruler seemed likely to grant privileges. This environment allowed a partial resurgence of local self-rule, though not in the form of a restored Frisian kingdom as in Redbad's time. Instead, it was more a patchwork of local power vacuums and opportunistic alliances.

8.2 Continuing Christian Influence

Despite the political uncertainty, the Church remained a stabilizing force. By now, many Frisian communities had well-established parishes, and monastic institutions were recognized landholders. Even if counts changed or royal decrees shifted, the religious calendar and local clerical structures continued. This consistency gave the Church an influential position in local affairs. Priests and bishops often mediated between fractious nobility or carried messages between rival Carolingian claimants.

At the same time, some local pagan customs still survived in pockets, especially in more remote areas. Missionary texts from the early 9th century occasionally mention "pagan superstitions" among the coastal folk, suggesting that the Christianization process was not fully uniform. Nevertheless, official support for Christianity was never stronger: each Carolingian prince, seeking legitimacy, portrayed himself as defender of the Church, thereby encouraging deeper religious integration.

8.3 Trade Shifts and the Decline of Dorestad

By the early 9th century, Dorestad began to decline for a combination of reasons: silting in the rivers changed navigational routes, shifting trade patterns; internal Carolingian power struggles caused instability; and new external threats (which we will discuss in Chapter Eight) disrupted shipping. As Dorestad's prominence faded, other ports and emporia rose, sometimes further north or along different river mouths. This shift altered the economic focus of Frisia, dispersing trade across multiple smaller hubs rather than one dominant center.

Merchants adapted by seeking alternative markets, possibly dealing with new partners in the British Isles or Scandinavia. Some historians note that Frisian traders appear in documents from towns like Quentovic in northern Gaul, or even from emerging Scandinavian emporia like Hedeby. The result was a more decentralized commercial landscape, which might have reinforced local independence. Counts had a harder time controlling a single major trade hub if commerce was scattered among many smaller ports.

---

9. Seeds of Future Challenges

9.1 The Looming Viking Raids

While not yet at full force in the early 9th century, Viking activity from Scandinavia was already a concern along Europe's coasts. Occasional raiding parties tested defenses in the British Isles and along the Frankish shore. Frisia, with its maritime networks and relative wealth, lay within easy reach of Viking ships. Although large-scale attacks were not yet commonplace in the early 9th century, small raids hinted at a growing menace. Coastal communities began to hear stories of Viking incursions, which would become a major disruptive force by the mid-9th century.

Aware of these dangers, Carolingian rulers sometimes ordered fortifications at river mouths or around key towns. Yet political fragmentation often meant such directives were inconsistently followed. Frisia's scattered settlement pattern—combined with dependence on water routes—made it vulnerable. Soon, local leaders would have to organize their own defenses or bargain with Viking bands. These pressures would reshape Frisian society in ways we will detail in the next chapter.

9.2 Erosion of Central Authority

As the Carolingian dynasty moved toward fragmentation—culminating in the Treaty of Verdun (843)—the once-unified empire split into separate kingdoms. Frisia became part of the middle section (Lotharingia) or the eastern section (East Francia) depending on the exact boundaries drawn by each settlement among Louis the Pious's heirs. Shifting allegiances at the top level made consistent governance of far-flung regions difficult. In the short term, local counts gained more freedom, and certain Frisian districts leveraged this to claim privileges or reduce obligations.

The church in Frisia also navigated a tricky path. Bishops remained nominally loyal to whichever Carolingian branch held sway, but they had to manage local powerbrokers who might or might not respect a distant king's authority. Records mention pleas for help against raiders, or for confirmation of church land rights, sent to kings in far-off palaces who had limited means to enforce decisions. The stage was set for a more turbulent 9th century, where outside threats coincided with weakened central power, leaving ordinary Frisians uncertain about their future.

9.3 Cultural Continuity Amid Change

Amid political flux, many elements of Frisian life continued unaffected on a daily basis. Farmers still plowed fields, built dikes, and held local assemblies. Family ties and clan-based customs persisted, although Christian rites now shaped key life events such as baptism, marriage, and burial. A blending of old and new was evident in everything from house construction (traditional timber-framed dwellings) to festival practices (saint's feasts with local flair).

Coastal identity remained strong, reinforced by the shared necessity of water management and the communal challenge of living by the sea. Even if a Carolingian count sat in a distant fortress, villagers still had to unify for seasonal dike repairs. These communal rhythms served as a stabilizing force, bridging differences and ensuring that the fundamental tasks of survival—and commerce—continued. In that sense, the early medieval challenges faced by Frisia did not uproot its core identity. Rather, they shaped it into a form more attuned to outside powers and new economic opportunities.

CHAPTER 8: THE VIKING THREAT AND FRISIAN ADAPTATIONS

1. Introduction: A New Era of Turbulence

By the mid-9th century, the Viking onslaught had become a dominant concern for many parts of Europe's coastline and river systems. Scandinavian raiders appeared suddenly in longships, attacking monasteries, towns, and farmsteads. The Carolingian empire—already weakened by internal splits—struggled to mount an effective defense along all fronts. Frisia, with its navigable waterways, trade wealth, and scattered settlements, was a tempting target.

In this chapter, we explore how Viking raids impacted Frisian society throughout the 9th and early 10th centuries. We examine the tactics used by these Scandinavian warriors, the defensive responses by local Frisian communities, and the broader political changes triggered by this chaos. Despite suffering repeated attacks, Frisia also found ways to adapt: local leaders fortified certain areas, made deals with Viking bands, or even joined in maritime ventures that blurred the line between defense and opportunism. Through these upheavals, Frisians demonstrated resilience, preserving key aspects of their culture and economic life, yet inevitably transforming as they faced a new wave of external pressure.

2. The Rise of Viking Raids in Frisia

2.1 Scandinavian Expansion

The Vikings were not a single, unified people but a collection of Norse-speaking communities from what is now Denmark, Norway, and Sweden. Motivated by various factors—population pressures, political rivalries, or the lure of treasure—they set forth in sleek, maneuverable ships. Starting with coastal raids in the British Isles in the late 8th century, their reach soon expanded across the

North Sea. By the 830s and 840s, Viking fleets began probing the Frisian coast, testing defenses.

Their targets were strategic: monasteries or churches rich in silver, towns with trade goods, and river mouths that provided inland access. In Frisia, the major rivers like the Waal, Lek, and IJssel were gateways to Carolingian heartlands. A successful raid could net substantial loot, including slaves, and quickly retreat to sea if threatened by local militias or a royal army. This pattern made them a scourge for coastal dwellers, who could never be sure when a Viking fleet might appear on the horizon.

2.2 Early Attacks and Local Reactions

The first major Viking raids in Frisia are recorded in the 830s, with attacks on trading centers and monasteries. These events caught many Frisians off guard. Although local leaders had heard rumors of Viking activity elsewhere, the Carolingian state had provided little in the way of preemptive naval defenses. When the raiders landed, they often met minimal organized resistance, sacked their targets, and sailed away before a response could be mustered.

Local communities quickly realized they needed immediate defensive measures. Towns hastily constructed palisades or ramparts. Wealthy churches hid relics and valuables or moved them inland. Some areas raised militias of armed peasants and local nobles to watch the coast. Yet, the scattered nature of Frisian settlements made a unified response challenging. In some cases, villages opted for a policy of paying tribute—buying off the raiders rather than fighting. This practice created a cycle: once the Vikings knew a region would pay, they might return for more.

2.3 Weakening Imperial Protection

At this same time, the Carolingian empire continued to fragment. After the Treaty of Verdun (843), Frisia lay mostly under the rule of Lothair I (in Lotharingia) or his heirs, but effective royal intervention was rare. Rival claimants to the Carolingian throne focused on their own power struggles rather than mounting coordinated naval defenses. While some kings or dukes did attempt to repel Viking forces, these efforts were sporadic and often underfunded.

This lack of centralized authority left Frisia to fend for itself. Local counts, theoretically obligated to protect the populace, lacked sufficient forces to drive off larger Viking fleets. The mismatch between small local militias and well-armed

Norse bands, sometimes hundreds strong, was stark. Raiders capitalized on that advantage, planning seasonal expeditions that struck coastal or riverine sites before retreating north or west to safer harbors.

3. Viking Impact on Frisian Trade and Economy

3.1 Disruption of Coastal Commerce

Even before the Viking Age, Dorestad had begun to decline, but the raids hastened its downfall. Repeated attacks in the mid-9th century devastated the once-bustling emporium, leading merchants to abandon it for safer ports or inland markets. Viking marauders pillaged warehouses and took hostages, crippling trade. This was a blow not only to local Frisian merchants but also to the Carolingian economy, which relied on coastal trade routes for revenue and supplies.

Other smaller ports also suffered. Some never fully recovered, while others adapted by relocating to more defensible locations. Local trade continued but in a more decentralized fashion. Villages that relied on shipping goods across the North Sea had to scale back or pay tribute to Viking parties for safe passage. Over time, a portion of Frisian commerce shifted to new or less-exposed routes, reducing the region's role as a central trade hub.

3.2 Shifts in Merchant Strategy

Frisian merchants did not simply surrender to fate. Some turned to convoys, banding together for mutual protection, or sought armed escorts. Others negotiated directly with Viking leaders, arranging "protection" deals akin to modern extortion rackets. While morally dubious, such payments might be cheaper than losing entire cargoes. A few entrepreneurial traders even engaged in commerce with Vikings themselves, bartering supplies or goods in exchange for safe conduct or shared profits.

These adaptive strategies revealed the resourcefulness of Frisian traders. They were accustomed to operating in changing political environments; dealing with Vikings was a new challenge, but not insurmountable. In some cases, local elites might partner with merchants to finance defensive measures—a small flotilla of ships or fortified outposts—to guard shipping lanes. Though these local solutions were patchwork, they allowed commerce to survive, albeit on a smaller scale and with higher risks.

3.3 Economic Consequences for Local Communities

At the local level, Viking raids often led to the destruction of farms and the seizure of livestock. Coastal communities that had once prospered from trade and cattle farming faced sudden impoverishment. Surviving peasants might relocate inland or become tenants of lords who offered protection. Wealthy families who retained resources might fortify their homesteads or pay mercenaries, thus entrenching social hierarchies further.

Monasteries, which had served as economic engines in some areas, also declined under repeated assaults. The flight of monks or the loss of manuscripts disrupted the cultural life of Frisia. While some monasteries were rebuilt, others vanished altogether, their lands transferred to lay nobles or left abandoned. Such upheavals accelerated a shift in land ownership patterns, with power consolidating in the hands of those who could protect property—often local lords or Viking chieftains who established bases in the region.

---

4. Political Realignments and Leadership Responses

4.1 Fragmented Carolingian Authority

As Viking raids intensified, the descendants of Louis the Pious fragmented the empire further. Lotharingia, which included much of Frisia, was contested by different Carolingian branches and sometimes by external forces like East Francia or West Francia. In this climate, the official "kings" who claimed Frisia under their domain could offer only partial relief. Royal decrees to fortify coastal defenses were seldom fully implemented; local powerbrokers had to fend for themselves.

This breakdown of central authority spawned small-scale warlords or local counts who stepped into the power vacuum. Some cooperated with the Vikings to secure short-term gains, while others tried to rally resistance. Records from the late 9th century mention local leaders forging temporary alliances with raiding parties, or even using Viking muscle to eliminate political rivals. Such deals, although pragmatic, further destabilized the region, blurring lines between friend and foe.

4.2 Emergence of Coastal Defense Lords

In some districts, individuals or families rose to prominence by organizing defense. They collected taxes specifically for building or maintaining watchtowers along the coast. They might commission small fleets of fast ships to intercept raiders. These "defense lords" often gained loyalty from local communities grateful for protection. Over time, they accrued considerable influence, sometimes recognized as quasi-independent rulers.

Such developments laid a foundation for later medieval claims of local authority that did not strictly align with distant kings. We see the seeds of this phenomenon in the ways that Frisian local assemblies or noble families negotiated their own pacts, minted small coinage for paying defenders, or set up local courts to handle disputes quickly. While not fully severed from the Carolingian or post-Carolingian political structure, these local leaders capitalized on imperial weakness to carve out spheres of authority that were essentially self-ruled enclaves.

4.3 Church Leadership in Crisis

In the face of Viking raids, bishops and abbots also assumed new roles. Once confined to spiritual duties, they now had to consider fortifications around churches and monasteries. Bishops might gather militias to protect relics and property. Some even engaged directly in diplomacy with Viking chieftains, offering gifts or ransoms to preserve sacred sites. This involvement in secular defense blurred the lines between spiritual and temporal power.

Moreover, the church hierarchy in Frisia was not immune to political fragmentation. When the bishopric of Utrecht was endangered, the bishop might relocate relics to safer inland areas. Some records mention entire religious communities fleeing during raids. Clerical authorities also had to manage the moral questions raised by negotiations with pagans who sacked Christian sites. Over time, these crises forced the Church to become more pragmatic and entwined with local power structures, sometimes losing the idealistic zeal of earlier missionary eras.

5. Viking Settlements and Long-Term Influence

5.1 Wintering Over and Semi-Permanent Camps

Initially, Vikings conducted hit-and-run raids. But as they realized the region's strategic value, some groups began overwintering, establishing camps near river mouths. By staying beyond a single season, they could launch raids into the interior more easily. These encampments sometimes evolved into semi-permanent settlements, where Norse chieftains reigned over mixed populations that included captured slaves and local collaborators.

Frisia's marshes and navigable waterways offered good locations for such bases. Viking ships could be moored along tidal flats, hard to approach by land-based armies. Over time, some Viking leaders minted coins in conquered areas or collected tribute systematically. A few intermarried with local families, creating dynastic ties that blurred the boundary between "raider" and "resident." This phenomenon was parallel to what happened in parts of England (the Danelaw) or along the Seine in West Francia (Normandy).

5.2 Cultural Exchanges

Viking presence inevitably led to cultural exchange. Though raiding was brutal, everyday contact in semi-settled areas included trade and social interaction. Norse craftsmanship—especially in metalwork—could influence local styles. Conversely, Vikings in Frisia encountered Carolingian coinage systems, Christian liturgy, and architectural methods. Some Norse individuals adopted elements of local dress or technology, while local people might pick up Norse words or maritime skills.

Archaeological finds reveal objects of Scandinavian origin—such as jewelry, amulets, or weapons—turning up in Frisian settlement layers dating to the 9th or early 10th century. Written accounts, though sparse, mention occasional alliances or personal friendships bridging cultural gaps. At times, a Viking warlord might sponsor the rebuilding of a local church in exchange for acceptance as a quasi-legitimate ruler. While this did not erase the violence of raids, it added nuance to the overall picture: Vikings were not always outsiders passing through but sometimes new settlers shaping local dynamics.

5.3 The Formation of Mixed Communities

In places where Vikings stayed for extended periods, new communities emerged with hybrid identities. Children born of Norse fathers and Frisian mothers grew up speaking both languages. Over a generation or two, some families might gravitate toward Christianity, especially if it offered social or political advantages. The local assembly or Thing (a Norse tradition) could sometimes blend with the Frisian concept of local gatherings, forging new legal customs.

These mixed communities might remain small pockets, overshadowed by the bigger realm of shifting alliances. But they illustrate that the Viking Age in Frisia involved more than just destruction. It also created cross-cultural connections that would linger long after major raids subsided. Whether these pockets identified as "Frisian" or "Norse" varied by place and time, reflecting the fluid nature of identity in an era of migration and intermarriage.

---

6. Defensive Innovations

6.1 Fortifying Towns and Monasteries

Repeated Viking attacks prompted a wave of fortification across Europe, and Frisia was no exception. Even smaller settlements realized the necessity of walls or earthen ramparts. Where funds allowed, stone or brick elements were added, though wood and earth were more common due to local resources. Monasteries, having historically been open spiritual centers, transformed into fortified enclaves with gates and watchtowers.

These defensive measures did not guarantee safety, but they could deter quick raids. Vikings preferred easy targets, so a well-defended community might avoid the worst if the raiders deemed the risk too high. Some local lords also placed watchposts at river mouths to warn of incoming fleets. Such posts would light beacons or send riders to surrounding areas, giving farmers time to hide valuables or flee to refuge. This warning system, while not foolproof, improved survival rates.

6.2 Naval Responses

One of the most direct ways to combat sea-based raiders was to form local navies. Although the Carolingian empire had sporadically tried to maintain a navy, it was often insufficient. In Frisia, some ambitious counts or local leaders built small fleets of shallow-draft vessels. Crewed by Frisian sailors who understood the tides and channels, these ships could engage Viking longships in local waters.

However, naval battles were risky, requiring disciplined crews and effective leadership. Vikings were experienced fighters on ships. If local forces were outnumbered or poorly coordinated, they could suffer heavy losses. Still, a few recorded instances mention Frisian defenders successfully repelling small raiding parties at sea, indicating that maritime strategy was evolving. Over time, these local naval efforts contributed to a sense of self-reliance, reinforcing the idea that Frisians needed to defend their home waters independently.

6.3 Coastal Alliances

Realizing that no single district could stand alone, some Frisian communities formed defensive alliances. These might involve mutual pacts between coastal towns or between local nobles and bishops. Resources were pooled for building communal fortifications or stationing watchmen. In certain areas, alliances extended beyond Frisia to neighboring Saxon or Frankish regions, recognizing that Vikings threatened everyone in the North Sea basin.

Such alliances were informal compared to a modern state military structure, but they represented a new level of regional cooperation. Through combined efforts, a larger militia or naval squadron might be assembled to confront a Viking host. Success varied widely, depending on leadership, resource availability, and the size of the Viking threat. Nonetheless, the very existence of these alliances signaled a shift from fragmented local defense toward coordinated regional action—a critical adaptation in an era of relentless raids.

7. Shaping the Political Future: Counts, Dukes, and Margraves

7.1 Growth of "Frontier" Titles

As the Carolingian empire splintered, new titles emerged for those who governed frontier regions—margrave (markgraf), for instance, was used to designate a count with special responsibilities for defense. In parts of Frisia threatened by Vikings, certain counts or lords might receive expanded authority from a king or emperor in East Francia, the realm that eventually encompassed the Low Countries. This recognition gave them the right to raise larger armies, collect higher taxes, and enact swift justice.

These frontier counts or margraves were, in essence, local strongmen who balanced their loyalty to a distant ruler with the immediate necessity of defending coastal lands. Some became quite powerful, overshadowing other local nobility. Over time, families that held these offices gained dynastic control, passing down titles that gave them significant autonomy. Their success or failure in repelling Vikings determined their reputation and legitimacy in Frisian eyes.

7.2 Rivalries and Power Struggles

The power vacuum created by weakened central authority led to local rivalries. Different counts or margraves might claim overlapping jurisdictions in Frisian territories, leading to feuds or even brief civil wars. While the Vikings remained a common enemy, these aristocratic disputes sometimes impeded a united defensive effort. Written sources hint at alliances formed by one count with a Viking warlord to undermine a neighboring rival, a brutal example of realpolitik overshadowing communal safety.

Such rivalries could be devastating to ordinary people caught in the middle. Villages might be forced to pay taxes to two competing lords or provide conscripts to rival forces. The Church, too, might be compelled to pick sides. Some bishops tried to stay neutral, focusing on spiritual duties, but neutrality was difficult when each faction demanded allegiance. Over time, stronger leaders emerged victorious, consolidating control and setting the stage for the region's future political divisions.

7.3 Transition Toward Post-Carolingian Realms

By the late 9th and early 10th centuries, the Carolingian lineage in East Francia was transforming into what would become known as the Ottonian dynasty (starting with Henry the Fowler and Otto the Great). Frisia, though not the center of Ottonian power, was gradually drawn into the sphere of a reorganized German kingdom. Counts in Frisia who acknowledged the new kings were granted charters confirming their lands and defensive roles. This formalized their status, though the daily challenges of Viking incursions persisted.

In time, these evolving structures laid foundations for medieval principalities in the Low Countries. While we are not yet at the stage of formal duchies and counties fully recognized in the High Middle Ages, the seeds of later developments were sown in this period of turbulence. Frisia's unique combination of local assemblies, water management, and strong communal traditions would interact with these rising dynastic powers in complex ways, ensuring that the region never fully conformed to feudal norms found elsewhere.

---

8. The Decline of Viking Raids and the Aftermath

8.1 Changing Dynamics in Scandinavia

By the early 10th century, Scandinavian politics were shifting. Some Viking leaders established more permanent realms in England, Ireland, or Normandy, redirecting their energies from raiding to governance. Internal consolidation in Denmark and Norway also meant fewer large fleets roving abroad. While raids did not cease overnight, their frequency and intensity in Frisia diminished compared to the mid-9th century peak.

Frisian leaders took advantage of this lull to rebuild. Churches were rededicated, trade routes reopened, and farmland ravaged by earlier raids was reclaimed. However, the memory of Viking attacks lingered, influencing local culture and fortification practices. Even in relative peace, communities stayed vigilant, maintaining watchtowers or local naval patrols in case future raiders emerged.

8.2 Recovery of Trade Networks

As Viking pressure receded, Frisian commerce began to recover in new forms. Dorestad was largely a memory by then, but other ports, such as those near modern-day cities like Utrecht, Tiel, or Deventer, gained importance for river trade. Coastal markets also revived, albeit cautiously. Frisian merchants ventured once again across the North Sea, trading with Anglo-Saxon England, which was itself undergoing consolidation under kings like Alfred the Great and his successors.

In a broader sense, Europe in the 10th century was starting to experience a modest economic upswing. Agricultural methods improved, and populations grew, creating demand for trade goods. Frisians, with their maritime traditions, were well-placed to take part in this recovery. Some historians suggest that the painful lessons of the Viking Age—such as the need for better defenses and alliances—actually made Frisian ports more robust and prepared for future commercial expansions.

8.3 Long-Term Cultural Effects

Though the Viking raids brought destruction, they also contributed to cultural blending. Norse words entered local vocabularies, especially in maritime or military contexts. Legends and stories about heroic defenses or tragic defeats became part of Frisian folklore. Some genealogies in aristocratic families quietly acknowledged Norse roots. Church records mention baptisms of individuals with Scandinavian names, hinting at assimilation over time.

Meanwhile, local governance had permanently changed. The power of certain counts, who had proven capable in defending against Vikings, endured. This contributed to the growing stratification of Frisian nobility. But the communal spirit remained strong, especially regarding dike-building or town fortifications. The combination of strong local assemblies and emergent noble lines set the stage for subsequent centuries of Frisian history, where unique regional freedoms would sometimes clash with the ambitions of feudal overlords.

9. Lasting Legacies of the Viking Era in Frisia

9.1 Fortified Settlements and Maritime Tradition

The 9th and 10th centuries left Frisia with a network of fortified sites that would continue to evolve. Some, originally built as wooden stockades against Vikings, later became full-fledged towns with walls and moats. Others fell into disuse once raids subsided, leaving only faint traces in the archaeological record. In either case, these structures reflect a period where maritime defense was critical to survival.

Frisian sailors also expanded their navigational skills, adapting to the challenge of confronting Viking ships. Over generations, they would turn this proficiency to more peaceful pursuits, eventually becoming known as expert traders and seafarers in the High Middle Ages. The harsh lessons of defending coastal waters instilled an enduring maritime mindset, one that valued agility, knowledge of tides, and quick communication among coastal communities.

9.2 Political Fragmentation and Future Autonomy

The Viking Age accelerated the fracturing of Carolingian authority in Frisia. Local counts, margraves, and assemblies stepped up when royal armies could not arrive quickly. While some recognized overlordship from East Francia or Lotharingia, real day-to-day control lay in local hands. This environment fed the notion—later famously expressed as "Frisian freedom"—that no external ruler should dominate the region without consent from local assemblies.

That said, the seeds of feudal structures also took root, as protective lords claimed greater rights over lands and populations. Thus, by the end of the 10th century, Frisia stood at a crossroads: on one hand, it possessed strong local traditions that resisted full feudal subjugation; on the other, powerful local magnates and bishops were embedding themselves in a broader aristocratic hierarchy. This tension would define Frisian politics for centuries.

9.3 Cultural Memory and Identity

The saga of Viking attacks became part of Frisian collective memory, retold in chronicles and oral traditions. Stories of heroic defenses or cunning escapes shaped local identity, emphasizing resilience and unity in the face of foreign threat. In some accounts, Viking brutality was highlighted to illustrate the suffering endured, while in others, there was a begrudging respect for Norse seamanship and courage.

Over time, the immediate trauma of the raids diminished, replaced by a sense of shared history that included both conflict and adaptation. For the Frisians, the 9th–10th centuries served as a crucible, forging stronger communal bonds. The cultural memory of this era reinforced local pride in surviving repeated invasions—a pride that would later underlie claims to special rights and freedoms when dealing with emerging powers in the High Middle Ages.

10. Conclusion

The 9th and early 10th centuries were a tumultuous chapter for Frisia, defined by relentless Viking incursions, political fragmentation, and far-reaching change. Yet, through hardship, the region demonstrated notable adaptability. Frisians built defenses, formed alliances, and in some cases negotiated or even cooperated with their erstwhile enemies. Viking influence left its mark on the culture, economy, and political landscape, but it did not destroy Frisian identity.

As we move forward, the Viking threat gradually recedes, opening space for new developments in the High Middle Ages. In subsequent chapters, we will explore **how Frisia transitioned into more stable regional structures**, contended with emerging feudal authorities, and continued to refine its water management and trade practices. The foundations laid in the wake of Viking turbulence would shape Frisia's medieval destiny—preserving an enduring sense of local autonomy and communal solidarity well into later centuries.

CHAPTER 9: INDEPENDENCE, FRISIAN FREEDOM, AND REGIONAL CONFLICTS

1. Introduction: A New Phase in Frisian History

By the close of the 10th century, Frisia had survived the disruptive Viking era. Although many coastal communities had been raided or forced to pay tribute, the frequency of large-scale attacks began to decline. Political conditions across Europe also shifted, as the Carolingian Empire gave way to a patchwork of successor states. In what we now call the Low Countries, various counts, bishops, and emerging local dynasties contended for influence. Meanwhile, many Frisian districts had come to rely on their own assemblies, water-management traditions, and networks of local defense.

From the 11th to the 12th century, these changes coalesced into what later generations called "Frisian freedom." While modern scholars debate the exact meaning and scope of that term, medieval references point to a distinct sense among Frisians that they owed feudal obedience to no single overlord. Instead, they prized local autonomy under community-based law and saw themselves as uniquely free compared to surrounding regions. This chapter explores how that freedom evolved: the role of local assemblies, the interactions with powerful neighbors, and the internal conflicts that sometimes tested Frisian unity. We will also see how new economic patterns and the ongoing demands of coastal life shaped the politics of freedom, leading to alliances and feuds within Frisia itself.

2. Political Landscape After the Viking Age

2.1 Rise of New Dynasties

After the fragmentation of the Carolingian realm, new dynasties rose in regions adjacent to Frisia, each aiming to extend authority over the coastal zones. To the south, the County of Holland emerged under the House of Holland (also referred to in some sources by family names like Gerulfing), gradually consolidating power. To the east, the Saxon dukes and various local counts eyed Frisian territory for expansion, hoping to control trade routes along the Wadden Sea and the lower Ems or Weser Rivers.

Within Frisia, the older system of Carolingian counts did not entirely disappear. In certain coastal districts, individuals continued to style themselves as counts, margraves, or viscounts, albeit with precarious authority. Local assemblies often determined whether these titles carried real power or were simply nominal. Overlapping jurisdictions became common, as multiple figures might claim the same region under vaguely defined charters or inherited rights. This confusion set the stage for frequent political struggles.

2.2 Influence of the Ottonian and Salian Kings

In East Francia (soon to be recognized as the Holy Roman Empire), the Ottonian dynasty (919–1024) followed by the Salian dynasty (1024–1125) shaped broader politics. While neither line established tight, day-to-day control over Frisia, they did grant official titles to supporters who nominally ruled certain Frisian lands. For example, an emperor might name a loyal noble as "Count of Friesland," expecting that person to collect taxes and uphold imperial law. In practice, the noble often found it difficult to enforce authority on the fiercely autonomous local communities.

Still, the imperial connection had benefits for some Frisian elites. If a local leader wanted outside military backing or official recognition of property claims, appealing to the emperor in distant German courts could help. This relationship cut both ways: emperors sometimes demanded that Frisians provide men for imperial campaigns or pay special levies. Resistance to such demands fed into the emerging narrative that Frisians were exempt from feudal obligations—a stance that would become more explicit in subsequent centuries.

2.3 Decline of Viking Settlement

While the 11th century was not completely free from pirate activity, the large-scale Viking presence had mostly dissipated. Some Norse-descended families remained in coastal enclaves, gradually blending with the Frisian population. These hybrid communities, formed from earlier raider settlements, were now recognized as part of the local tapestry. They participated in assemblies and contributed to regional trade. The crisis mentality of the Viking era gave way to a renewed focus on rebuilding towns, churches, and farmland. This relative stability provided the backdrop for evolving political structures in Frisia, grounded less in emergency defense and more in debates over lawful governance and autonomy.

3. Foundations of Frisian Freedom

3.1 Communal Water Management and Collective Action

One hallmark of Frisian society was the communal approach to coastal protection. Centuries of living in tidal lowlands had fostered traditions of cooperative dike building and terp (dwelling mound) maintenance. Such large-scale projects were impossible without broad participation. Local assemblies, sometimes called "upstalsboom" gatherings in later sources, allocated labor quotas, resolved disputes, and enforced communal rules. People had to work together, or floods would destroy farmland and homes.

These communal efforts bred a sense of equality among participants, at least in theory. Even if one family was wealthier, it still depended on neighbors for dike repairs. Over time, this spirit of equality contributed to the idea that no single individual had the right to command the region without consent. The concept of "Frisian freedom" thus partly arose from the daily reality that survival depended on collective decision-making, not top-down feudal structures.

3.2 Legal Traditions and Oral Law

Frisia's legal landscape was shaped by customary law—rooted in Germanic tradition yet evolving over centuries of adaptation. In many places, laws were transmitted orally by designated law-speakers (or local judges) who recited rules on property boundaries, inheritance, wergild (compensation for injury or death), and the obligations each person owed to the community. While influences from Carolingian and Ottonian decrees existed, local practices remained dominant.

During the 11th and 12th centuries, some of these laws began appearing in written form, often referred to collectively as the "Lex Frisionum" (though that label sometimes applied earlier to partial codifications). These texts show a continued emphasis on personal freedoms. For instance, a free Frisian could not be compelled to become someone's vassal without explicit agreement. Land tenure also differed from typical feudal holdings: many small farmers held property as allods (independent ownership) rather than as fiefs from a lord. This legal tradition was a powerful factor in sustaining Frisian claims of independence.

3.3 The Symbolic Role of the Emperor's Exemptions

A recurring theme in medieval Frisian lore is that some emperor—often Charlemagne in legends—had granted the Frisians special privileges or exemptions from feudal burdens. While historians debate the authenticity of specific charters, the stories reveal how Frisians explained their unique status. They believed they owed allegiance only to the emperor (and, in some accounts, only if they chose to reaffirm it), not to intermediary counts or dukes. Local assemblies would proclaim that their liberties dated back to ancient times, upheld by legendary charters.

Such claims, whether rooted in actual imperial documents or mythic tradition, fueled local resistance when foreign lords tried to impose taxes or feudal dues. Frisians would argue, "We are free people under the emperor, and none else can command us." This stance gave them a moral and legal rationale to reject or limit outside interference. Over the 11th and 12th centuries, these beliefs crystallized into the concept that all Frisians, from small landholders to local nobles, were fundamentally unbound by standard feudal obligations.

---

4. Conflicts with Neighboring Powers

4.1 The County of Holland and Its Expansion

South of Frisia lay the County of Holland, centered around the regions near the mouths of the Rhine and Meuse. In the 11th century, counts of Holland sought to expand northward to control more of the coastal trade and farmland. This expansion inevitably led them into disputes with Frisian communities that considered themselves independent. Holland's counts might attempt to place a bailiff or castellan in a Frisian town, only to face organized resistance from local assemblies.

One notable figure was Count Dirk III of Holland, active in the early 11th century. He famously clashed with the Bishop of Utrecht (a major landowner in the area) and various local Frisians who resisted demands for tolls on shipping routes. Dirk III's successes and failures exemplify the fractious politics: he could sometimes coerce a Frisian district to pay tolls, but other times local militias or allied forces from neighboring Frisian communities drove his men out. This pattern of struggle continued under Dirk's successors, shaping the region's political map for decades.

4.2 Bishops of Utrecht and Episcopal Claims

The Bishopric of Utrecht had inherited extensive lands in the coastal and riverine zones from Carolingian times. The bishop held both spiritual and secular authority in these domains—an arrangement often called a "prince-bishopric." For Frisians, however, the bishop's claim to temporal rule was frequently unwelcome. Many recognized the bishop's spiritual role but refused to pay feudal homage or dues for the bishop's estates unless forcibly compelled.

During the 11th and 12th centuries, several bishops of Utrecht tried to assert control over parts of Frisia to secure income and bolster the bishopric's political clout. They encountered stiff opposition. Local assemblies might withhold rents, block bishop's officials, or ally with rival secular lords to keep Utrecht at bay. In response, some bishops formed alliances with the counts of Holland or other regional powers, hoping combined force would bring Frisia in line. This maneuvering led to ongoing disputes, occasionally erupting into open conflict.

4.3 Eastern Neighbors and Saxon Influence

To the east, Saxon dukes and local counts (for example, those of Eastphalia or Westphalia) had their eyes on the trans-Ems territories. A number of Frisian districts east of the Ems River, sometimes called "East Frisia," had cultural ties to the rest of Frisia but were geographically closer to Saxon realms. This proximity meant Saxon lords often pressed claims of overlordship, especially if they could produce imperial charters granting them theoretical rights over border regions.

As with the Bishop of Utrecht, Saxon lords found it hard to enforce paper claims against coastal communities proficient in local self-defense. Some Saxon dynasties, like the Billungs and later the Welfs, attempted to place local chieftains under vassal obligations. They faced a mixture of compliance and resistance. Certain Frisian families cooperated, gaining titles or privileges in Saxon courts, while others remained staunchly independent, fueling a patchwork of alliances and enmities across the region.

4.4 Maritime Tensions and Naval Encounters

Conflicts over trade routes also played out at sea. The mouth of the Zuiderzee (a large inlet in what is now the Netherlands) and the Wadden Sea islands were strategic zones for commerce. Rival powers sometimes tried to blockade Frisian ships or impose tolls on passing vessels. In response, Frisians formed ad hoc fleets, either to protect their shipping or to raid the shipping lanes of a hostile neighbor. Chronicles from the 12th century mention skirmishes at sea involving Frisian craft that used shallow-draft boats, well-suited to navigate tidal flats.

These maritime tensions underscored Frisia's significance as a coastal trade hub. Control of key ports and safe navigation routes could yield wealth from tolls. Likewise, local communities recognized that if they lost the right to move goods freely, their economy would suffer. Thus, the fight to remain free from external tolls was not merely ideological—it directly affected livelihoods. Whenever an outside lord tried to collect maritime dues without permission, Frisians saw it as a threat to their economic survival.

---

5. Internal Divisions and Family Feuds

5.1 Emergence of Local Lineages (Geslachten)

While Frisians collectively championed the idea of freedom from feudal overlords, they were not monolithic. Over the 11th century, powerful families (sometimes referred to as geslachten) rose within various districts, each seeking to extend its local influence. Some families aligned with outside counts or bishops for support, while others relied on strong community backing to maintain autonomy. Rivalries between these families could lead to violent feuds, overshadowing external threats.

One example is the feud between the van Groningen family and the van Coevorden family in the northeastern districts of Frisia. Both lineages claimed extensive rights and mobilized local allies. Periodically, one side might call upon outside help—such as a bishop or a Saxon count—offering them concessions in return for military support against their Frisian rivals. Ironically, these internal feuds sometimes opened the door to external domination that the families claimed to oppose.

5.2 Town vs. Rural Assemblies

Another source of internal tension emerged between growing urban centers—small though they were—and rural assemblies. Certain Frisian towns, spurred by trade growth, wanted privileges that set them apart from the countryside. Urban merchants or guild leaders might support the notion of a count or bishop granting them a charter, as it could formalize market rights and offer legal protections. In contrast, rural assemblies feared such charters would introduce feudal constraints or outside taxation.

This dynamic contributed to friction within Frisia itself. A town's leaders might be more inclined to negotiate with a regional power if it ensured stable commerce. Meanwhile, farmland communities insisted on the principle of local independence, resisting any step that looked like subjugation. Though these differences did not always erupt into open conflict, they illustrate the diverse interests that existed under the broad banner of "Frisian freedom."

5.3 Arbitration and Local Courts

To manage these internal disputes, Frisians often relied on arbitration by local notables, law-speakers, or occasionally neutral parties from a neighboring district. Formal court gatherings, sometimes called "redjeven" or "ding," sought to resolve feuds before they escalated into wider violence. The authority of these courts stemmed not from a king's decree but from communal respect for custom.

In principle, if both sides agreed to the arbitration, the verdict was binding. Offenders might owe fines, hostages, or land concessions. However, strong families could ignore the ruling if they had enough armed support. This sometimes forced rival clans into protracted vendettas. Over the 11th and 12th centuries, the repeated cycles of feuding and arbitration shaped how Frisians balanced local freedom with the need for stability. Each conflict that spilled into open bloodshed underscored the fragility of their cherished autonomy.

6. Economic Developments in the 11th–12th Centuries

6.1 Agricultural Expansion and Reclamation

As population gradually rose after the Viking age disruptions, Frisians expanded farmland along the coastal marshes. Techniques for drainage improved, with more sophisticated sluices and dike networks. Monastic institutions, especially those that survived earlier turbulence, also played a role in land reclamation. A monastery might invest in new dikes, draining areas of peat or marsh to create arable fields. Local labor financed by either communal effort or monastic endowment powered these efforts.

The result was a slow but steady increase in cultivated acreage. Cattle remained central to the rural economy, providing both meat and dairy, but crop diversity improved—wheat, rye, oats, and barley were grown where soil conditions allowed. Some communities specialized in flax or hemp cultivation for textiles. These developments underpinned the region's relative prosperity in many districts. Although floods remained a constant threat, the constant drive to push the dike line further seaward testified to confidence in communal engineering skills.

6.2 Trade Continuity and Shifting Routes

Frisian traders continued to sail to England, the Baltic, and along the North Sea coast to Flanders and Normandy. While the heyday of Dorestad was long gone, new or revitalized ports emerged, such as Staveren (Stavoren) and later, towns along the Zuiderzee. Salt production from coastal marshes was also an important commodity; salt not only preserved food but was essential in tanning leather. Thus, Frisians found a ready market for salt in inland regions that lacked access to the sea.

In the 11th and 12th centuries, the broader European economy was gradually picking up, driven by population growth and renewed urbanization. Flemish towns like Bruges and Ghent boomed, and English ports prospered under stable monarchies. Frisians benefited from this upswing, though competition from other maritime groups, such as the emerging Hanseatic towns in the Baltic region, began to appear. Still, Frisian seafarers maintained a reputation for skill in navigating tricky coastal waters. This reputation helped them secure shipping contracts for merchants from inland areas who needed reliable transport of goods.

6.3 Coinage and Market Rights

In the 11th century, the Holy Roman Emperors and local counts minted coins of varying quality. Frisia itself had no single centralized mint that controlled coin production, though certain powerful lords or towns might produce local coinage under imperial license. This decentralized approach meant that many coins circulated, some minted in Holland, some in Saxony, some in distant imperial cities. Local traders learned to assess coin weight and silver content carefully, a skill that influenced everyday commerce.

Granting "market rights" was a significant step for a developing settlement. A local lord or bishop might issue a charter allowing a weekly market or annual fair, granting merchants certain privileges and protections. In some Frisian areas, local assemblies themselves could declare a market if enough support existed, bypassing the need for a feudal grant. Though a contentious process, these new markets helped unify local economies, making them more attractive to distant traders. Over time, a handful of Frisian towns gained enough commercial prominence to shape regional trade patterns, though never as dominantly as older centers like Utrecht or new rising ports in Flanders.

---

7. The Church's Evolving Role

7.1 Monastic Revival and Cistercian Influence

After the challenges of the Viking age, monasteries and convents in Frisia underwent revival and sometimes reorganization. An important development was the arrival of Cistercian monasticism in the 12th century. The Cistercians were known for strict discipline, agricultural innovation, and land reclamation. They established houses in coastal regions, introducing advanced drainage methods and improving local farming efficiency.

These Cistercian monasteries also served as spiritual and economic hubs, employing laborers (both free and bound) to expand farmland. By draining additional marshes, they contributed to the region's prosperity. At the same time, their monastic ideals influenced the local religious culture, emphasizing piety, manual labor, and communal work—values that resonated with many Frisians who already believed in cooperative dike maintenance. Though friction sometimes arose over monastic land claims, the overall effect was an infusion of new techniques and spiritual energy.

7.2 Parish Life and Lay Involvement

As villages continued to grow, so did parish structures. Local priests often came from Frisian families, bridging the gap between ecclesiastical authority and communal traditions. Church festivals integrated into the agricultural calendar, with blessings for dikes or fields, forging a blend of Christian rites and older local customs. Laypeople had a significant voice in parish matters, choosing or endorsing priests who represented community interests.

In some districts, families vied for the right to present priests to the local bishop, a privilege that conferred influence. This patronage system could be a source of tension if the bishop tried to appoint a priest from outside. But it also confirmed how deeply local communities valued religious life on their own terms. The Church in Frisia, therefore, walked a line: it sought to uphold canonical norms while accommodating local assemblies. The parish became a forum where spiritual needs intersected with social and economic realities.

7.3 Pilgrimages and Connections to Broader Christendom

The 11th and 12th centuries also witnessed a surge in pilgrimages across Europe, sparked in part by the relative peace established in some regions and the rise of new monastic orders. Frisians joined these movements, traveling to shrines like Santiago de Compostela, Rome, or even the Holy Land. Such journeys broadened cultural horizons: returning pilgrims brought stories, relics, and knowledge of other lands.

In turn, the outside world learned more about Frisia. Monastic chroniclers from distant abbeys sometimes commented on Frisian visitors, noting their distinct customs or clothing. This cross-cultural contact made Frisia a small, but recognized, participant in the wider Christian community. Over time, philanthropic donations from wealthy Frisian pilgrims helped fund churches or hospices near pilgrimage routes, enhancing spiritual ties beyond the coastline. Yet, these international contacts seldom undermined the local sense of freedom; if anything, they gave Frisians more prestige and a broader network of potential allies or patrons.

---

8. Conflicts, Alliances, and the Shaping of Frisian Autonomy

8.1 Major Confrontations in the 11th Century

Throughout the 11th century, flashpoints erupted as neighboring rulers challenged Frisian districts. One notable example was the conflict between the Bishop of Utrecht and certain Frisian communities near the Lauwers area (in present-day Groningen). The bishop tried to enforce feudal dues, claiming rights granted by an imperial charter. A coalition of Frisian assemblies defied him, seizing or expelling his officials. Utrecht responded with a military expedition, but the bishop's forces struggled in the watery terrain. Eventually, a truce was reached, acknowledging limited bishop control but preserving local assembly powers—typical of the compromises that characterized Frisian disputes.

Another key dispute flared when the Count of Holland sought to impose tolls on Frisian ships passing the southern Zuiderzee. The towns reliant on shipping vigorously objected, forming a defensive pact. Skirmishes at sea followed, with small Frisian fleets intercepting Holland's toll collectors. Peace was only restored after an imperial mediator stepped in. This outcome further cemented the Frisian stance that external tolls were illegitimate unless freely agreed upon by local assemblies.

8.2 Internal Alliances: The Upstalsboom Idea

By the late 11th century, references appear (in somewhat legendary form) to a "central assembly" or meeting place known as Upstalsboom, often located near what is now Aurich in East Frisia. According to tradition, representatives from different Frisian districts gathered there annually to discuss mutual concerns, settle disputes, and proclaim laws. Whether this meeting was formalized at the time or fully realized only in the 13th century remains debated. However, the notion that Frisians coordinated region-wide decisions—beyond the scope of single villages or families—was increasingly recognized.

Such assemblies attempted to unify the fractious local groups. If an external power threatened one district, the others might pledge support. If two Frisian families were locked in a feud, assembly mediators worked to restore peace. This emerging structure did not eradicate local rivalries, but it showed that a shared identity could overcome internal strife when major external challenges loomed. The upstalsboom concept would later gain symbolic significance as the embodiment of Frisian freedom and unity.

8.3 Growing Diplomatic Sophistication

Frisians also became more adept at diplomacy. Rather than merely repel outside aggression, they learned to negotiate beneficial treaties or alliances. If a powerful count or bishop offered commercial privileges or recognized local autonomy in exchange for partial cooperation, many Frisian communities were willing to bargain. They might allow an outside lord to build a fortress or maintain a minimal garrison, as long as that lord upheld Frisian laws and refrained from imposing serfdom or heavy taxes.

In some instances, Frisian communities even sought alliances with foreign princes in times of crisis. For example, if East Frisia faced a threat from a Saxon noble, local leaders might send envoys to the Count of Holland or the Bishop of Bremen, proposing mutual defense. The result was a fluid web of pacts, shifting as each generation's circumstances changed. This diplomatic skill set, combined with local militias and maritime prowess, helped Frisians maintain a degree of autonomy that stood out in an era when feudal structures dominated much of Europe.

---

9. The Emergence of Written Claims to Freedom

9.1 Early Charters and Codifications

In the 12th century, we begin to see more surviving written records that codify Frisian laws and privileges. Among these are references to "liberties" that local communities insisted were ancient. Sometimes, these claims were formalized in charters witnessed by outside authorities, such as bishops or imperial commissioners. Although the authenticity of each document varies—some might have been rewritten or forged for strategic purposes—they provide evidence that Frisians felt a collective need to document their rights.

For instance, a late 12th-century text might outline the boundary of a district, stating that only the local assembly could levy taxes for dike building and no external count could demand tribute. Another might confirm that free Frisians could not be tried outside their district without the assembly's consent. The process of writing these provisions, and having them sealed by a notary or recognized by a bishop, gave them weight in medieval legal culture. Over time, these documented rights solidified the concept that Frisian freedom was a legitimate, legally grounded status.

9.2 Influence of Canon Law and Imperial Courts

Medieval Europe saw the growing importance of canon law (the law of the Church) and the revival of Roman law in scholarly circles. While these trends often bolstered hierarchical authority, they also provided new legal tools for local communities to defend their rights. A skilled advocate could argue in an imperial court that a prior grant or a long-standing custom was inviolable under Roman legal principles of prescription or established usage. Meanwhile, Church law could condemn the abuse of power by secular lords, if it infringed on moral or ecclesiastical principles.

Frisians who traveled or sent representatives to imperial diets or synods might harness these arguments. They emphasized the unique coastal conditions, the historical necessity of communal water management, and past imperial exemptions. Although the Holy Roman Emperor was, in theory, the supreme overlord, many within the imperial structure recognized the practical difficulties of subduing a region so physically and culturally distinct. Thus, imperial courts often issued compromises or partial rulings that left substantial autonomy in Frisian hands.

9.3 Growing Sense of Collective Identity

All these legal codifications, assemblies, and external negotiations contributed to a stronger collective Frisian identity by the end of the 12th century. Local families still feuded, but they often invoked the broader cause of Frisian freedom as a rallying point. Monks and chroniclers, writing local histories, began praising the region's proud heritage and the notion that its people had never been fully enslaved by foreign powers. In some narratives, the ancient times under King Redbad were romanticized, depicting him as a symbol of stubborn independence—despite his era being centuries removed.

This heightened sense of unity did not erase local differences. West Frisia (roughly corresponding to modern North Holland), Middle Frisia (the area around Leeuwarden and the Frisian Lakes), and East Frisia (across the Ems) each maintained nuances in law and custom. Nevertheless, outside observers started referring to "Frisians" collectively, noting their refusal to accept feudal norms and their reliance on collective assemblies to govern. By the threshold of the 13th century, this reputation was well established in Northern Europe.

---

10. Conclusion

The 11th and 12th centuries were transformative for the Frisians. In the aftermath of Viking upheavals, they navigated a complex political environment in which the Holy Roman Empire, neighboring counts, and prince-bishops all sought to assert authority. Yet, thanks to centuries of communal dike building, distinct legal customs, and a growing sense of shared heritage, many Frisian communities managed to resist full subjugation. They voiced an evolving doctrine of "Frisian freedom," claiming exemptions from feudal burdens and emphasizing local assemblies' power.

This period also saw a mix of internal feuds, alliances with external powers, and cautious attempts at diplomatic bargaining. Economic life advanced through agricultural reclamation, maritime trade, and the slow rise of new towns. Monasteries, particularly the Cistercians, reinforced communal labor traditions in coastal reclamation while the local Church balanced spiritual leadership with political realities. By the end of the 12th century, Frisia stood out as a coastal region maintaining local autonomy in a feudal age.

Chapter Ten will delve into the **social and economic structures** of medieval Frisia in more detail, focusing on how communities were organized, how people earned their livelihoods, and how cultural expressions solidified Frisian identity. This examination will underscore the ways daily life, communal institutions, and shifting markets interacted with the broader political transformations we have explored.

CHAPTER 10: SOCIAL AND ECONOMIC STRUCTURES OF MEDIEVAL FRISIA

1. Introduction: The Fabric of Frisian Life

Having tracked the political evolution of Frisia through the 11th and 12th centuries, we now turn our attention to the **social and economic structures** that underpinned Frisian communities. While the notion of "Frisian freedom" often takes center stage in historical narratives, it was the daily routines of farming, fishing, trading, and communal cooperation that made this freedom viable. Families living on terpen or behind dikes shaped how land was owned, how labor was organized, and how conflicts were resolved.

In this chapter, we explore the diverse aspects of medieval Frisian society: class distinctions between nobles, free peasants, and dependent laborers; the significance of maritime activities in local culture; the roles of women and family structures; the interplay of religious institutions with everyday life; and the ways in which legal customs evolved to handle economic disputes. By examining these facets, we gain a clearer picture of how Frisians maintained a distinctive regional identity, balancing communal autonomy with gradual integration into broader European trends. No single factor can explain Frisian society—it was a tapestry woven from environmental challenges, legal traditions, external influences, and local innovation.

2. Landholding Patterns and Class Structure

2.1 Allodial Ownership and Feudal Tensions

One key feature of medieval Frisian society was the prevalence of **allodial ownership**—land held free of feudal obligations. In many parts of Europe, a typical farmer held land as a fief, owing rent or service to a lord. In Frisia, numerous landholders possessed small plots outright, enabling them to manage their property without paying homage or labor dues. Such allods often passed down through families, reinforcing the independence of local kin groups.

However, this system coexisted with pockets of feudal tenure, especially where powerful local lineages or external lords had managed to establish feudal claims. A bishop or count might hold certain estates, expecting rent from peasants there. This patchwork created tension between those living under feudal constraints and those who prided themselves on allodial freedom. Sometimes entire villages were allodial, forming a tight-knit community that resisted any attempt by an outside noble to impose rent. Elsewhere, a strong local noble family had converted surrounding farmland into feudal holdings, especially if they once protected that land from Viking raids or invested in dike construction.

2.2 Nobility, Chieftains, and Proto-Aristocracy

Although large-scale feudalism was less dominant in Frisia than in many regions, a **proto-aristocracy** did exist. Wealthy families—often called chieftains or geslachten—emerged as local leaders. They owned larger tracts of land, possibly spanning multiple terpen or villages. Their authority came not only from property but from the respect or fear they commanded within local assemblies. Such families could trace their lineage to past heroes or successful warlords, using that history to justify leadership roles.

The word "chieftain" can be misleading, as these figures were not necessarily tribal leaders but local aristocrats who combined the old Germanic tradition of personal loyalty with newly introduced feudal elements (if it suited them). They might serve as guardians of local law, sponsors of a church or monastery, and patrons of local craftsmen. Some even minted local coins or sealed documents with personal crests, showcasing aspirations akin to continental nobility. But they still had to navigate communal assemblies that insisted on their own voice in governance. A chieftain who ignored local consensus risked losing influence or provoking violent retaliation.

2.3 Freemen and Dependent Laborers

Below the nobility were the **freemen**, smallholders who owned or leased plots of land, participated in assemblies, and contributed labor to communal dike projects.

Freemen formed the backbone of Frisian society, as they maintained a sense of shared responsibility for water management and local defense. Their right to bear arms, attend assemblies, and have a say in local law set them apart from peasants in many other European regions, where strict feudal stratification curtailed such freedoms.

However, not all inhabitants enjoyed this status. A segment of the population lived as **dependent laborers** or cotters, working on lands owned by chieftains, monastic communities, or wealthier freemen. Though not exactly serfs in the classical feudal sense—Frisia's legal environment often prohibited outright servitude—these laborers had limited autonomy. They might owe part of their harvest as rent or be contractually bound to remain on a certain estate. Social mobility for dependent laborers was possible if they saved enough to purchase a small allod or married into a freer family, but it was not common.

---

3. Water Management: Dikes, Terpen, and Communal Efforts

3.1 Evolving Dike Technology

Frisia's coastal geography demanded advanced water management techniques. While terpen—artificial mounds—had protected individual farmsteads for centuries, population growth necessitated larger dikes to reclaim and safeguard extensive tracts of marsh. By the 11th and 12th centuries, earthen dikes were built in continuous lines along the coast, reinforced with wooden piles or fascines where needed. Some areas experimented with tidal sluices, allowing water to drain at low tide but closing against high tide. These improvements expanded cultivable land, fueling economic growth.

Each dike segment required significant labor. Communities gathered periodically for dike-raising seasons, hauling earth in wicker baskets or on carts. High-ranking families sometimes financed major sections, earning them prestige and influence. Monasteries also played a pivotal role, using their organizational capacity and spiritual motivation to muster laborers. Despite these cooperative efforts, dike maintenance was an ongoing challenge: storms or floods could break sections of dike, and if repairs were neglected, entire fields might revert to marshland.

3.2 Terpen: Adaptive Housing

Even with substantial dikes, many families continued to live on **terpen**. Built up over generations, these mounds rose several meters above the surrounding fields, offering a refuge when water levels soared. Some terpen evolved into small villages with a central church and cluster of houses. Archaeological layers reveal how, over centuries, inhabitants added material (earth, clay, refuse) to raise the mound further.

Terpen made Frisian settlement patterns distinctive: rather than neat villages or a single castle overshadowing farmland, one often found dispersed mounds, each home to a few extended families. When a strong storm broke through a dike, people and livestock could temporarily crowd onto a terp until the waters receded. This resilience shaped attitudes toward communal life. Even if an outside lord claimed ownership of the land around a terp, the mound's inhabitants typically felt self-sufficient, reinforcing local traditions of autonomy.

3.3 Community Organization and Dike Laws

Water management required strict rules. Many Frisian districts developed **dike laws** that stipulated how labor was apportioned, how costs were shared, and how disputes were resolved. These laws were proclaimed in local assemblies, ensuring that each landholder contributed according to their acreage or livestock. Penalties for neglecting dike work could be severe, since a single unmaintained segment threatened the entire region. Fines or forced labor might be imposed on defaulters.

Enforcement of dike law reflected Frisian communal principles. Instead of a single lord commanding the workforce, an elected or appointed official—often called a **dike reeve** or "dijkgraaf" in later sources—oversaw the project. The reeve reported back to the assembly, ensuring accountability. This structure also curbed aristocratic overreach, as a powerful chieftain still needed assembly approval to direct communal resources. Over time, water management institutions grew in sophistication, eventually forming the basis of the "waterschappen" (water boards) that would persist into much later centuries.

4. Maritime Economy and Trade Networks

4.1 Coastal Navigation and Shipbuilding

Frisia's identity was deeply intertwined with the sea. Besides farmland, the region's wealth also came from fishing, shipping, and maritime commerce. Fishing families used small vessels to harvest herring, flatfish, and shellfish from the North Sea. Inland waters and estuaries also teemed with fish. Over generations, Frisians improved boat designs to handle shallow tidal zones, crafting robust yet agile craft that could navigate sandbanks and mudflats.

For long-distance trade, larger seagoing ships (often referred to in broad terms as "cogs" by the 12th century) were built in small shipyards along the coast. These ships had flat bottoms or minimal keels, suitable for loading and unloading in harbors without deep wharves. They carried cargoes of grain, salt, timber, wool, and hides to markets around the North Sea basin. English wool, for instance, was in high demand on the Continent, and Frisian merchants acted as middlemen, ferrying bales from English ports to Flanders or the Rhineland.

4.2 Major Trading Routes and Partners

By the 11th century, the North Sea was a busy commercial corridor linking England, Flanders, northern France, the Rhineland, and Scandinavia. Frisians took advantage of these routes, forging trade links that offset their relatively small local market. Partnerships with Flemish and English merchants proved especially lucrative. Flemish cloth towns needed raw wool, some of which could be sourced from English estates transported by Frisian ships. Conversely, continental products—wine, metal goods, or luxury textiles—could be carried back to English ports.

Some Frisian traders also ventured into the Baltic, interacting with emerging towns like Lübeck. Although the Hanseatic League would formalize Baltic trade networks later in the 13th century, the seeds of that development were planted during the 12th century. Frisians laid initial groundwork, learning the routes and forging local contacts. Over time, competition from Saxon and Wendish merchants in the eastern Baltic grew, but Frisians retained a niche, especially in shipping cargoes through shallow waters.

4.3 Port Towns and Market Centers

While no single Frisian port dominated trade as Dorestad once did, a series of **port towns** grew in importance. Examples include Staveren (Stavoren), eventually overshadowed in the late medieval period by newer Zuiderzee towns; and coastal settlements near the mouth of the Vlie or the Lauwers. Some were protected by wooden palisades or stone walls, financed by local chieftains or merchant guilds. A typical town might feature a modest harbor, a market square, a church, and a scattering of workshops—blacksmiths, coopers, rope-makers—serving the shipping trade.

Fairs and market days drew rural folk who sold surplus grain, dairy, or wool. In turn, they purchased tools, salt, fish, and foreign imports. Guilds formed among craftsmen or merchants, regulating quality and prices. Over time, these guilds exerted influence within local assemblies, pressing for roads, bridges, or harbor improvements. Thus, towns became catalysts for social and economic change, introducing more specialized trades and shifting the balance of power away from purely rural assemblies.

---

5. Social Life, Family, and Gender Roles

5.1 Household Structure and Marriage Customs

Medieval Frisian households varied in size. Wealthier families living on large terpen might incorporate multiple branches of an extended clan—grandparents, married sons, unmarried daughters, and possibly laborers under the same roof. Smaller farms housed nuclear families, occasionally supplemented by hired hands. **Marriage** was both a personal and economic alliance. Parents often arranged unions to consolidate land or forge alliances with neighboring kin groups. Dowries or bridewealth (in the form of livestock, land, or cash) were common.

In a culture prizing family lineage, genealogical memory was strong. Oral tradition recounted ancestors who supposedly defended the region from invaders or contributed to local dike building. Women typically managed household tasks—cooking, weaving, childcare—while men tended fields or fished. However, in many families, women also engaged in trade or helped with farm labor, especially if a husband was away at sea. Among the chieftain class, noblewomen might oversee estate finances or act as regents for young heirs, showcasing their capacity for leadership in times of crisis.

5.2 Role of Women in Assemblies and Property Rights

While medieval societies generally limited women's public roles, Frisian customs sometimes offered them greater latitude than feudal norms elsewhere. **Property rights** for Frisian women could be relatively generous, especially if land was allodial. A widow might inherit a portion of her husband's farm and continue managing it until remarriage or passing it to children. A married woman's dower portion could remain under her control, preventing total economic dependence on her husband.

Yet, participation in assemblies was mostly reserved for adult males recognized as freemen. Rare exceptions occur in records of widows or noblewomen representing a family line, possibly when no adult male was available. Even then, such appearances were unusual and typically required prior agreement by the assembly. Though not equal by modern standards, these limited openings for women to be heard or to control property contributed to a social environment less rigidly stratified than in many feudal regions.

5.3 Social Gatherings, Feasts, and Folk Traditions

Frisian communal life included **seasonal celebrations** tied to the agricultural cycle—spring sowing feasts, harvest festivals, and winter gatherings. Church holidays overlapped with or replaced older pagan customs, but remnants of pre-Christian beliefs sometimes lingered in local superstition or folklore. Feasting served as a key social glue: families invited neighbors, forging bonds that reinforced communal ties. Beer and mead were staples at these gatherings, often brewed locally. Music, storytelling, and competitions (e.g., wrestling, archery) created a sense of shared culture.

Folk traditions also appeared around maritime life. Sailors and fishermen observed rituals or invoked patron saints for safe voyages. Local chapels might display votive offerings—small wooden ships or tokens—given in thanks after surviving storms. Storytellers recounted legendary sea heroes or recast older Germanic sagas in a Frisian context. Over generations, these communal events and narratives forged a strong collective spirit. The emphasis on shared feasts, neighborly help, and respect for local custom undergirded the broader concept of Frisian unity.

6. Law and Conflict Resolution

6.1 Customary Law and Its Flexibility

Frisians relied on **customary law** that evolved to meet the region's changing needs. Unlike Roman-based legal codes that sought uniformity, Frisian law gave weight to local precedent and oral tradition. Judges or law-speakers recited established rules, but assemblies could adapt them through discussion. This fluidity allowed the system to accommodate new realities, like maritime trade disputes or the introduction of minted currency.

Yet, the same flexibility could lead to inconsistencies. A dispute resolved one way in East Frisia might be handled differently in West Frisia. For cross-district matters—such as shipping conflicts or homicide cases involving individuals from separate areas—representatives might convene a special moot, aiming for a consensus. In this environment, personal relationships and clan alliances mattered significantly. Skilled negotiators could sway the assembly's ruling, which might otherwise favor the more influential party.

6.2 Wergild, Blood Feuds, and Mediation

Wergild—the compensation owed for killing or injuring someone—remained central in Frisian law. The amount varied by the victim's social rank, with free Frisians typically commanding higher wergild than dependent laborers. If a family felt the wergild was insufficient or was not paid, they could pursue a **blood feud**, seeking personal vengeance. This system was an ancient Germanic custom, but it coexisted uncomfortably with Christian teachings about forgiveness.

Over time, local assemblies and church leaders worked to mediate or discourage feuds, fearful they would escalate into larger clan wars. Monasteries sometimes offered "holy ground" for negotiations, persuading warring families to accept a settlement. Chieftains or bishops also acted as mediators if they had enough prestige. Avoiding feuds was critical for preserving community harmony, and successful mediation reinforced the principle that law, not raw violence, should govern conflicts.

6.3 Oaths and Procedural Ordeals

In the 11th and 12th centuries, **oath-taking** was a common legal procedure. A defendant, accused of theft or wrongdoing, could swear an oath of innocence, backed by "oath helpers" who vouched for their character. If the assembly doubted these oaths, they might require an **ordeal**—like carrying hot iron or plunging a hand into boiling water—to test guilt or innocence based on divine judgment. Although the Church increasingly frowned on ordeals as the century progressed, they remained embedded in local practice.

Frisian assemblies sometimes adapted these ordeals to local conditions. For instance, a water-based ordeal could be used, though it was less common than in other parts of Europe. The logic was that if a person sank (supported by God's will), they were innocent, and if they floated, they were guilty—a grim test that risked drowning. Over time, external church reforms discouraged such methods, pushing Frisians toward more rational inquiry. Yet tradition died slowly, illustrating how local communities balanced Christian influences with inherited customs.

---

7. The Church as a Social Institution

7.1 Rural Priests and Community Ties

In many Frisian parishes, the **village priest** was a linchpin of social life. He officiated baptisms, marriages, funerals, and feast-day masses. A local priest might be from the community itself or from a neighboring district, and his personal ties could shape how actively he engaged in local disputes. A supportive priest could mediate conflicts, while a priest allied with a powerful family might appear partisan.

The church building, often on a raised terp beside the village graveyard, doubled as a communal meeting spot. Assemblies might gather in its yard (or even inside in bad weather) to discuss urgent issues, bridging spiritual and civic spheres. Tithes were expected—usually one-tenth of produce—but enforcement varied. If a priest or bishop demanded too strict a tithe policy, local freeholders might resist, citing older exemptions or threatening to withhold labor on church lands.

7.2 Monastic Outreach and Charity

Monasteries, especially Cistercian outposts, played a vital role in **charitable work** and social welfare. They often hosted travelers, pilgrims, or the poor. In times of flood or crop failure, monasteries could distribute stored grain or fodder, alleviating famine in surrounding villages. Such acts increased the monastery's standing, fostering goodwill. In turn, local families might donate land or wealth in gratitude, strengthening the monastic community's influence.

Cistercians, in particular, emphasized labor and discipline, sometimes setting an example for the broader region. They cultivated new farmland meticulously, draining bogs and building drainage ditches. This practical demonstration appealed to Frisians, who appreciated collaborative water management. Monastic annals from this period occasionally describe cooperative projects: laypeople constructing a dike under the guidance of monks, forging a bond that transcended feudal conflicts and further linked religious institutions with everyday economic life.

7.3 Pilgrimage, Relics, and Regional Identity

As pilgrimages grew in popularity, certain Frisian churches claimed special relics or shrines. Pilgrims traveling along the North Sea coast might stop to venerate a local saint or see an alleged relic. While these shrines never matched the fame of great European pilgrimage sites, they did attract some traffic, bringing coins and donations. A few local legends grew around holy figures reputed to protect Frisia from storms or floods, blending older coastal beliefs with Christian hagiography.

Additionally, returning Frisian pilgrims brought foreign relics, icons, or architectural ideas, spurring church renovations or expansions. Some coastal churches adopted Romanesque or early Gothic elements in building design, reflecting broader European trends. Despite these external influences, the local spin on religion remained strong. Saints were often depicted in local attire, and liturgical celebrations might incorporate Frisian folk songs or references to water-based miracles. Through such adaptations, the Church in Frisia became a fusion of universal Christian themes and regional identity.

8. Cultural Expressions and Daily Life

8.1 Language and Literature

While Latin dominated church writings, **Old Frisian** remained the spoken language for daily affairs and local legal texts. Over time, scribes started writing some documents in Old Frisian, creating a modest corpus of charters, legal codes, and even fragments of poetry. These texts preserve the distinctive vocabulary used to describe dike law, maritime matters, and communal assemblies. To modern linguists, they reveal how closely related Old Frisian was to Old English, reflecting shared roots in the North Sea Germanic family.

Literary output was limited, focusing on practical or religious texts rather than epic poetry. Oral storytelling, however, thrived. Minstrels or traveling singers recounted local legends, war tales, or saintly miracles. Households also passed down genealogical stories highlighting ancestors' feats in building dikes or repelling invaders. Thus, while we lack a grand Frisian literary canon from this period, an oral tradition preserved community memory and shaped local identity across generations.

8.2 Clothing, Crafts, and Material Culture

Frisians dressed in garments adapted to a damp climate. Common folk wore woolen tunics or dresses, with cloaks to protect against rain and wind. Dyes derived from local plants produced earthy colors—browns, grays, muted blues, and greens. Footwear often consisted of leather shoes or boots, sometimes treated with grease to repel moisture. Wealthier families might wear finer fabrics—linen undergarments or embroidered wool—trading for these materials via maritime connections.

Craftsmanship centered on practical goods, though decorative items did exist. Potters made sturdy earthenware for cooking and storage. Woodworkers built boats, furniture, and tools. Metalworkers forged agricultural implements and weapons; certain villages specialized in iron smelting using peat bog iron. Jewelry, when worn, typically included simple brooches or rings. Among the chieftain class, silver or gold brooches with filigree or gem settings indicated status. Archaeological finds show that some designs were influenced by contacts with Anglo-Saxon or Scandinavian artisans.

8.3 Feasting, Music, and Games

Beyond life's necessities, Frisians enjoyed leisure in the form of **feasting** and communal entertainments. Large gatherings often followed important events like weddings, church consecrations, or harvest completions. Meat—pork, beef, mutton—took center stage, supplemented by bread, cheese, and local produce. Beer was the staple drink, brewed from barley and flavored with herbs (hops became more common later). Musical traditions featured stringed instruments akin to lyres or early fiddles, wooden flutes, and rhythmic drums.

Board games, such as tafl-like variants (related to the Norse "hnefatafl") or simpler dice games, were played in communal houses or taverns. Wrestling and archery contests tested physical prowess. On the coast, net casting competitions or boat races might mark festival days. These amusements fostered social cohesion, bridging the gap between wealthy chieftains and small farmers. Though disputes could arise—especially if gambling was involved—organized festivities generally reinforced communal identity.

---

9. Changing Frameworks: Towards the High Middle Ages

9.1 Shifts in Power and External Influences

By the close of the 12th century, Europe as a whole was entering the **High Middle Ages**. Kings consolidated power in England and France, monastic orders expanded, and commercial hubs thrived in Flanders and the Rhine. Frisia felt these influences: trade volume increased, new technology like the heavy plow and windmill began to appear, and alliances with neighboring counts grew more formal. While the essential structures of Frisian society—communal dikes, local assemblies, allodial farms—remained intact, external pressures to conform to feudal norms persisted.

In some cases, chieftains adopted aspects of chivalric culture from abroad, building small stone towers or wearing more advanced armor. They might host jousts or sponsor minstrels who sang of knightly deeds. This cultural borrowing did not necessarily erode Frisian freedom but introduced new social symbols. A tension grew between older traditions of local equality and the aristocratic desire for recognized nobility across Europe.

9.2 Incremental Legal Reforms

At the same time, law codes were being refined. With better record-keeping, local assemblies codified rules on inheritance, property disputes, and water governance. Some codes recognized women's property rights in clearer language, reflecting practical realities. Others standardized procedures for oath-taking and evidence assessment, edging away from ordeals. Church synods also pressed for changes that aligned local practice with canonical law, such as banning certain marriages deemed incestuous by broader medieval standards.

These legal refinements helped Frisia function more coherently as an economic region. If merchants from distant lands could trust that Frisian courts would uphold fair processes, trade was more likely to flourish. Moreover, the presence of a clearer legal framework gave local leaders a stronger hand when negotiating with outside lords or bishops. They could point to written codes proving that certain taxes or obligations were not recognized in Frisian law, thus reinforcing the independence narrative.

9.3 Evolving Identity and Preparing for Future Struggles

As the 12th century drew to a close, Frisians had navigated centuries of external threats—Roman overshadowing, migrations, Frankish expansions, Viking raids—and forged a distinctive social system. Communal dike management, robust assemblies, partial feudal elements, a thriving maritime trade, and a deep-rooted sense of local law all combined to create a resilient culture. The concept of "Frisian freedom" was now more than a vague tradition: it was embedded in how farmland was owned, how people worshipped and governed themselves, and how they negotiated with powerful neighbors.

But the story was far from over. The High Middle Ages would bring **new challenges**: intensifying territorial ambitions from the Counts of Holland, attempts by princes in the Holy Roman Empire to unify the region, evolving feudal structures in adjacent lands, and even crusading fervor that might draw off some Frisian fighters. These changes would shape the next chapters of Frisian history. The social and economic structures we have examined here provided the foundation for future centuries of adaptation and conflict.

CHAPTER 11: TRADE NETWORKS AND CITY GROWTH

1. Introduction: Frisia in a Changing Economic World

By the late 12th century, Europe was entering a period of dynamic economic expansion often referred to by historians as the **Commercial Revolution** of the High Middle Ages. Populations were on the rise, agriculture was more productive, and international trade routes—by land and sea—became increasingly reliable and profitable. In this atmosphere, Frisia's position along the North Sea coast offered prime opportunities for merchant ventures. Local traders, shipbuilders, and port towns benefited from the region's maritime expertise, linking continental markets to the wider North Sea world and, gradually, the Baltic as well.

At the same time, inland regions were also experiencing transformations. Improvements in road networks, the spread of minted coinage, and the emergence of new fair towns opened novel routes for goods. Frisia adapted to these shifts, merging its traditional focus on sea-based commerce with growing inland connections. This chapter explores the forces driving Frisian trade and the rise of new towns, showing how local communities capitalized on regional and transcontinental demand. We also examine the social transformations sparked by city growth, such as the emergence of urban elites, craft guilds, and the interplay between town charters and traditional Frisian freedom.

2. Contextualizing the 12th-Century Boom

2.1 Europe's Broader Economic Expansion

Medieval Europe's economic upswing in the 12th century was driven by multiple factors. Improved agricultural yields (due to better plows, crop rotations, and clearing of new lands) supported larger populations. More people meant greater demand for everyday goods—from grain and fish to textiles and metal wares—leading to increased production and trade. Furthermore, evolving monetary systems, including more consistent silver coinage, smoothed commercial transactions. Large fair towns like Champagne in France became epicenters of exchange, attracting merchants from as far as Italy and England.

Maritime trade also flourished, as coastal shipping routes supplemented land-based caravans. The North Sea, Baltic Sea, and Atlantic coasts saw a surge of vessels carrying bulk goods: salt, fish, timber, metals, and wool. Ports grew in importance, some forming loose alliances to protect mutual trading interests. Eventually, a more formal confederation would develop in the Baltic (the Hanseatic League), but the seeds of that structure were already visible in the late 12th century. Frisia sat at an intersection of these routes, bridging the Rhine delta and the Zuiderzee with direct sea lanes to England and Flanders.

2.2 Post-Viking Stability and Regional Politics

In Frisia, the relative stability following the Viking age allowed for economic renewal. Though occasional feuds among local families continued, large-scale destruction of port facilities had subsided. Neighbors such as the County of Holland or the Bishopric of Utrecht still contested Frisian autonomy, yet these powers also recognized that stable trade yielded tax revenue and tolls. As a result, while political conflicts didn't disappear, they often took a back seat to commercial cooperation in port towns.

Additionally, the Holy Roman Empire's gradual shift of focus to southern and eastern frontiers meant that imperial interference in northern coastal affairs was somewhat sporadic. Emperors might still grant charters or confirm privileges for Frisian communities, but they rarely imposed direct administration. This gave local leaders—both rural chieftains and rising urban elites—room to shape economic structures that suited them, further entrenching Frisian practices of self-governance and local decision-making in maritime affairs.

3. Evolution of Frisian Maritime Commerce

3.1 Merchant Ships and Innovations

Frisian merchants and shipbuilders drew upon centuries of local seafaring expertise. During the 12th century, vessel designs evolved to carry heavier cargoes and to navigate both rivers and coastal waters. Early medieval ships, like small cogs, began to incorporate design features that improved capacity: stouter hulls, higher sides, and sturdier rudders. Single-masted with square sails, these ships were not especially fast but proved durable in rough North Sea conditions.

For shallow Frisian inlets and mudflats, specialized craft called **"praams"** or similar flat-bottom boats were used. Such boats could land cargo directly on sandy shores or riverbanks without needing deep harbors. This flexibility made it easier for smaller Frisian settlements to engage in trade, bypassing large port monopolies. Over time, some Frisian shipwrights experimented with improved rigging techniques—borrowing ideas from English or Scandinavian mariners—and built relationships with foreign merchants who needed ships capable of handling local waters.

3.2 Primary Commodities: Salt, Fish, Wool, and Grain

While Frisia produced various goods, several key commodities dominated its export scene:

1. **Salt**: Derived from coastal peat or saline marshlands, salt was indispensable for preserving meat and fish in a pre-refrigeration age. Frisian salt works dotted certain coastal areas, employing laborers to boil or evaporate brine. This salt found a ready market in inland Europe.
2. **Fish**: Herring, cod, and flatfish formed much of the catch. Processed (salted or dried) fish traveled widely, feeding urban populations that observed meatless days or simply needed a cheap protein source. In addition, local fishermen supplied fresh catch to emerging Frisian towns, fueling both domestic consumption and small-scale export.
3. **Wool**: While English wool overshadowed continental production in some markets, Frisia's smaller flocks still contributed to local textiles. More importantly, Frisian merchants carried English wool from East Anglia or Yorkshire, shipping it to Flemish cloth centers. Acting as middlemen, they profited from bridging the English-Flemish trade corridor.

4. **Grain**: Coastal and reclaimed lands yielded cereals—rye, barley, oats, and some wheat. These grains fed local populations, but surplus could be exported to regions facing shortages. With the population boom, bread demand soared across Europe, making grain a staple in commercial traffic.

3.3 Routes and Partnerships

The main shipping lanes connected Frisian ports to:

- **England**: Particularly East Anglian ports (like King's Lynn or Boston), from which wool and other items were procured.
- **Flanders**: Key destinations included Bruges and Ghent, epicenters of cloth-making and general trade.
- **Lower Rhine**: Overland or river routes extended goods to Cologne or further inland, linking with Central Europe.
- **Scandinavia**: Sporadic voyages to Norway or Denmark for timber, iron, or cod (especially the thriving stockfish trade).

These routes were not monopolized by a single Frisian port. Instead, a web of smaller coastal towns facilitated the flow of goods, occasionally forming ad hoc alliances. Merchants might band together in convoys for protection against piracy—though piracy had diminished since the Viking era, raiders or rogue knights still posed a threat on poorly guarded seas. Over time, Frisian merchants established reputations for reliability in shallow waters, encouraging foreign traders to hire Frisian crews or lease Frisian-built vessels for coastal navigation.

4. Growth of Frisian Towns and Market Centers

4.1 Emergence of New Urban Hubs

Unlike some parts of Europe where a single city (like Venice or Lübeck) dominated trade, Frisia's urban development was more diffuse. **Staveren (Stavoren)**, once significant in earlier centuries, continued as a moderate trade hub, though silting and changes in shipping routes sometimes hampered growth. Along the Zuiderzee coast, towns like **Harlingen** or **Workum** expanded modestly, hosting weekly markets and attracting artisans. Further east, near the Ems River, places like

Emden (though sometimes considered East Frisian) garnered attention for its strategic location.

Some of these towns were not large by modern standards—perhaps a few thousand inhabitants—but in the medieval context, they were bustling centers. Wooden docks, warehouses, and small stone or timber homes clustered behind protective dikes or ramparts. Merchant families often lived close to the quayside, storing goods in attached sheds. Streets could be narrow and muddy, with occasional attempts at paving near key market squares. Over time, as trade profits accrued, wealthier citizens funded modest public works, like improved market halls or watchtowers to guard the harbor.

4.2 Town Charters and Autonomy

As trade flourished, many Frisian towns pursued **charters**—documents granting them specific privileges. These could include:

- **Market Rights**: The legal authority to hold weekly or annual markets free from certain tolls.
- **Self-Governance**: Permission to elect their own aldermen or a local council, often in tandem with existing Frisian assemblies.
- **Fortification**: The right to build walls or maintain a militia for defense.
- **Judicial Freedoms**: The ability to try local cases under town law rather than deferring to a distant count or bishop.

Often, such charters were confirmed by a bishop, a neighboring count, or (less frequently) an imperial authority. Yet in true Frisian fashion, obtaining a charter didn't necessarily mean accepting feudal subjugation. Instead, towns aimed to codify their existing freedoms and protect themselves from external overlords demanding tribute. Thus, a tension emerged: outside authorities might see charters as a means to incorporate towns into a feudal hierarchy, while towns saw them as a shield bolstering local autonomy.

4.3 Guilds, Crafts, and Merchant Brotherhoods

With growing urban populations came **guilds**—associations of artisans or merchants that regulated trades, set quality standards, and protected members' interests. Crafts like baking, brewing, smithing, and carpentry each formed guilds. These groups negotiated with town councils on matters such as fair pricing, apprentice training, and public works. Guilds also served mutual aid purposes, offering financial help to members facing illness or family crises.

Merchant brotherhoods arose among those engaged in long-distance shipping, facilitating joint ventures and risk-sharing. Members might pool resources to fund a voyage, splitting profits according to their shares. The brotherhood might maintain a common warehouse or arrange group transport. Disputes between merchants were settled internally, sometimes in the presence of local magistrates. This cooperative approach helped reduce the financial perils of maritime trade, fostering a sense of unity among trading houses.

---

5. The Interplay of City and Countryside

5.1 Tensions with Rural Assemblies

Though towns contributed to Frisian prosperity, they did not always harmonize seamlessly with the rural communities. Many farmers worried that city councils might impose new market rules or tolls that infringed on old freedoms. Rivalries flared when towns sought to extend jurisdiction over surrounding countryside, perhaps to secure food supplies or protect trade routes. Rural assemblies, deeply attached to the ideal of local autonomy, resisted such encroachments.

In some districts, the tension escalated into outright conflict. For example, if a town tried to regulate fishing rights on nearby waters, local fisherfolk might sabotage the town's regulatory offices. Alternatively, city-based elites who acquired farmland around the settlement might claim authority to collect rents. This tug-of-war between urban and rural interests was a microcosm of a broader theme in medieval Frisia: balancing the newly consolidated wealth and power found in towns with the longstanding traditions of decentralized governance in the countryside.

5.2 Mutual Dependencies

Despite these frictions, towns and countryside needed each other. City merchants relied on rural produce—grain, dairy, hides—to supply both local consumption and export markets. Likewise, farmers benefited from a secure place to sell surplus. Towns also offered specialized goods: better tools from blacksmith guilds, varied cloth from textile workshops, or advanced milling services. Over time, collaborative customs formed. A rural assembly might grant a town exclusive rights to host a large seasonal fair in exchange for guaranteeing fair treatment of rural vendors.

Moreover, the communal approach to water management frequently unified both spheres. Whether city or village, all needed robust dikes and drainage. Town councils contributed funds or manpower to dike repairs that protected farmland feeding the town's population. Conversely, rural dwellers recognized that a thriving port could sponsor major water-control projects. When a severe storm threatened, these mutual dependencies often overcame day-to-day disagreements.

5.3 Formation of District Alliances

In parts of Frisia, alliances formed among multiple towns and their surrounding rural districts. These alliances sought to create stable conditions for trade and shared defense against external threats. They sometimes formalized under a collective name or assembly, akin to later "urban leagues" found in the Low Countries or northern Germany. While never as centralized as the famous Hanseatic League, these Frisian alliances demonstrated the region's capacity for cooperative problem-solving.

A typical alliance might delineate each participant's obligations: how many soldiers or ships they must provide in wartime, how to handle trade disputes, and how tolls or dike maintenance costs were shared. Town representatives and rural chieftains jointly oversaw these agreements, forging a balance between new urban interests and older communal traditions. Although not always permanent (feuds or leadership changes could unravel them), these alliances provided a glimpse into how Frisia adapted medieval governance models to its own context.

---

6. Cultural and Social Shifts in Town Life

6.1 Urban Elites and Social Stratification

As Frisian towns matured, **urban elites** emerged: merchant dynasties, wealthy guild masters, and sometimes chieftain families who relocated to the city for better commercial opportunities. They built larger houses, invested in multiple trade ventures, and played leading roles in town councils. Their power did not go unchallenged—less affluent guild members or day laborers sometimes accused them of monopolizing resources. Nonetheless, the broad prosperity allowed many craftspeople and small merchants to achieve relative comfort compared to peasants in feudal areas elsewhere in Europe.

This new urban stratification paralleled the older rural distinctions between freemen, dependent laborers, and nobility. Despite the rhetoric of Frisian freedom, a merchant patriciate could wield heavy influence, shaping market regulations to suit their interests. Tensions periodically flared if the poorer inhabitants felt overtaxed or excluded from governance. While local assemblies provided a voice for ordinary citizens, the elites often steered decisions by virtue of wealth and patronage networks.

6.2 Urban Religious Life

Town churches and chapels became focal points for social gatherings, religious festivals, and charity. Merchant guilds adopted patron saints—often associated with seafaring (e.g., Saint Nicholas or Saint Clement)—and funded chapels dedicated to them. Processions on saints' days, attended by townspeople in their guild livery, showcased communal pride. Pilgrimage shrines within certain towns also drew visitors from across the region, boosting local commerce.

Monasteries increasingly took root near towns, where they could minister to urban populations, operate schools or hospitals, and maintain scriptoriums. Orders like the Cistercians or Premonstratensians extended their landholding from rural reclamation projects into urban real estate. Sometimes, friction arose if monastic privileges exempted them from certain taxes or if their competition in brewing or milling undercut local guilds. Nonetheless, the spiritual and practical benefits they provided generally ingratiated them with city dwellers.

6.3 Urban Culture and Entertainment

Compared to rural villages, Frisian towns offered a livelier cultural scene. Minstrels, jugglers, and traveling actors sometimes performed in market squares. Seasonal fairs might feature acrobatic displays or comedic plays. Feasting in guild halls became grander, celebrating profitable trade deals or religious festivities. Certain towns developed reputations for specialized crafts—like fine leatherwork, pottery with distinctive glazing, or embroidered textiles—fostering local artistic flair.

Literacy also edged upward among the urban populace, especially the merchant class who needed to keep accounts and read contracts. Some wealthier families hired tutors or sent sons to cathedral schools in Utrecht or elsewhere, creating a class of literate merchants who could correspond with distant partners. This growing literacy, while still limited, contributed to the eventual compilation of more detailed town records, charters, and even early civic chronicles. Over time, these records would offer historians deeper insights into medieval Frisian urban life.

---

7. External Influences and Challenges

7.1 Rivalry with Holland and Utrecht

The expanding County of Holland continued to cast an ambitious eye northward, hoping to annex or at least influence wealthy Frisian towns. Holland's counts recognized the economic potential of controlling trade routes along the Zuiderzee and the Wadden Sea. They attempted to impose tolls on Frisian shipping, or to place Holland-friendly bailiffs in key ports. Frisian towns sometimes fought back, forming alliances or paying lumpsum tributes only if the count recognized local autonomy.

Simultaneously, the Bishopric of Utrecht maintained claims in certain Frisian districts, including the region around the lower Ems and parts of northern Overijssel. Utrecht's bishops, functioning as prince-bishops, often needed revenue from Frisian commerce to maintain their seat. They might bestow market privileges on selected towns in exchange for loyalty, prompting those towns to accept partial overlordship. Other communities, suspicious of episcopal interference, invoked Frisian legal traditions to avoid subjection. This push-and-pull defined the 12th and 13th centuries, with no side achieving outright domination.

7.2 Emerging Hanseatic Connections

Though the **Hanseatic League** would not fully formalize until later in the 13th century, precursors of Hanseatic cooperation already existed among German and Scandinavian towns. Lübeck, Hamburg, Bremen, and other rising Baltic/North Sea ports sought secure trade with inland Germany and beyond. Frisian cities, smaller in scale, recognized potential advantages of collaborating with these powerful mercantile centers. Some Frisian merchants established branches or trading posts in Hanseatic cities, forging personal relationships.

However, friction could arise if Hanseatic towns tried to monopolize certain routes. Frisians cherished free trade principles and disliked heavy-handed regulation from foreign associations. Even so, a measure of mutual benefit kept them engaged. Joint agreements on coinage standards or piracy control surfaced in sporadic treaties. Over time, the relationship between Frisian ports and the Hanse would oscillate between cooperation and competition, depending on shifting economic interests.

7.3 Environmental Hazards: Storm Surges and River Changes

During the 12th and 13th centuries, climatic fluctuations led to occasional severe storms in the North Sea. **Storm surges** could breach dikes, flooding farmland and damaging port facilities. Major disasters, such as the devastating storm floods recorded in certain chronicles, reshaped coastlines—sometimes creating new inlets or destroying old ones, altering trade routes. Towns that once flourished might find their harbors silted up, forcing relocation of shipping activities.

For example, historians note repeated floods that battered the Zuiderzee region, eventually expanding the body of water's extent. Communities unable to fund quick dike repairs sometimes abandoned vulnerable sites. Others rebounded thanks to coordinated efforts and the resources of wealthy merchants or monastic landholders. Such environmental volatility underscored the fragility of Frisian prosperity. Despite robust communal water management traditions, the sheer force of nature could reorient economic fortunes overnight.

---

8. Social Transformations and Legal Codes

8.1 Town and District Laws

As Frisian towns gained prominence, they produced more **written legal codes**. These codes supplemented older oral traditions, focusing on commercial disputes, maritime regulations, and civic administration. Influenced partly by Roman and canon law, they offered standardized rules for contracts, loans, and property conveyances. Merchants appreciated the clarity, reducing the risk of ambiguous or biased rulings by local chieftains.

However, tension arose when these urban laws clashed with traditional Frisian district law. Rural assemblies sometimes saw town ordinances as infringing on their prerogatives, especially if city courts claimed authority over regional trade routes or farmland near the town. Negotiations to delineate jurisdictional boundaries became common, with some districts creating formal compacts specifying how far town law extended beyond city walls. These compacts represented innovative approaches to governance, balancing new legal frameworks with older communal systems.

8.2 The Concept of "Keurnoten" and Codification

In certain Frisian areas, references to **"keurnoten"** (law codes or sets of decrees) appear in the late 12th and early 13th centuries. These documents summarized local customary law, including water management obligations, inheritance guidelines, and procedures for public assemblies. The impetus for writing them down came from both internal desire for consistency and external pressure—bishops, counts, or even imperial envoys often required a tangible reference when disputes arose.

By codifying their laws, Frisian districts strengthened the argument that they were governed by ancient, recognized customs rather than arbitrary whim. This bolstered their stance against feudal claims. If a foreign lord demanded new obligations, the local representatives could point to the keurnoten, demonstrating that no such duties existed in established law. While no single codex unified all Frisian lands, these partial compilations laid the foundation for more comprehensive law collections in later centuries.

8.3 Shifts in Local Leadership

As towns matured and commerce thrived, some chieftains evolved into **urban patricians**, blending feudal and mercantile privileges. Wealthy families might retain rural estates while also running shipping ventures or holding seats on city councils. Their status derived from both lineage and capital, reshaping the idea of nobility. Meanwhile, new families that made fortunes in trade could ascend socially, marrying into older noble lines. This fluidity distinguished Frisia from strictly feudal territories where noble birth was paramount.

At the same time, smaller landholders—long the backbone of Frisian freedom—faced growing economic pressures. They contended with competition from monastic estates or large-scale reclamation projects funded by wealthy investors. Some less prosperous freemen sold or mortgaged their property, slipping into semi-dependent status. While the ideal of a broadly free Frisian society persisted, economic stratification in the 12th and 13th centuries did create pockets of wealth and poverty, challenging older egalitarian myths.

9. Cultural Continuity and Adaptation

9.1 Language and Identity

The growth of written records in towns—charters, guild documents, shipping manifests—brought more Old Frisian texts into being. Yet Latin often remained the language of official or ecclesiastical documents. Bilingualism became common among educated elites, who used Latin for formal matters and Frisian for local dealings. Over time, contact with Low German speakers (especially from Saxony and Hanseatic cities) introduced linguistic influences into spoken Frisian, especially in commercial settings.

Still, a core sense of Frisian identity thrived, linked to the region's unique legal traditions and communal water management. Poets or minstrels who performed in local dialects contributed to cultural cohesion, celebrating legendary ancestors or praising communal feats like dike construction. This evolving identity encompassed both maritime trade towns and inland farmland, unifying them under the banner of shared language and historical memory.

9.2 Religious Expression

The Catholic Church's presence in Frisia continued to deepen. Parishes in growing towns built larger churches, sometimes with Romanesque or early Gothic elements. Stained glass windows might depict maritime themes—ships, fish, or anchors—reflecting the local economy. Feast days for patron saints became major communal events. Some wealthy towns erected belfries or church towers that also served as lookout points, bridging sacred and security functions.

Cistercian monasteries, having expanded farmland through drainage, influenced cultural life with their emphasis on contemplation and liturgical rhythms. They sometimes introduced architectural styles or decorative motifs from France or other regions of Europe. Lay brotherhoods formed around popular saints or devotions, reinforcing social bonds beyond guild lines. Meanwhile, the old tension between local independence and hierarchical church authority persisted—parishioners expected their priests to reflect community values, not just bishop directives.

9.3 Festivities and Local Customs

Urban festivals mingled older rural customs with new influences. Processions might include guild floats depicting scenes of local industries—salt making, fishing, weaving—alongside religious tableaux. Jousting tournaments were rare (since full-blown chivalry never took deep root in Frisia), but simpler pageants, contests of archery or wrestling, and comedic plays performed in the town square were frequent highlights. Drinking houses multiplied, catering to merchants and sailors passing through.

Local folk traditions—like lighting beacons on high ground at certain times of year—took on an urban flavor as watchtowers replaced natural hills. Tales of sea spirits or drowned lands circulated, a reminder of the environment's volatility. Chroniclers mention beliefs that certain storms were divine punishment, or that particular saints protected vessels in dangerous waters. These narratives entwined spiritual convictions with the day-to-day realities of living in a low-lying coastal region.

CHAPTER 12: EXPANSION OF LOCAL POWERS AND EXTERNAL PRESSURES

1. Introduction: Frisia at the Crossroads of Power

By the dawn of the 13th century, Frisia was a tapestry of independent-minded districts, growing port towns, and entrenched noble or chieftain families. These local powers balanced precariously between the larger ambitions of neighboring states—especially the County of Holland and the Bishopric of Utrecht—as well as broader currents within the Holy Roman Empire. Internally, the interplay between wealthy merchant patricians in rising towns and traditional rural assemblies continued to evolve. Externally, new attempts at consolidation by regional counts or prince-bishops threatened to undermine the cherished principle of Frisian freedom.

In this chapter, we delve into the **13th and 14th centuries**, a time when alliances shifted more frequently, and the stakes grew higher. Holland's counts advanced north with renewed vigor, certain Frisian lineages grew into near-dynastic powers, and emperors or imperial princes sporadically intervened in local disputes. These entanglements produced both armed conflicts and diplomatic settlements, shaping the trajectory of Frisian autonomy. By examining the key political players, economic undercurrents, and the persistent role of communal law, we understand how medieval Frisia continued to adapt—or, at times, resist—encroaching feudal structures.

2. The County of Holland's Renewed Ambitions

2.1 The House of Holland Strengthens

In the early 13th century, the **House of Holland** (the dynasty of the counts) experienced a series of capable rulers who expanded their influence. Figures like **Count Floris IV** and **Count William II** recognized the economic promise of controlling Frisian trade corridors. William II even became elected King of the Romans (a stepping stone to being Holy Roman Emperor) in 1247, briefly giving him broader leverage.

For these counts, securing Frisia meant more than just collecting tolls. It promised direct access to the North Sea, thereby bolstering Holland's maritime standing. They also had their eyes on farmland reclaimed from the sea—a source of wealth through rents and taxes. The counts typically claimed ancient charters or imperial grants that, in their view, entitled them to rule Frisia. Their approach alternated between military aggression, strategic alliances (often via marriage or treaties with local chieftains), and attempts to bestow official titles on Frisian towns, hoping to bind them into feudal vassalage.

2.2 Conflicts and Armistices

Unsurprisingly, most Frisian communities did not welcome feudal overlordship from Holland. While some towns might sign short-term pacts—especially if the count offered privileges—rural assemblies remained firmly opposed. Periodic **skirmishes** erupted, especially when Holland's representatives tried to station garrisons or impose new tolls on shipping lanes. Chronicles mention smaller battles where Frisian militias, benefiting from local terrain knowledge, ambushed Holland's forces in marshy areas or behind dike lines.

Still, outright warfare was not constant. Both sides recognized that extended conflict jeopardized trade and farmland. Thus, negotiations yielded temporary **armistices** or "truces," where Frisia might concede minimal tribute or symbolic homage in exchange for being left largely self-governing. Over time, these armistices codified the uneasy relationship: the counts of Holland enjoyed nominal claims over certain Frisian districts, yet real local authority often remained in the hands of assemblies or chieftain families. Tensions simmered, ready to flare up whenever a new count tested the boundaries.

2.3 The Impact of William II's Reign

When **William II** ascended as King of the Romans, he sought to leverage his imperial position to enforce claims over Frisia. In 1256, while attempting to subdue Frisian resistance, William was killed during a campaign in the wintry marshes, famously said to have perished after falling through ice. This dramatic event reverberated through the Low Countries, demonstrating the difficulties even an imperial figure faced in quelling Frisia's stubborn autonomy.

William's death temporarily weakened Holland's push northward, providing a respite for Frisian communities. Yet, the House of Holland persisted in its ambitions under subsequent rulers like **Floris V**. The cycle of conflict and compromise would continue into the late 13th century, shaping the precarious balance of power in coastal territories.

---

3. The Rise of Powerful Frisian Chieftains

3.1 Local Families as Regional Powers

Throughout the 13th century, certain Frisian families, once mere local notables, expanded their wealth and influence to rival any external count or bishop. They combined farmland ownership, control of strategic dike segments, and alliances with merchants or monastic landholders to build quasi-principalities. In East Frisia, for instance, the **tom Brok** family and later the **Cirksena** lineage would exemplify how a chieftain clan could dominate multiple districts, forging personal armies and establishing small "court" centers.

Such chieftains often adopted noble customs—like forging alliances through intermarriage, maintaining retinues of knights or men-at-arms, and constructing stone fortresses on raised terpen. Yet they did so within a Frisian framework, proclaiming they upheld local freedoms and law. Their support among free peasants could be strong if they were seen as protectors against foreign invasion or mediators in local feuds. Alternatively, if they grew too oppressive—demanding rents or labor—assemblies might turn against them, sparking violent internal disputes.

3.2 Feuds and Land Disputes

As these chieftain families rose in power, **feuds** became a frequent method of settling scores. A killing, property encroachment, or insult might trigger a chain reaction of retaliation between rival clans. Each side mustered allies from various districts or even sought backing from external players like Holland or Utrecht. Some feuds dragged on for years, devastating farmland and trade routes.

Chroniclers lamented the chaos, suggesting that endless vendettas weakened Frisian unity at a time of looming external threats.

In many cases, these feuds also revolved around **land disputes** tied to water control. A family controlling a key dike or sluice could hamper a rival's farmland, effectively turning water management into a weapon. Recognizing the risk, local assemblies strove to keep dike law neutral—insisting that essential waterworks remain outside personal feuds. Success varied. In some places, communal pressure forced warring families to respect the greater good of flood protection; in others, entire areas were submerged when one side intentionally sabotaged a dike section.

3.3 Attempts at Broader Confederations

The growth of these powerful chieftain families sometimes spurred attempts to form **broader Frisian confederations** to end feuds and present a united front against outside powers. Legends and partial records reference gatherings at the "Upstalsboom," a traditional assembly site, where representatives from West, Middle, and East Frisia supposedly met to affirm collective principles. Some of these assemblies tried to codify peace treaties among feuding families, employing religious ceremonies to sanctify them.

While these confederations rarely achieved long-term, centralized governance, they underscored a desire for region-wide cooperation. Periodically, charters declared that all Frisians would stand together if Holland or another external force attacked. Yet each district guarded its local prerogatives, and the strong chieftains resented any supra-regional body restricting their autonomy. This tension prevented Frisia from forming a cohesive medieval "state," leaving it open to piecemeal encroachments by powerful neighbors.

---

4. The Role of the Bishopric of Utrecht

4.1 Prince-Bishops and Their Claims

Parallel to Holland's ambitions, the **Bishopric of Utrecht** maintained territorial claims in parts of Frisia, especially near the Overijssel region and the Ems. The bishop, as a prince of the Holy Roman Empire, wielded both spiritual and temporal authority. Monastic foundations and ecclesiastical estates dotted these areas, providing the bishop with revenue and manpower. In theory, these estates owed him fealty, but in reality, local assemblies often made direct decisions about tithes and water management.

Conflict arose when bishops demanded feudal homage from Frisian communities that considered themselves free. Ecclesiastical lords might send bailiffs to collect rents, only to find local militias refusing entry. At times, the bishop allied with the count of Holland or local chieftains to press claims. At other times, the bishop might attempt to strike separate deals with towns, offering to confirm their market privileges if they recognized Utrecht's overlordship.

4.2 Church Influence in Political Affairs

Beyond feudal claims, the bishop also carried **moral and spiritual weight**. By excommunicating rebellious leaders or placing entire districts under interdict, the bishop could theoretically pressure communities into submission. However, Frisian assemblies often challenged such tactics, claiming the bishop's spiritual authority did not override their ancient liberties. Some chieftains openly defied excommunication, gambling that local priests would still administer sacraments under communal pressure.

Occasionally, a bishop tried a more conciliatory approach—supporting local monastic projects or endorsing communal water-management initiatives. By presenting himself as a protector of the common good, a bishop hoped to earn goodwill among free peasants. Such gestures sometimes succeeded in forging alliances, but they were fragile. The fundamental tension remained: Utrecht saw the region as part of its temporal jurisdiction; Frisians saw themselves as free from external lords, whether secular or ecclesiastical.

4.3 Synods and Ecclesiastical Courts

Ecclesiastical courts handled issues like marriage disputes, moral infractions, or clerical discipline. In Frisian contexts, the bishop attempted to extend these courts' jurisdiction into more secular realms—property conflicts, inheritance for land under church ownership, or even minor crimes committed on ecclesiastical estates. Frisians contested many of these encroachments, insisting that local assemblies or district courts retained final say. This led to protracted legal wrangling, with each side citing different charters or customary laws.

Synods, convened by the bishop, brought together clergy from across the region to discuss canon law, discipline, and church reforms. Frisian parishes, used to a high degree of local autonomy, sometimes resisted new regulations—like standardized tithes or mandatory feast day observances. While many priests dutifully attended, they also channeled their parishioners' concerns. The result was a delicate dance where the bishop strove to unify church practice, but local Catholic identity in Frisia remained entwined with the region's sense of independence.

---

5. Economic Underpinnings: 13th–14th Century Trade and Shifts

5.1 Continued Maritime Prosperity

Despite the political turbulence, Frisian trade generally continued to flourish into the early 14th century. Merchant fleets sailed regularly to English and Flemish ports, carrying cereals, fish, and other goods. The towns that had grown in the 12th century—Staveren, Harlingen, Emden, and others—retained or expanded their roles as commercial nodes. Some chieftain families invested in shipping enterprises, further linking their fortunes to maritime commerce.

Guild structures matured in the port towns. Merchant guilds expanded membership, while craft guilds—such as ship carpenters, sail-makers, and rope-makers—professionalized their trades. Urban guild leadership often overlapped with local government, reinforcing the power of an emerging merchant-patrician class. Meanwhile, peasants in reclaimed farmland produced surpluses for trade. Profits from exports sometimes funded additional dike building, creating a cycle of expansion and investment.

5.2 The Growth of the Hanseatic League

During the 13th century, **the Hanseatic League** coalesced, dominated by northern German towns like Lübeck, Hamburg, and Bremen. Though its center of gravity lay in the Baltic, the Hanse also encompassed North Sea commerce. Frisian ports found themselves in a tricky position: cooperating with the Hanse could open broad markets, but membership often required accepting certain rules about pricing, competition, and dispute resolution, which clashed with local autonomy ideals.

Nevertheless, some Frisian towns formed limited agreements or joined smaller "Hanse" circles within the region. They recognized the value of mutual defense and standardized trading practices. But full integration into the Hanseatic League was rare, as it might undermine the independence that Frisian assemblies cherished. Hence, while practical collaboration existed—joint efforts against pirates or standardizing weights and measures—Frisian communities often stopped short of surrendering local judicial sovereignty to a broader confederation.

5.3 Market Challenges and Economic Diversification

From the late 13th century onward, several economic **challenges** emerged. England grew more protective of its wool trade, at times restricting exports to favor its own cloth industry. Flanders, once dependent on English wool, faced internal rebellions and power shifts, occasionally disrupting the cloth markets that Frisian merchants supplied. Simultaneously, the climate exhibited signs of cooling (a precursor to the "Little Ice Age" in later centuries), affecting harvest yields. Periodic harvest failures in parts of Europe could slash demand for certain imports or spark inflation.

In response, Frisians diversified. Some turned to local cloth production, though not on the same scale as Flemish towns. Fishing communities explored different catches or salting methods to target new markets. Town councils built stronger relationships with inland trade routes, forging deals to deliver goods deeper into the Holy Roman Empire. The coastal location remained a key advantage, but prudent adaptation became essential to maintain prosperity in an increasingly competitive environment.

6. Urban and Rural Frictions Deepen

6.1 Town Autonomy vs. District Assemblies

As port towns matured, their councils sought greater control over roads, tolls, and local justice. This ambition brought them into conflict with rural assemblies that insisted on shared governance. A town might, for instance, levy a fee on every cart of grain entering the city gates—funding new defensive walls. Nearby villages cried foul, arguing such fees violated long-held customary exemptions. Sometimes, the dispute escalated to physical blockades or sabotage, reminding towns that they relied on rural produce.

In regions where a strong chieftain dominated both a town and its surrounding countryside, he or she might try to unify interests or forcibly quell rural dissent. In other cases, a bishop or count stepped in as a mediator, hoping to gain political capital from either the town or the assembly. These conflicts revealed the friction inherent in Frisia's dual identity: commercial towns forging ahead with new administrative practices, and traditional farmland districts guarding older communal freedoms.

6.2 Class Tensions Within Towns

Inside the towns themselves, **class tensions** became more pronounced. Wealthy merchant families (the patriciate) held key positions on town councils. Lesser artisans or day laborers often felt excluded from political decisions that shaped commerce and taxation. Guilds provided some channels for expressing grievances, but certain trades—especially unskilled laborers—remained outside guild structures. Occasionally, populist revolts flared if councils imposed harsh taxes or restricted guild membership, though full-blown urban revolutions were rare.

Another conflict area was property speculation: affluent merchants might buy up multiple houses, renting them at prices the poor struggled to afford. Chroniclers mention instances where city dwellers unable to pay rent ended up seeking refuge with relatives in rural districts or turning to crime. Town authorities responded by expanding poor relief or hospital services, often run by religious brotherhoods. While these measures helped alleviate hardships, the underlying social stratification persisted.

6.3 Religious Factions and Reform Movements

During the 13th and early 14th centuries, various **religious reform movements**—including the Beguines, Beghards, and other lay fraternities—gained followers in the Low Countries. These movements emphasized simple piety, charity, and sometimes a critique of clerical wealth. In Frisian towns, such groups found fertile ground among artisans and smaller merchants who disliked the opulence of certain monastic orders or the close ties between bishop and nobility.

Local priests and some chieftains worried that these lay groups could undermine traditional church hierarchies and social norms. They sought to regulate their activities, leading to conflicts over property rights for Beguine houses or whether members owed taxes. In some places, city councils recognized these communities under strict guidelines, acknowledging their charitable contributions to the poor. Elsewhere, heated debates raged, occasionally resulting in forced dispersal if the movement was branded heretical by church authorities.

---

7. Intensifying Pressures from Holland and Beyond

7.1 The Late 13th Century: Floris V and Others

Count Floris V of Holland (reigned 1256–1296) played a particularly aggressive role in Frisian affairs. Nicknamed "der Keerlen God" (the God of the Peasants), he initially cultivated a reputation for championing common folk's interests against higher nobility. However, in relation to Frisia, Floris V aimed to assert firm control. He launched military campaigns to enforce Holland's claims, constructing or rebuilding fortresses near contested areas. Some Frisian districts resisted fiercely, while others, weary of internal feuds, temporarily accepted Floris's overlordship for stability.

Yet Floris V's policies sparked resentment. Even some local collaborators felt the count's demands for tribute and men-at-arms were excessive. Rebellions erupted, culminating in violent confrontations. Ultimately, Floris V was captured and killed in 1296 by a group of disaffected nobles in Holland, an event tied to broader political machinations. His demise once again disrupted Holland's northward drive, offering Frisia another temporary reprieve.

7.2 Influence of the German Princes

Within the Holy Roman Empire, power was becoming more decentralized. Various German princes—like the dukes of Brunswick-Lüneburg or the archbishops of Bremen—showed sporadic interest in East Frisian territories. They eyed trade tolls on the Ems and Jade rivers. Some tried to grant imperial fiefs to East Frisian chieftains in exchange for loyalty. But friction remained: local assemblies balked at such feudal formulas, insisting any relationship must respect communal rights. Indeed, many deals ended up as polite paper agreements with little practical effect.

Occasionally, an emperor or leading prince might intervene in a Frisian dispute if appealed to by a powerful chieftain or bishop. They issued diplomas reaffirming or denying certain claims. Yet they rarely dispatched large forces to enforce them. Hence, while these formal ties connected Frisia to the broader empire, enforcement on the ground was minimal. This half-in, half-out status reinforced the region's unique blend of local autonomy under a nominal imperial umbrella.

7.3 Conflicts with the Prince-Bishop of Münster

An additional external pressure came from the **Prince-Bishopric of Münster**, lying to the east of Frisia. Münster's bishops also carried secular power over broad Westphalian lands, occasionally pressing claims into East Frisian zones. They sought control of trade routes along the Ems or recognition of feudal rights in certain border districts. As with Utrecht, Münster combined spiritual threats (excommunication) with secular means (alliances, small armies).

Some East Frisian chieftains, eyeing an opportunity to outmaneuver rivals, allied with Münster, offering fealty in exchange for military backing. This alarmed neighboring Frisian families who saw it as a betrayal of communal freedom. Feuds escalated, with the bishop sometimes fueling one side. Over time, these entanglements created a complex mosaic of allegiances: a single Frisian chieftain might owe partial allegiance to Münster while simultaneously claiming membership in a "Frisian freedom" confederation. Such contradictory commitments ensured a near-constant state of tension.

---

8. Environmental Catastrophes and Their Political Effects

8.1 The St. Lucia Flood (1287)

One of the most devastating floods mentioned in medieval Frisia is the **St. Lucia flood** of December 1287. Chronicles describe how a storm surge overwhelmed dikes along the Zuiderzee and Wadden Sea coasts. Thousands reportedly died, farmland was submerged, and entire villages vanished. The flood also reconfigured portions of the coastline, forming new channels or expanding existing inlets. In some areas, saltwater contamination ruined cropland for years.

In the wake of this disaster, local assemblies struggled to gather resources for dike repairs on a massive scale. They turned to wealthy families, monasteries, or even external powers like the count of Holland for financial aid. This gave powerful benefactors leverage; offering funds in return for political concessions. Some communities accepted new feudal obligations or heavier tolls, believing survival outweighed autonomy. Others refused, leading to conflict between reconstruction supporters and those who saw external funding as a Trojan horse.

8.2 Other Major Storm Surges

Subsequent centuries saw multiple catastrophic floods, including the **Grote Mandränke** (Great Drowning of Men) in 1362, which also struck broad swathes of the North Sea coast. These events repeated the pattern: abrupt devastation, frantic calls for solidarity, and the threat that unscrupulous leaders might exploit a crisis to assert control. Some historians argue that these environmental catastrophes accelerated the centralization of water management in certain districts, as local independence had to be partially surrendered to finance large-scale dike reconstruction.

Nonetheless, many assemblies retained a strong communal ethos. They used the floods' aftermath to reaffirm that water management must remain free from personal or feudal feuds. Temporary alliances formed across fractious lines to rebuild defenses, demonstrating that no single lord or chieftain could handle such disasters alone. These cycles of destruction and rebuilding reinforced a collective memory of resilience, integral to the Frisian identity.

---

9. Cultural and Legal Developments in the 14th Century

9.1 Codifications of "Frisian Freedom"

As pressures mounted from Holland, Utrecht, Münster, and Saxon or German princelings, Frisian districts increasingly invoked a concept of **"Frisian freedom"** as a legal principle. We see more references in documents—some contemporary, others possibly retroactive—forging claims that the emperor (often said to be Charlemagne, in legendary accounts) had exempted all Frisians from feudal bondage. The exact authenticity of these charters is debated, but the belief they expressed was potent.

By the 14th century, local scribes compiled or expanded older law codes, such as the so-called **"Upstalsboom Statutes."** While incomplete and sometimes contradictory, these texts symbolized a supra-local attempt to unify Frisian legal identity. They asserted that Frisians owed allegiance to no count or bishop except the emperor himself—and even that loyalty was often framed as conditional upon the emperor's recognition of local customs. The repeated copying and circulation of such texts solidified the notion that "Frisia was free, by ancient right."

9.2 Emergence of Official Seals and Symbols

To bolster their standing in diplomatic contexts, various Frisian assemblies, towns, or chieftains began using **official seals** on treaties and letters. While heraldry was more common among European nobility, Frisians adapted these customs to represent communal bodies. Some seals depicted a stylized eagle or lion referencing supposed imperial connections, while others showed dikes, ships, or local saints. The symbolism underscored that Frisia was an entity recognized by law and tradition, not just a scattering of villages.

Additionally, certain chieftain families adopted coats of arms or personal badges, mimicking feudal aristocrats. Over time, these heraldic images helped clarify allegiances in the swirl of feuds and alliances. A retinue flying a particular crest signaled loyalty to a specific family or district confederation. Meanwhile, critics argued that adopting feudal trappings contradicted the spirit of Frisian freedom. This tension between tradition and adaptation to European aristocratic norms remained an undercurrent through the 14th century.

9.3 Intellectual and Spiritual Currents

While the High Middle Ages saw rising literacy in Europe's urban centers, Frisia remained somewhat peripheral to major intellectual movements. However, traveling scholars, Dominican or Franciscan mendicants, and occasional university-educated clerics introduced new theological and philosophical ideas. Some monasteries in Frisia maintained scriptoria, copying religious texts or local chronicles. These recorded genealogies of chieftain families, the outcomes of feuds, and notable natural disasters, shaping a rudimentary historiographical tradition.

Spiritually, the mendicant orders (Franciscans, Dominicans) made modest inroads into Frisian towns. Their emphasis on preaching and serving the poor resonated with certain urban dwellers disillusioned by wealthier monastic orders. Nonetheless, local church practices—saint veneration, communal festivals, water-blessing rites—remained quite traditional. In some quarters, friction arose between mendicant preachers who condemned extravagance and chieftains who flaunted wealth in feasts or building projects. But overall, religious life integrated new impulses with older coastal piety.

---

10. Conclusion

The **13th and 14th centuries** saw Frisia confronted by intensifying external pressures from the County of Holland, the Bishopric of Utrecht, and neighboring German principalities. Internally, powerful chieftain families and emerging towns struggled over land, water rights, and social hierarchies. Yet despite intermittent defeats or partial subjugations, the core principle of Frisian freedom endured. Assemblies and local leaders deftly negotiated with or resisted outside claims, leveraging communal law codes and the region's formidable tradition of water-management cooperation.

Catastrophic floods highlighted the fragility of life in the coastal lowlands, compelling unity at times but also providing opportunities for stronger players—whether external counts or wealthy chieftains—to expand influence. Culturally and legally, Frisians codified their customs, circulated seals, and honed a collective identity. By the end of the 14th century, Frisia was still a patchwork of semi-independent districts, each bound by a common ethos yet facing a precarious future. The next chapters—**Thirteen and Fourteen**—will address **how the late Middle Ages** continued to transform Frisia, from ongoing internal rivalries to evolving ties with foreign powers, setting the stage for future struggles in the centuries ahead.

CHAPTER 13: THE LATE MIDDLE AGES AND INTERNAL RIVALRIES

1. Introduction: Frisia in the Late Middle Ages

By the early 14th century, Frisia had evolved into a region of small port towns, strong chieftain families, and rural communities still devoted to local autonomy. Yet this period was hardly peaceful. Throughout the 14th and early 15th centuries, **internal rivalries** deepened, fueled by competition over land, trade routes, and political influence. Factionalism flared, fracturing Frisian unity just when external forces—like the County of Holland, the Bishopric of Utrecht, and emerging Burgundian power—were becoming more assertive in the Low Countries.

This chapter focuses on how these **internal conflicts** shaped Frisian society. We will explore the roots of the famous **Vetkopers (Fat Buyers) and Schieringers** factions, the roles of chieftains who turned local feuds into wider wars, and the consequences for ordinary Frisians trying to safeguard farmland and livelihood. We also examine how storms, economic changes, and evolving alliances influenced the trajectory of these rivalries. While the doctrine of "Frisian freedom" remained a unifying ideal, the actual political landscape in the 14th and 15th centuries was splintered by personal ambition, clan feuds, and shifting loyalties.

2. Background: Frisia's Fragmented Political Scene

2.1 Dispersed Power Structures

From earlier chapters, we know that Frisia lacked a centralized monarchy or duchy in the late Middle Ages. Instead, real authority lay in the hands of:

- **Local chieftains** (or petty lords), who controlled clusters of villages, farmland, and occasionally small fortresses on raised terpen.
- **Urban elites** in port towns, often wealthy merchants who governed through councils and guilds.

- **Rural assemblies**, upholding traditions of communal law and water management.

These groups did not always cooperate. A powerful chieftain might attempt to extend authority over a nearby town, while the town's council resisted or made alliances with rival chieftains. Meanwhile, rural farmers insisted on preserving local assemblies, seeing any strong lord—local or foreign—as a threat to their freedoms. This decentralized mosaic created a breeding ground for feuds, especially in prosperous or strategically valuable districts.

2.2 Economic and Environmental Pressures

The 14th century brought **economic volatility**: periodic harvest failures, fluctuating trade with England and Flanders, and competition from new Hanseatic ports in Germany. Although Frisia's maritime commerce continued, some towns struggled to adapt to shifting markets. In parallel, repeated storm surges and floods ravaged dikes, draining local coffers as communities scrambled to rebuild.

These strains often translated into political tension. A chieftain might raise tolls to finance dike repairs; local farmers might resist, claiming custom forbade new levies. Or a town might impose fees on rural goods entering its gates, angering nearby villages. In such disputes, old grudges quickly reignited, turning a simple conflict over dike maintenance or toll collection into a broader feud that drew in neighboring districts.

2.3 The Prelude to Deep Factionalism

By the early 14th century, many of these feuds coalesced into broader factions—some region-wide, some localized. Alliances that once had been purely local or family-based began to adopt **collective names** and identities. Historians see this as a major turning point: internal rivalries became more formalized, intensifying the scale of conflicts. As chieftains built small armies, the potential for destructive civil strife loomed large. Into this unsettled climate arose two factions that would define Frisian politics for decades to come: the **Vetkopers** and the **Schieringers**.

3. The Rise of the Vetkoper and Schieringer Factions

3.1 Origins and Naming

The exact beginnings of the **Vetkopers** and **Schieringers** are steeped in legend. The terms themselves—"Vetkoper" often translated as "Fat Buyer" (or "Greasy Buyer"), "Schieringer" sometimes as "Grey" or "Clean"—have prompted various theories. Some say "Vetkoper" linked to wealthy, well-fed landowners or traders, while "Schieringer" might refer to simpler, more austere folk. However, the names probably arose from local insults or symbolic references that then stuck as labels for opposing sides.

What is clearer is that these factions were not purely economic or social categories. Both groups cut across lines of wealth and class. A powerful chieftain might lead a Vetkoper alliance in one district, while a different chieftain in another area pledged loyalty to Schieringers. Town councils, too, might align with one faction or the other. Over time, the Vetkopers and Schieringers each claimed to represent the "true" Frisian values—though ironically, their struggles often plunged the region into violent chaos.

3.2 Underlying Motives and Alliances

At heart, these **factions** reflected deep-seated political and personal rivalries. Chieftains sided with one or the other based on longstanding feuds, marriage ties, or local disputes. Town officials might choose a faction if it safeguarded their trade privileges or offered protection against a hostile neighbor. Rural assemblies might back whichever faction respected their water management laws or promised to keep new taxes low.

Over time, each side built **networks of supporters** across multiple districts. This enabled conflicts to spill far beyond their starting point. A minor quarrel in East Frisia could draw in Vetkoper allies from West Frisia, who then clashed with Schieringer partisans near the Zuiderzee. Chroniclers describe a near-endless cycle of shifting alliances, betrayals, and short-lived truces. By the mid-14th century, these factional lines dominated Frisian politics.

3.3 Key Early Confrontations

Although records are fragmentary, we know of several notable clashes that set the tone:

- **Feud over Dike Tolls** (c. 1340s): A Vetkoper-aligned chieftain demanded tolls on a new dike segment, prompting local farmers (backed by Schieringer leaders) to refuse. Armed raids ensued, culminating in a brief occupation of the chieftain's terp fortress.
- **Town vs. Chieftain Standoff** (c. 1350s): A coastal town declared itself Schieringer, raising a militia to expel Vetkoper tax collectors. A nearby Vetkoper warlord attacked, only to be repelled by the town's walls and arrow-firing guild archers.
- **Marital Alliances** (ongoing throughout the 14th century): Vetkoper and Schieringer families intermarried either to consolidate local power or, occasionally, to broker peace. But such unions could also be exploited, as one spouse turned against the other's family in a sudden betrayal.

In each case, the pattern repeated: a local spark triggered a factional blaze, drawing in allies from across Frisia. Bloodshed became all too common, and the repeated feuding sapped resources, even as external threats loomed on the horizon.

---

4. Impact on Daily Life and Governance

4.1 Civil Strife and Insecurity

Ordinary Frisians suffered under these **factional wars**. Farmers feared losing crops and livestock to roaming bands of warriors. Town merchants dreaded blockades that halted trade. Coastal dike repairs sometimes fell behind schedule if a district aligned with one faction refused to cooperate with neighbors of the other persuasion. Chronicles lament entire harvests ruined and villages deserted, as local families fled repeated violence.

To defend themselves, some communities built or reinforced **palisades** around villages, stationed armed guards at key dike points, and stockpiled grain. However, no settlement was entirely safe. Alliances shifted quickly: a chieftain who once protected a village might become an enemy if he switched factions. This pervasive insecurity eroded trust in the old communal ethos, intensifying local self-reliance and suspicion of outsiders.

4.2 Assemblies and Arbitration Attempts

Amid the turmoil, **traditional assemblies** still convened, attempting to mediate feuds. In principle, each faction recognized the authority of communal law. But in practice, faction leaders often manipulated assemblies or refused to abide by decisions. Arbitrators—sometimes neutral chieftains or respected monastic figures—sought to impose wergild payments or land restitution to resolve disputes. Yet enforcement proved difficult. The same retinues that waged feuds could intimidate local judges.

Repeatedly, we see references to large assemblies called at neutral sites—sometimes near the Upstalsboom—where hundreds of representatives from both factions debated peace terms. These gatherings offered fleeting hope. They might produce a "perpetual peace" document, sealed by faction leaders. But soon after, a new provocation would ignite fresh hostilities, rendering the accords meaningless. Over time, the cycle led to deep cynicism about the assemblies' ability to halt feuding.

4.3 Role of the Church and Monasteries

Monasteries, originally havens of stability, found themselves caught in the crossfire. Some monastic estates had links to certain families or factions. Vetkoper supporters might attack a monastery rumored to shelter Schieringer refugees, or vice versa. Several abbeys built **defensive walls** or small towers, a testament to how entrenched the violence became.

Church leaders repeatedly called for peace. Bishops or abbots threatened excommunication for those who broke truces. But local acceptance of excommunication was mixed—Frisians often valued their clan allegiances above ecclesiastical censure. Even so, some friars and parish priests bravely served as go-betweens, delivering messages or trying to negotiate local ceasefires. Occasional successes highlight that religion still carried moral weight, though it was overshadowed by secular feuding.

5. External Players Exploit the Factions

5.1 Holland's Interventions

The County of Holland, under successive counts, saw the Vetkoper-Schieringer divide as a chance to penetrate Frisian politics. Holland might secretly fund one faction, hoping to secure loyalty if that side triumphed. In a particular district, the count might supply weapons to Vetkopers in exchange for their oath of fealty. If that arrangement turned sour, the count would pivot to Schieringers next door. This cynical approach aimed to divide and conquer, forging pockets of direct Holland influence.

Not all Frisian leaders fell for such tactics. Some recognized the risk of letting the count's forces in. But others, desperate for support in a local feud, accepted outside help. Over time, small enclaves in Frisia effectively became puppet zones of Holland, paying tribute or following the count's edicts. This creeping infiltration undercut Frisian unity, as one faction's "victory" might come at the cost of partial subservience to an external lord.

5.2 Bishopric Maneuvers

Bishops of Utrecht or Münster also exploited the factions. A bishop might anoint a Schieringer-friendly chieftain as an official "vicarius" (representative) in a disputed area, giving him religious legitimacy. In return, the chieftain promised certain taxes or recognized the bishop's feudal overlordship. Alternatively, if that arrangement soured, the bishop switched support to Vetkopers in a rival district. By fueling factional chaos, the bishopric hoped to expand its secular domain.

Yet, these alliances were inherently unstable. The faction reliant on episcopal backing could lose local credibility—some free Frisians would claim they were betraying "Frisian freedom" by selling out to a foreign bishop. So while bishops could glean short-term gains, long-term consolidation proved elusive. The minute a chieftain felt strong enough, he might renege on bishopric ties, reverting to full autonomy or forging a new external partnership.

5.3 Broader Imperial and Regional Context

Beyond Holland and the bishoprics, other powers occasionally ventured into Frisian factional politics. The Holy Roman Emperor typically had bigger concerns elsewhere, but might confirm a chieftain's "imperial fief" if it served to check Dutch expansion. Meanwhile, East Frisian families with connections to Saxon dukes or the Hanseatic towns sometimes leveraged external trade agreements or military pacts. The result was a **complex web of influences**: Vetkoper or Schieringer alliances, partial feudal acknowledgments of distant princes, and shifting deals with neighbors.

For common folk in Frisia, these outside entanglements felt like layers of confusion. One year, your local chieftain might brandish an imperial diploma to claim freedom from Holland. Next year, the same chieftain might ally with Holland for personal advantage. The swirl of external deals rarely stabilized local life; instead, it prolonged the cycle of feuds, since each faction could tap foreign backers for arms or mercenaries.

---

6. Consequences for Towns and Trade

6.1 Town Councils Caught Between Factions

Frisian towns, which thrived on commerce, suffered whenever faction fights spilled into **urban streets** or blockaded harbor access. Yet many towns were forced to pick a side. A council might lean Schieringer if a majority of guild leaders favored that faction, or if a local Vetkoper chieftain had extorted them previously. Conversely, some towns turned Vetkoper to avoid losing farmland supplies controlled by allied chieftains.

These alignments led to periodic **urban uprisings**. If townsfolk believed their magistrates had sold out to a disliked faction, they might riot, overthrow the council, and invite the opposing faction's champions. The new regime might tear down houses of known faction loyalists, seize property, or punish prominent supporters. In extreme cases, entire families fled, seeking refuge in friendlier towns or countryside enclaves. This instability hampered trade: merchants wanted secure ports and predictable governance, but they seldom found it in faction-riven Frisia.

6.2 Disruption of Maritime Commerce

As Vetkoper and Schieringer warbands patrolled the coastline, **piracy and privateering** rose. Factions authorized their ships to seize enemy vessels—often under flimsy pretexts. Foreign merchants, confused by the fractal nature of these conflicts, hesitated to risk their cargoes in Frisian waters. Some sought safer routes through Hanseatic or Dutch-ruled harbors. The resulting decline in sea traffic undercut local economies. Towns that once profited from trade tolls saw revenues shrink, intensifying internal strife over scarce resources.

Moreover, repeated blockades of key waterways—like the Lauwers or Ems estuaries—disrupted grain shipments and fish exports. A Vetkoper-held fortress at a strategic river mouth could effectively starve a Schieringer-aligned town upstream, or vice versa. Chroniclers record desperate pleas from city councils to warring factions, asking them not to cripple vital trade routes. But the feuding parties often prioritized military advantage over commercial well-being.

6.3 Efforts to Maintain Neutral Zones

Amid these disruptions, some districts attempted to declare **neutrality**—no Vetkoper or Schieringer allegiance, just peaceful commerce. Certain towns tried to form "peace leagues," pledging to remain open to all merchants. Others threatened to collectively expel any faction that violated local neutrality. These efforts sometimes succeeded briefly, offering safe havens for trade.

However, neither Vetkopers nor Schieringers liked neutral enclaves that gave respite to their opponents. A powerful faction might brand a "neutral" town as covertly supporting the other side, thus justifying an incursion. Still, a few port towns managed to sustain neutrality by skillfully balancing alliances or paying tribute to both factions. In doing so, they preserved a semblance of commerce and stability, though always at risk of betrayal.

7. Attempts at Reform and Unity

7.1 Peace Conferences and Truces

Throughout the 14th century, **reform-minded chieftains** or monastic leaders occasionally called for broad peace conferences. Their logic: the Vetkoper–Schieringer feud had drained Frisia of wealth and men, while external lords advanced ever closer. These gatherings, sometimes arranged at recognized neutral sites, sought a lasting settlement. Delegates drafted elaborate treaties pledging an end to "fratricidal war," the release of prisoners, and mutual aid in dike repairs.

Alas, such truces typically dissolved. One side or the other soon claimed the terms favored their rivals, or a local spark reignited hostilities. Chroniclers mention more than one carefully negotiated peace undone by the assassination of a chieftain who had brokered it. Still, the repeated attempts show that many Frisians recognized how damaging the feud had become—and how vulnerable the region was to external conquest if unity could not be achieved.

7.2 Ecclesiastical Mediators

A few bishops or abbots, alarmed by the chaos, tried to broker internal Frisian peace from a spiritual angle. They declared communal fasts, processions for divine mercy, or threatened to excommunicate any faction leader who violated a newly minted peace covenant. Sometimes these efforts worked on a local scale, especially if a revered abbot was personally respected by both sides. Yet large-scale success eluded them, since the underlying political and economic rivalries ran deeper than spiritual appeals could remedy.

One notable effort occurred in the 1390s, when a group of monastic leaders in Middle Frisia organized an extensive **"Peace of the Fields,"** urging all chieftains to sign. Many did so publicly. But within two years, an old boundary dispute flared up in East Frisia, and the fragile pact collapsed. Recriminations flew, with each faction accusing the other of acting in bad faith.

7.3 The "Great Frisia" Vision

Amid the disarray, some idealists promoted a vision of a **"Great Frisia"**—a unified, self-governing entity stretching from the Zuiderzee to the borders of Denmark, all free from feudal oppression. They pointed to historical legends (and partially mythic charters) stating that Emperor Charlemagne had granted perpetual freedom to the Frisian people. Advocates of "Great Frisia" argued that the Vetkoper–Schieringer feud was a self-inflicted wound, preventing real independence.

Although inspiring in theory, this vision lacked practical impetus. Too many local power brokers benefited from the status quo or doubted their rivals' sincerity. Nonetheless, the "Great Frisia" idea resonated with ordinary folk, fueling a persistent undercurrent of longing for unity. It would reemerge in the 15th century when new external threats galvanized certain factions, and calls for a broader Frisian alliance temporarily grew louder.

8. Key Figures and Notable Families

8.1 The Haro, Galama, and Donia Clans

Among the many chieftain lines were families like **Haro**, **Galama**, and **Donia**, each controlling pockets of Middle or West Frisia. Chroniclers detail their genealogies: how marriages linked them to rival clans, or how a son might break from his father's faction, igniting intrafamily wars. These clans often built stone houses or small castle-like structures for defense, overshadowing local villages.

- **Haro Family**: Known for cunning alliances, sometimes switching from Vetkoper to Schieringer if it promised advantage. Their frequent negotiations with Holland indicated ambitions to carve out a mini-territory under partial Dutch patronage.
- **Galama Family**: Longtime supporters of Schieringer ideals, at least officially. They claimed to champion "true Frisian freedoms," although adversaries accused them of hypocrisy when they taxed peasants in their domain.
- **Donia Family**: Staunch Vetkoper partisans in several districts, famed for fierce militias. One Donia leader boasted a warband of hundreds, deployed to raid Schieringer farmland or to guard the coast from external incursion.

8.2 East Frisian Dynasties: Tom Brok and Cirksena

In East Frisia, families like the **tom Brok** clan rose to notable power in the 14th century. They expanded farmland, maintained armed forces, and brokered deals with Hanseatic merchants. Their conflicts with other East Frisian chieftains sometimes overshadowed the Vetkoper–Schieringer framework, though eventually they, too, took sides. Later, the **Cirksena** family emerged, marrying into or defeating rivals to become a dominant East Frisian house.

These East Frisian dynasties typically styled themselves as **"Upstalboom chiefs"** or even "counts," aspiring to unify local districts. Sometimes they invoked an imperial grant for legitimacy. Their success varied. Some momentarily controlled large swaths of East Frisia, but feuds or external interventions frequently shattered such proto-state formations. Nonetheless, the Tom Brok and Cirksena lines signaled a future shift toward more consolidated rule in East Frisia, anticipating the 15th-century transformations.

8.3 Women in Chieftain Families

While male chieftains occupied the limelight in warfare, **women** from these families could wield significant influence behind the scenes. Marriages arranged alliances, but women themselves negotiated dower lands, presided over estates in their husbands' absence, or even led local militias in dire circumstances. Chroniclers provide occasional glimpses of formidable "chieftain's widows" who defended fortresses or managed trade concessions. Though barred from official assembly roles, these women shaped faction politics through strategic counsel and resource management.

---

9. The Transition into the 15th Century

9.1 Growing Fatigue with Endless Feuds

By the early 1400s, many Frisians were **exhausted** by the Vetkoper–Schieringer strife. Chronicles lament entire generations growing up amid raids and shifting alliances. Economic stagnation in some districts, combined with mounting foreign threats, pushed local leaders to seek any path to stability. While neither faction vanished, calls for a broad, lasting peace gained momentum.

Simultaneously, some chieftains realized that indefinite feuding kept Frisia too divided to resist the growing might of the **Burgundian dukes**, who were consolidating lands throughout the Low Countries. Rumors swirled that Burgundy's interest in coastal trade was expanding. If Frisia presented a weak, bickering front, it risked falling under Burgundian rule or becoming a battleground in larger conflicts.

9.2 The Influence of External Changes

Political upheavals beyond Frisia also shaped local fortunes. In the Holy Roman Empire, emperors sought to strengthen direct control over certain regions, yet their energies were often diverted to Italian campaigns or internal German rivalries. Meanwhile, the County of Holland underwent dynastic shifts, eventually falling under the sway of the powerful House of Bavaria-Straubing and then drifting toward Burgundian orbit. Each transition offered new openings or threats to Frisian autonomy.

For many Frisian towns, the 15th century dawned with uncertainty. Would the factions continue to tear the region apart? Or would a new external power step in to impose order, at the cost of local freedom? Some Vetkoper or Schieringer leaders believed they could harness the ambitions of a foreign prince to defeat their rivals. Others warned that once a foreign lord established a foothold, Frisian liberties would be lost.

9.3 Seeds of Larger Conflict

As we will see in the next chapter, these internal tensions and external transformations set the stage for **major upheavals in the 15th century**. Faction leaders, desperate for advantage, invited alliances with outside powers that eventually overshadowed them. The Burgundian dukes, in particular, had the wealth and military clout to reshape the entire region. By the end of the 14th century, Frisia stood on the threshold of a new era in which foreign rulers—backed by large armies and sophisticated bureaucracy—could attempt to end the chaotic factional status quo once and for all.

CHAPTER 14: INFLUENCE OF FOREIGN RULERS AND SHIFTING ALLIANCES

1. Introduction: A Century of Transformations

The **15th century** was pivotal for Frisia. This era witnessed the dramatic expansion of **Burgundian power** in the Low Countries, the complex realignment of the Holy Roman Empire's influence, and the final transformations of the medieval world. For Frisia, still riven by the Vetkoper–Schieringer divide, these external forces presented both dangers and opportunities. Some local leaders sought Burgundian backing to crush their internal foes, only to discover that alliances with mighty foreign dukes came at a steep price. Others tried to maintain strict autonomy, battling both rival factions and Burgundian armies.

This chapter explores the **shifting alliances** that defined Frisia's 15th century. We will examine how the Burgundian dukes, in particular, extended their reach into the coastal region—sometimes through diplomacy, sometimes by force. We will also see the continuing interplay of local chieftains, towns, and rural assemblies striving to navigate a rapidly changing political landscape. Ultimately, the 15th century set in motion long-lasting changes in Frisian governance, concluding the medieval chapter of fractious independence and laying groundwork for new power structures.

2. The Burgundian Dukes Enter the Scene

2.1 Burgundy's Ascendancy in the Low Countries

Beginning in the late 14th century, the **Dukes of Burgundy** from the Valois-Burgundy line acquired vast territories in the Netherlands region—through inheritance, marriage, and conquest. By the early 15th century, they controlled

Flanders, Brabant, Holland, Zeeland, and other principalities, forging a powerful state that rivaled even the French and the Holy Roman Emperor in influence. Under dukes like **Philip the Good (r. 1419–1467)** and **Charles the Bold (r. 1467–1477)**, Burgundian ambitions extended to every corner of the Low Countries, including Frisia.

The Burgundian court in cities like Dijon or later in Brussels boasted immense wealth, refined culture, and advanced administrative methods. They deployed sophisticated diplomacy to bring fractious lords under their umbrella. When diplomacy failed, they had well-equipped armies. This combination of strategic skill, economic power, and military force made Burgundy a formidable presence—and a direct threat to Frisia's tradition of local autonomy.

2.2 Burgundy's Initial Approaches to Frisia

At first, the Burgundian dukes tested the waters diplomatically. They recognized that **Vetkopers and Schieringers** were locked in self-destructive conflict. If one faction requested outside help, the duke could step in as a "peacemaker," granting privileges in return for fealty. Indeed, as early as Philip the Good's reign, some chieftains sent emissaries to the Burgundian court. They offered to acknowledge the duke as overlord if he assisted them against their local enemies.

Meanwhile, Burgundian envoys quietly sounded out major Frisian towns. If city councils could be convinced that Burgundian rule would bring peace and stable trade, they might open their gates. Towns battered by decades of factional violence were tempted, though they feared losing their ancient freedoms. The dukes, ever pragmatic, hinted that they would preserve local laws while simply adding Burgundian oversight. In truth, once Burgundian administration took root, real autonomy often diminished.

2.3 Competing Claims and Imperial Sanction

The Burgundian dukes often **invoked imperial authority** when laying claim to places like Holland or parts of Frisia. By mid-century, they had inherited or purchased rights from the House of Wittelsbach (Bavaria-Straubing line), which ruled Holland and Zeeland. Since the Holy Roman Emperor recognized these transfers, the dukes argued that "Frisia is part of our rightful domain." Local assemblies countered with references to their own imperial charters of freedom.

But the Burgundians, backed by a more robust relationship with the emperor, found it easier to present their stance as legitimate in imperial diets.

Still, the emperor did not always intervene directly. Much depended on the broader German political climate. When the emperor needed Burgundian support against France or rival princes, he might endorse Burgundian claims. If a crisis flared up elsewhere, the emperor might ignore Frisian pleas. Thus, the stage was set for a methodical Burgundian encroachment, aided by local feuds that kept Frisia disunited.

---

3. Internal Factions Seek Burgundian Support

3.1 Vetkoper Alliances with Philip the Good

Early in **Philip the Good's** reign, certain Vetkoper chieftains approached the Burgundian court, hoping to crush Schieringer rivals once and for all. They argued that they alone could deliver a stable Frisia to the duke's rule—if he provided troops and recognized them as local governors. Philip, eager to extend his domain, listened. In a series of covert deals, Burgundian arms arrived in selected districts, giving Vetkoper forces a decisive edge. Towns historically aligned with the Schieringers sometimes fell quickly to these joint invasions.

Yet the alliance was not purely beneficial for the Vetkopers. Burgundian advisors insisted on establishing administrative offices, collecting taxes, and placing garrisons in conquered towns. Over time, Vetkoper leaders realized they had effectively traded one external meddler (like Holland or Utrecht) for a more powerful one. Meanwhile, Schieringers in other districts recognized the existential threat of a unified Vetkoper-Burgundian front. They searched for alternative external allies or made desperate stands behind town walls.

3.2 Schieringer Hopes for Imperial or Hanseatic Aid

The **Schieringers**, for their part, tried forging alliances with other powers to counter the Vetkoper-Burgundian threat. Some approached the Holy Roman Emperor directly, petitioning for a reaffirmation of "imperial freedom" that would block Burgundian takeover. Others turned to the Hanseatic League, hoping that shared trade interests might prompt Baltic or North German cities to protect

Frisian autonomy. However, neither approach yielded a robust defense. The emperor was preoccupied, and the Hanseatic League was reluctant to commit resources to a purely political conflict.

Still, in certain East Frisian districts, Schieringer chieftains found limited success forming alliances with Saxon or Eastphalian lords who disliked Burgundian influence. A handful of border skirmishes erupted, but the Burgundians proved formidable. Without a unified Schieringer front or consistent foreign sponsorship, their resistance struggled. Internal rifts among Schieringer families, plus the longstanding suspicion of any feudal overlord, further undercut efforts at cohesive alliance-building.

3.3 Shifting Loyalties

In the fluid 15th-century landscape, alliances were seldom fixed. Some Vetkoper chieftains, disillusioned by Burgundian demands, secretly reached out to Schieringers or alternative princes, hoping to preserve independence. Similarly, certain Schieringer leaders, cornered by Vetkoper aggression, might sign an accord with Burgundian envoys if it promised immediate relief. The net effect was a patchwork of deals, betrayals, and short-lived coalitions. Burgundian diplomats skillfully exploited these divisions, offering carrots (privileges, local lordships) or sticks (military intervention) to coax different players into submission.

---

4. Burgundian Military Campaigns in Frisia

4.1 Philip the Good's Conquest Strategy

By the mid-15th century, **Philip the Good** had consolidated Holland, Zeeland, and other provinces, freeing him to focus on stubborn Frisia. He dispatched experienced commanders with well-equipped forces, including artillery—an increasing advantage in an era where many Frisian strongholds were just walled terpen. Some towns capitulated upon seeing Burgundian artillery train on their gates, fearing destructive sieges.

Philip also used **naval power** along the Zuiderzee and Wadden Sea, blockading rebellious coastal enclaves. Overland, Burgundian cavalry cut supply lines to Schieringer or independent Vetkoper pockets. While not all campaigns succeeded immediately—Frisians were adept at guerrilla tactics in marshy terrain—step by step, Burgundian armies established footholds. They installed governors, demanded tribute, and pressed local assemblies to swear fealty. In some areas, the dukes recognized a cooperative chieftain as "hereditary captain," effectively bridging feudal titles with local customs. The more flexible approach worked in certain towns, which preferred submission to ongoing factional bloodshed.

4.2 Notable Sieges and Battles

Contemporary chronicles highlight a few major sieges:

- **Siege of Dokkum (mid-15th century)**: Dokkum, a Schieringer-aligned port, resisted Burgundian forces until heavy bombardment. The battered defenders finally negotiated surrender, with terms letting some local leaders flee. Burgundian officials installed a new council, proclaiming an end to Schieringer misrule.
- **Battle near Workum**: A Vetkoper contingent, supported by Burgundian cavalry, routed a Schieringer force that attempted to cut off supply lines. This victory solidified Burgundian authority in southwestern districts.
- **Coastal Skirmishes**: Smaller harbors faced naval blockades, prompting local fishermen to join or resist the Burgundian cause. Historians mention occasional "pirate" raids where outnumbered Frisian vessels ambushed Burgundian transports, scoring limited tactical victories that had little strategic effect.

Despite pockets of fierce resistance, the Burgundian war machine was too organized and well-funded for a divided Frisia to repel indefinitely.

4.3 Gradual Subjugation and Rebellions

Over the course of the century, Burgundian officials extended their grip. Certain chieftains accepted Burgundian suzerainty—**they paid taxes and recognized the duke** in exchange for retaining local authority. Others fled or were deposed. Town councils, exhausted by faction violence, often complied if the Burgundians promised stable governance and reopened trade routes. However, discontent smoldered. Some communities launched **rebellions** after a few years, outraged by new taxes or forced labor on ducal fortifications. Burgundian garrisons suppressed these uprisings harshly, discouraging further revolt in the short term.

Still, complete pacification remained elusive. Large stretches of East Frisia, dominated by powerful families like the Cirksena, retained significant autonomy. Even in West or Middle Frisia, local revolts occasionally flared. Thus, Burgundian "control" was partial—strong in certain towns or coastal highways, weaker in rural backwaters. By century's end, the region was locked in a cycle of uneasy Burgundian rule punctuated by local insurgency.

---

5. Changing Social and Economic Dynamics

5.1 Decline of Old Feuds—or Their Transformation

With **Burgundian power** looming, the classic Vetkoper–Schieringer rivalry lost some of its earlier fervor. Many feuds were overshadowed by the question of resisting or accommodating the duke. Some local leaders, once sworn enemies under faction banners, found themselves cooperating to fend off Burgundian rule, or else jointly submitting to preserve status. Meanwhile, those who remained staunch factional partisans discovered the old lines blurred as new alliances formed around pro-Burgundian or anti-Burgundian sentiment.

This realignment, ironically, brought partial **reconciliation** among certain Vetkoper and Schieringer families. Their energies shifted from warring with each other to negotiating either with or against the Burgundians. Feuds did not vanish—personal grudges still flared up—but the overarching faction system gave way to a more complex tangle of local vs. Burgundian allegiances.

5.2 Towns Under Burgundian Administration

Wherever the Burgundians established firm control, they introduced **administrative reforms**. Town councils now had to coordinate with ducal bailiffs or governors who ensured taxes, tolls, and legal rulings aligned with Burgundian policy. The ducal bureaucracy required proper record-keeping, stable coinage, and standard weights and measures for trade. Some local merchants appreciated the potential for greater market integration into the expansive Burgundian network. Others resented the new constraints on their traditional freedoms.

Additionally, Burgundian officials tried to quell the worst factional violence by disarming private militias or demolishing certain urban fortifications. They also promoted Catholic orthodoxy, sometimes clashing with local religious customs. Over time, a **merchant-patrician class** in certain towns found it advantageous to cooperate, acquiring ducal favors or trade monopolies in return. This collaboration spurred economic growth in pockets but eroded local self-governance.

5.3 Rural Assemblies and Water Management Under Pressure

In rural areas, the communal dike boards and assemblies that had sustained Frisian society for centuries endured but faced new supervision from ducal officials. A Burgundian-appointed reeve might oversee dike finances, ensuring the crown's interests were protected. Some assemblies resisted, but the threat of armed intervention loomed large. Over time, these boards adapted, continuing day-to-day water management while acknowledging ducal oversight. The old sense of completely **"free" self-governance** faded, replaced by partial subordination to an external lord.

Still, local traditions proved resilient. Burgundian reeves, conscious of the region's uniqueness, often let communal water management proceed with minimal interference—provided taxes were paid. In that sense, the century brought partial integration but not total assimilation. Many farmers still clung to older customs, even as they grudgingly recognized new authorities collecting tribute.

---

6. Burgundian Rivalries and the Shadow of the Habsburgs

6.1 Duke Charles the Bold and His Ambitions

Under **Charles the Bold (r. 1467–1477)**, Burgundian expansion reached a zenith. Charles sought a grand Burgundian kingdom bridging the Netherlands, Lorraine, and beyond. Frisia was a small piece of that puzzle, but controlling the coastal zone secured maritime trade and completed the Low Countries mosaic. Charles tightened garrisons in rebellious Frisian towns, cracked down on local chieftains who refused homage, and imposed stricter tolls. While effective short-term, his heavy-handed rule bred resentment.

Outside Frisia, Charles's wars with Swiss cantons and the French crown ended in disaster. He died in 1477 at Nancy, leaving a precarious inheritance to his daughter,

Mary of Burgundy. This sudden shift in Burgundian fortunes again disrupted the political landscape. Some Frisian enclaves seized the chaos to rebel, hoping Burgundian power would collapse. But Mary's subsequent marriage to Archduke **Maximilian of Habsburg** introduced yet another formidable dynasty into the Low Countries equation.

6.2 Emergence of Habsburg Influence

With Mary of Burgundy's marriage in 1477, the Low Countries effectively entered the **Habsburg orbit**. Maximilian, soon to be Holy Roman Emperor, used his position to uphold Burgundian holdings. Frisia, caught in the flux, faced new imperial entanglements. Maximilian, like earlier emperors, invoked his authority to confirm or revoke local rights, but now with a personal stake in preserving the Burgundian legacy. This link to the Habsburgs eventually shaped early modern politics, though at the end of the 15th century, it was only beginning to show its force.

In practical terms, some Frisian towns had to reaffirm loyalty to Mary and Maximilian, while rebellious districts attempted to extricate themselves. Vetkoper–Schieringer distinctions blurred further; the real divide was increasingly between pro-Habsburg (or pro-Burgundian) interests and those clinging to older Frisian liberties. The next few decades would see escalations as Habsburg rule consolidated, culminating in future centuries when the entire region was drawn into the broader Habsburg realm.

6.3 Frisia in Broader European Diplomacy

Frisia's strategic coastline also factored into broader **European diplomacy**. France, England, and other states recognized that controlling or influencing the North Sea littoral had commercial and military implications. Some tried to woo Frisian towns as allies against Burgundian or Habsburg hegemony, offering naval protection. But these forays were limited, overshadowed by the main axis of Burgundian/Habsburg vs. local Frisian players. By the close of the 15th century, Frisia found itself less an independent actor on the European stage and more a contested region within the orbit of powerful dynasties.

7. Cultural and Legal Shifts Under Burgundian-Habsburg Pressure

7.1 Revised Law Codes and Feudal Titles

Where Burgundian rule took hold, officials revisited local **law codes**, merging them with ducal or imperial statutes. Some old Frisian customs were codified in new frameworks, ensuring continuity in matters like water management. However, ducal scribes often inserted clauses guaranteeing that ultimate authority lay with the duke or his governor. In a sense, the principle of "Frisian freedom" was gradually constrained, though not wholly erased. Local courts functioned, but final appeals might go to a Burgundian-appointed bailiff or a Habsburg magistrate.

Simultaneously, certain chieftains who cooperated with the new regime received **feudal titles** like "baron" or "lord" recognized by Burgundian nobility. This ironically completed their transformation from purely local strongmen into feudal aristocrats. Meanwhile, those who resisted sometimes saw their lands confiscated or given to loyal supporters. Over the century, a new landed class emerged, loyal to the external power that had legitimated their claims.

7.2 End of the Independent Terp Fortresses

During the earlier Middle Ages, chieftains fortified their **terpen** or built small castle-like structures. The Burgundian or Habsburg authorities systematically dismantled these if they posed a threat to ducal control. Some were repurposed as official residences for local governors. Others, especially those owned by rebellious families, were razed. This policy aimed to reduce local warlordism, which had fueled centuries of internal feuds.

Though it curbed Vetkoper-Schieringer conflicts, it also signaled the end of an era. The once-common sight of multiple petty strongholds across Frisia gave way to a handful of recognized manors under ducal oversight. This reduced local militarization but also meant less purely local autonomy in matters of defense, as foreign-appointed governors now directed larger fortifications.

7.3 Religious Continuity and Subtle Changes

Throughout the 15th century, the **Catholic Church** remained the spiritual backbone of Frisia. Burgundian dukes, staunch Catholics, generally respected the authority of bishops in Utrecht and across the Netherlands. They occasionally installed or supported bishops favorable to their policies, linking the Church more tightly to ducal aims. Parish life continued much as before, with festivals, pilgrimages, and monastic patronage. Yet, ducal oversight sometimes standardized religious practices, reducing the idiosyncrasies once tolerated under looser Frisian independence.

Some clergy welcomed Burgundian rule if it ended destructive feuds. Others lamented the erosion of local control. Monasteries that had navigated Vetkoper–Schieringer politics now had to balance loyalty to the new external lords. Overall, the Church in Frisia did not face major doctrinal upheaval in the 15th century—those changes would come with Reformation waves in the 16th century. For now, religion continued to unify communities, even as secular governance shifted dramatically.

---

8. Local Resistance and Attempts at Unity

8.1 Anti-Burgundian Revolts

Here and there, **revolts** erupted against Burgundian authority. Some were small-scale, led by a disgruntled chieftain who believed he could rally towns or villages. Others were broader uprisings, temporarily uniting Vetkoper and Schieringer partisans under the banner of restoring "true Frisian freedom." While a few rebellions achieved initial success—overrunning a ducal garrison or capturing a hated official—they typically fizzled under the weight of Burgundian reprisals. Superior organization, cavalry, and artillery, plus the capacity to impose blockades, gave the duke's forces the upper hand.

8.2 Calls for a Unified Frisian Movement

In the latter half of the 15th century, some intellectuals, minor nobles, and city notables again championed a "**Unified Frisia.**" They circulated pamphlets or public proclamations referencing legendary charters from Charlemagne or ancient Frankish times. The argument: all of Frisia should stand together to expel foreign rule. They exhorted old faction leaders to set aside grudges in favor of a common cause. A few conferences convened, but old suspicions lingered. Chieftains still worried about losing local power. Town councils feared anarchy if the Burgundians withdrew. Ultimately, these unification efforts proved too weak to overturn the entrenched structures.

8.3 Strategic Coexistence

Amid ongoing tension, a **strategic coexistence** emerged in many districts. Burgundian officials tolerated certain local customs, as long as taxes were paid and no rebellion stirred. Former Vetkoper or Schieringer warlords became mid-level administrators, quietly cooperating with the new order. Towns used formal charters to protect partial autonomy, forging a modus vivendi. Over time, younger generations in Frisian families grew accustomed to Burgundian presence, viewing it less as an occupation and more as an established fact. This pragmatic acceptance gradually reduced open conflict, though a latent desire for full self-rule still simmered beneath the surface.

---

9. The End of the Medieval Era in Frisia

9.1 The Death of Charles the Bold and Transition

Charles the Bold's death in 1477 marked a turning point in Burgundian expansion. His heir, Mary of Burgundy, and later her son Philip (the Fair), as well as Maximilian of Habsburg, carried on a policy of controlling the Netherlands, including Frisia. While occasional local revolts continued, the overarching trajectory was integration into the Burgundian-Habsburg sphere. By **1500**, the medieval tapestry of autonomous Frisian chieftaincies had mostly faded, replaced by a patchwork of ducal or imperial structures.

9.2 Shifting Social Fabric

This shift in governance accelerated social transformations. Some chieftain families adapted, acquiring official titles recognized across the Netherlands. Others fell into obscurity, stripped of lands or exiled. Towns that cooperated with ducal rule often thrived economically, at least in the short term, tying into broader markets. However, the old ethos of communal assemblies making all decisions gave way to formalized **burgundian/habsburg** administrative processes. Over the next century, these changes laid foundations for early modern statehood in the region.

9.3 Legacy of the 15th Century for Frisian Autonomy

In many respects, the 15th century concluded the **medieval story** of Frisia's fractious independence. The region entered the early modern era under a powerful external overlord, with local freedoms heavily curtailed. Yet the memory of "Frisian freedom," so passionately invoked during Vetkoper-Schieringer conflicts, did not vanish. In later centuries, that memory would resurface, shaping local identity and influencing how Frisians responded to new political upheavals. The 15th century thus stands as both an end—closing the book on purely autonomous medieval Frisia—and a beginning, planting the seeds of how Frisians would negotiate identity under evolving foreign powers.

---

10. Conclusion of Chapter Fourteen

The **15th century** brought **foreign rulers—especially the Burgundian dukes—into direct confrontation with a divided Frisia**. Vetkoper-Schieringer conflicts provided an opening for Burgundian intervention. Some Frisians, tired of endless feuding, welcomed the duke's promises of order; others fought bitterly to preserve local freedoms. Through a combination of diplomacy, military conquest, and administrative reforms, the Burgundians (and soon the Habsburgs) inserted themselves into Frisian affairs. The once-dominant internal rivalry was overshadowed by a broader contest between local autonomy and powerful external rule.

By century's end, Frisia was partially integrated into the Burgundian-Habsburg realm, though pockets of resistance and local identity endured. This period finalized the medieval trajectory of factionalism, feudal infiltration, and maritime commerce, transitioning Frisia toward a new era. In the **next chapters—Fifteen and Sixteen**—we will explore how **economic changes and cultural expressions** evolved under these altered power structures, and how **political restructuring** in the 16th and 17th centuries (including the Reformation's impact) would further transform Frisian society.

CHAPTER 15: ECONOMIC CHANGES AND CULTURAL EXPRESSIONS

1. Introduction: Frisia on the Threshold of a New Age

By the year 1500, Frisia had already undergone massive upheaval. The chaotic Vetkoper–Schieringer factional conflicts of the 14th and 15th centuries had opened the door for outside intervention, most prominently by the Burgundian dukes and, through inheritance, the Habsburg dynasty. Although large stretches of Frisia still maintained a measure of local autonomy, formal or informal rule by the House of Habsburg gradually became the norm across the Low Countries in the early 16th century.

Against this backdrop, the **16th century** proved a period of accelerated change, especially in **economic life** and **cultural expressions**. Trade routes shifted, agricultural techniques improved, and new markets emerged, partly driven by the discovery of the New World and an evolving global economy. Meanwhile, religious and cultural currents emanating from southern and western Europe—soon to be amplified by the Protestant Reformation—found their way into Frisian communities, influencing everything from local arts to conceptions of identity. This chapter explores how Frisians adapted to these transformations, highlighting both continuity with medieval traditions and the innovations that defined a new age.

2. The Habsburg Incorporation and Its Economic Consequences

2.1 Transition from Burgundian to Habsburg Rule

During the final decades of the 15th century, Frisia was partially integrated into the Burgundian state. When Mary of Burgundy married Maximilian of Austria (of the Habsburg family) in 1477, the Burgundian inheritance gradually passed to the

Habsburgs. Their son, **Philip the Fair**, and grandson, **Charles V**, presided over vast territories collectively known as the Habsburg Netherlands. Frisia, in turn, was subsumed into this larger entity—though local governance structures varied significantly from one district to another.

Early in the 16th century, **Emperor Charles V** (r. 1519–1556) sought to centralize administration across the Netherlands, including Frisia. He installed governors or stadtholders, standardized taxation where possible, and attempted to streamline legal codes. For Frisians long accustomed to local assemblies, these measures felt intrusive. Yet, Charles V also recognized the importance of local traditions in maintaining stability. Consequently, while new institutions (like the Council of State in the Netherlands) oversaw broader policy, local laws and communal water management systems often continued under partial self-direction. This balance of central oversight and local practice shaped Frisian economic life throughout the century.

2.2 Restructured Taxation and Trade Regulations

Under Habsburg rule, **tax policies** became more systematic compared to the fragmented feudal levies of the medieval era. Charles V's government introduced excises on goods like beer, salt, and cloth, as well as land-based taxes paid by wealthy property holders. For Frisia, these taxes were both a burden and an incentive for modernization: local officials, if they cooperated with Habsburg administrators, could secure privileges for their ports or commercial fairs, fostering growth in exchange for reliable tax revenue.

Similarly, **trade regulations** became more uniform. Whereas medieval Frisia saw each district or town levy its own tolls, the Habsburg regime worked to simplify commercial rules across the provinces, theoretically reducing internal barriers. Some Frisian towns welcomed these reforms, recognizing the potential for larger-scale trade integration with other Netherlands provinces (Holland, Brabant, Flanders) and even the German lands. Others worried that standardized tolls undermined local prerogatives. Still, on balance, the 16th century saw a modest rise in interregional trade flows, aided by greater political stability and improved administrative frameworks.

2.3 Agricultural Adjustments and Land Consolidation

By the 16th century, many Frisian farmers began **consolidating their landholdings**. While medieval Frisia featured a mosaic of small allodial plots, a more market-oriented mentality prompted some wealthier families or urban investors to acquire multiple parcels, merging them into larger, more efficient farms. This process was often spurred by better drainage and dike technology—larger landowners could finance improvements that smaller holders struggled to afford.

Such consolidation had social ramifications. Some small farmers, unable to compete, sold out and became tenant farmers or wage laborers. This shift echoed broader European trends, where emerging capitalist agriculture gradually replaced subsistence-based peasant holdings. Yet, the communal ethos of water management endured—dike boards still required broad cooperation to maintain flood defenses. Even wealthy landowners had to collaborate with peasant communities to keep the sea at bay. This interdependence tempered social conflict, though disparities in wealth grew more noticeable as the century advanced.

---

3. Trade Networks and Maritime Ventures in the 16th Century

3.1 Changing Global Context

The dawn of the **Age of Exploration** dramatically reshaped European commerce in the 16th century. While Portuguese and Spanish ventures to Africa, Asia, and the Americas took center stage initially, northern European powers also expanded their maritime ambitions. For Frisia, historically a maritime region, these developments had mixed implications. On one hand, direct involvement in transatlantic trade was limited at first—Frisian ports lacked the capital or navy to challenge Iberian supremacy. On the other hand, new opportunities arose to supply ships with essentials (grain, fish, timber) and to serve as regional transport hubs feeding into the bustling ports of Antwerp or Amsterdam.

3.2 Role of Frisian Ports Under Habsburg Influence

Under Habsburg rule, major Netherlands ports like Antwerp flourished, becoming continental Europe's principal trading hub. Though overshadowed by such giants, smaller Frisian ports found niches in:

1. **Coastal Shipping**: Transporting cereals, salt, peat, and fish around the North Sea and Baltic.
2. **Shipbuilding**: Some Frisian towns specialized in building smaller coastal vessels, known for shallow drafts that navigated the Wadden Sea's tricky tidal flats.
3. **Intra-Regional Trade**: Linking local farms to bigger Dutch or German markets, facilitated by improved roads and river routes.

Habsburg administrators occasionally granted charters to Frisian towns for annual fairs, where merchants from across the Low Countries converged. These fairs boosted local economies, encouraging artisanal growth (weaving, brewing, pottery) that met rising consumer demand. Yet competition from cities in Holland or the southern Netherlands was stiff, and many Frisian towns remained modestly sized. The best-connected ones—like Leeuwarden or Harlingen—gained prominence as administrative and commercial centers.

3.3 Baltic Connections and Hanseatic Decline

Throughout the late Middle Ages, the Hanseatic League dominated Baltic trade. By the 16th century, however, the Hanse's power waned due to internal conflicts and the rise of emerging maritime states like Denmark-Norway and Sweden. Frisian merchants benefited from this shift: as Hanseatic monopolies crumbled, new shipping routes to the Baltic opened, allowing direct or less-restricted trade in timber, hemp, and fish.

Additionally, the broader rivalry between the Habsburgs (ruling much of the Netherlands) and various German princes encouraged alternative commercial linkages. Some Frisian shipowners capitalized on carrying cargoes between the Baltic and the rapidly industrializing Low Countries. The ease of coastal navigation, plus the tradition of building sturdy yet shallow vessels, kept Frisian maritime enterprise viable, even as major port expansions in Amsterdam or Enkhuizen threatened to eclipse smaller Frisian harbors.

4. Cultural Expressions: Art, Architecture, and Learning

4.1 Artistic Influences in a Northern Renaissance Context

The **Northern Renaissance** that blossomed in Flanders and Holland also touched Frisia. Although local artistic production paled in scale compared to Antwerp or Bruges, Frisian patrons—noble families, wealthy merchants, or church institutions—commissioned works reflecting the era's new techniques and sensibilities. Portraiture became more common, capturing chieftains or town burghers with realistic detail. Religious art evolved, influenced by the devout yet humanized style of painters from the southern Netherlands.

In certain Frisian churches, altarpieces displayed refined craftsmanship, featuring biblical scenes in a more naturalistic manner than medieval iconography. While large-scale master artists rarely settled in Frisia, traveling painters or apprentices circulated, leaving behind smaller altarpieces, stained glass windows, or carved polychrome statues. These works demonstrated a blending of medieval religious tradition with Renaissance humanism—figures wearing local Frisian dress might appear in biblical narratives, grounding the sacred in everyday life.

4.2 Church Architecture and Secular Building

During the 16th century, many Frisian parishes embarked on **church renovations**, sometimes funded by rising commercial wealth or local noble sponsorship. Romanesque or early Gothic buildings gained late Gothic flourishes—taller spires, pointed arches, and more elaborate choir stalls. Although these expansions often preceded the Reformation, they revealed confidence in the parish community's identity, shaped by both medieval spirituality and emerging Renaissance styles.

Secular architecture also evolved. Town halls (or "Stadhuis") in places like Leeuwarden, Bolsward, or Dokkum took on more ornate facades, showcasing local pride. Gabled roofs and decorative stonework referenced architectural trends from Flanders and Brabant, filtered through simpler Frisian taste. Wealthy merchant families or minor nobles constructed larger brick residences in towns, reflecting status. Meanwhile, rural farmhouses slowly adopted more robust brick sections or expanded barns to accommodate larger herds and the shift toward commercial dairying. These changes signaled that Frisian society, while still rustic in many areas, was incrementally aligning with broader European developments in design and construction.

4.3 Growth of Literacy and Early Humanism

Though overshadowed by major university centers (like Leuven or Paris), the 16th century saw a **slow spread of literacy** in Frisia, fueled by merchant needs and the Catholic Church's educational initiatives. Some monasteries established small schools, teaching basic Latin grammar, arithmetic, and religious doctrine. Certain chieftains or town elites hired private tutors for their children, introducing them to Renaissance humanist writings that circulated widely after the invention of the printing press.

Over time, itinerant scholars or clerics brought ideas from Erasmus of Rotterdam or other Northern Humanists into Frisian intellectual circles. While advanced humanist scholarship never took deep root outside a few town notables or clerical reformers, the seeds were sown. By mid-century, these influences would resonate more profoundly as debates about religion and society intensified, setting the stage for shifts in faith and governance.

---

5. Religious Undercurrents Before the Reformation

5.1 Catholic Dominance and Local Devotions

Before the Protestant Reformation's open spread in the Low Countries, **Catholicism** remained the formal religion across Frisia. Bishops governed ecclesiastical affairs, though local parishes often ran with remarkable autonomy, drawing on centuries-old communal traditions. Lay confraternities and guilds sponsored altars or annual feasts, weaving religious devotion into the social fabric. Pilgrimages to regional shrines—some dedicated to Frisian saints or miracle stories—remained a common expression of faith.

Monasteries, notably Cistercian and Augustinian houses, still operated farmland expansions and charitable functions. Over time, however, corruption or lax discipline in certain monasteries generated murmurs of discontent. A few devout priests, influenced by early reformist ideas or the Devotio Moderna movement (which stressed personal piety), began urging spiritual renewal. Their critiques did not necessarily call for schism but demanded purification of Church life—foreshadowing deeper ruptures to come.

5.2 Early Reformist Echoes

Although Martin Luther's Ninety-Five Theses (1517) and the subsequent Protestant Reformation would soon shake Europe, the 16th century's first decades in Frisia saw only faint echoes of such dissent. A handful of traveling merchants or students brought back stories from Saxony or other German states where Luther's ideas spread rapidly. Small circles of literate townsfolk might read banned tracts, but official Church and Habsburg authorities cracked down on open heresy. Burning of illicit books or intimidation by local inquisitors kept most Frisians outwardly loyal to Catholic rites during the early Reformation years.

Nevertheless, seeds of questioning took root among select individuals—urban professionals, some minor clergy, or those influenced by cross-border trade with Lutheran areas. The region's maritime links to northern Germany, where Lutheranism thrived, made it only a matter of time before reformist ideas found deeper footholds. That shift would intensify in the mid-16th century, eventually reshaping Frisian culture, but it did not dominate the first decades of the century.

5.3 Ties Between Religion and Communal Identity

For many local communities, **religious life** remained inseparable from communal identity. Processions through fields for good harvests or blessings of dikes to prevent flooding carried both spiritual meaning and social cohesion. Priests or friars who participated in these collective rituals built trust. Meanwhile, hostility toward "foreign" bishops or absentee clerics persisted. Some rural assemblies grumbled about tithes sent to distant diocesan centers, echoing older medieval friction. In this sense, Catholic unity coexisted with local resentment of hierarchical structures.

Such tensions did not yet crystallize into a mass Reformation movement, but they weakened unwavering loyalty to the existing order. As the century progressed, economic and political pressures—tied to Habsburg control—would mingle with spiritual questions, preparing the ground for religious turmoil. For the moment, the 16th century's early decades were a transitional phase, bridging medieval devotions and emergent calls for reform.

6. The Dutch Revolt and Its Reverberations in Frisia

6.1 The Rise of Discontent

By the mid-16th century, **Emperor Charles V** ceded control of the Habsburg Netherlands to his son, **Philip II of Spain** (r. 1556–1598). Under Philip II's rule, religious and political tensions escalated across the Low Countries. Harsh persecution of Protestant "heretics," coupled with heavy taxation to finance Spanish wars, ignited widespread unrest. The Dutch Revolt (or Eighty Years' War) erupted in 1568, led by princes and nobles determined to end Spanish dominance. While the war's early stages centered on Holland and the southern provinces, Frisia could not remain untouched.

Though this conflict technically belongs to a broader 16th–17th century timespan (more fully addressed in Chapter Sixteen), its **initial shock waves** reached Frisia before the century closed. Rumors of Protestant preachers stirring congregations, Spanish troops garrisoned in certain Frisian towns, and the creation of rebel militias unsettled local communities. The seeds of rebellion found fertile ground among those resentful of Habsburg interference and rising religious persecution. Meanwhile, pockets of Catholic loyalists supported Spanish authority, hoping to preserve order and tradition. Thus, economic concerns intertwined with emerging religious divides, bringing a new phase of uncertainty.

6.2 Early Protestant Penetration

Although large-scale Calvinist or Lutheran congregations would only openly form later, the 1560s and 1570s saw clandestine **Protestant preaching** in certain Frisian towns. Some merchants or artisans, drawn by reformist doctrine and suspicious of Spanish taxation, gathered in secret "hedge services" to hear radical pastors. Repression was swift where Spanish officials held sway—arrests, fines, or forced recantations. Yet the climate of fear did not entirely halt the spread of new teachings. Smuggled pamphlets circulated, referencing a more direct relationship with God and criticizing the Church's corruption.

Farmers in remote districts encountered the new doctrines more slowly, and many remained Catholic or simply indifferent, focusing on survival in a fractious political environment. However, the infiltration of Protestant ideas among urban elites or chieftain families signaled that Frisian society was poised for deeper religious transformation. Economically, some Protestant-leaning merchants found allies among rebels in Holland, forging clandestine trade routes that bypassed Spanish controls. Tensions soared, setting the stage for greater upheaval in the final decades of the 16th century and beyond.

6.3 Shifting Loyalties at the Century's End

As the Dutch Revolt intensified, Frisia's position straddled allegiances. Some local leaders declared for William of Orange (the primary figure of the Dutch independence movement), aligning with the rebellious northern provinces. Others, especially Catholic nobles or Habsburg appointees, vowed loyalty to Philip II. Meanwhile, a large portion of the population tried to remain neutral or waited to see which side would prevail. This indecision hampered cohesive resistance but also prevented the swift imposition of Spanish martial law in every Frisian district.

The **economy** felt the strain. Naval skirmishes in the Zuiderzee or near the Wadden Sea disrupted shipping, raising insurance costs. Some towns quietly paid off rebel privateers or Spanish captains to spare their harbors. Agriculture continued, but war taxes or forced contributions to passing armies burdened peasants. Observers reported a sense of foreboding, as if Frisia stood on the brink of a massive conflagration. Indeed, the final decades of the 16th century foreshadowed the major religious and political realignments that would dominate the following century.

---

7. Cultural Continuities and Shifts by 1600

7.1 Enduring Folk Traditions

Despite the swirl of economic, political, and religious changes, many **folk traditions** persisted in Frisian villages well into the 16th century's close. Seasonal festivals tied to planting and harvest, communal feasting after successful dike repairs, and local saint's days with processions or fairs remained integral to communal identity. Even as the Reformation's ideas gained traction in some quarters, the majority still found comfort in these age-old rites, fusing Catholic elements with local customs. In remote coastal hamlets, everyday life continued much as it had centuries before—managing livestock, fishing, weaving, and celebrating communal milestones.

7.2 Literacy and Printing

One notable evolution was the **spread of printing**. Though major printing centers lay outside Frisia (in Antwerp, Leiden, or Cologne), smaller presses occasionally operated in Frisian towns. They produced devotional tracts, local ordinances, or pamphlets advocating particular religious or political views. Literacy, while limited to a minority, became more common among burghers and some wealthier farmers. This incrementally boosted political awareness and facilitated the clandestine spread of Protestant writings. Conversely, Catholic authorities also used print to disseminate counterarguments or official decrees.

By 1600, the printed word—whether in Latin, Dutch, or early modern forms of Frisian—had begun to shape public debate. Town magistrates might post printed edicts on church doors, bridging official governance and local assemblies. Over the next century, this new medium would profoundly impact how Frisians received and contested religious and political ideas.

7.3 Art and Architecture at a Turning Point

The late 16th century also saw artistic transitions reflective of the building religious tensions. A handful of church interiors—especially in areas leaning Protestant—quietly removed or whitewashed certain Catholic iconographies, anticipating more radical iconoclasm in the decades to come. Meanwhile, secular building projects in towns strove for more imposing, Renaissance-influenced facades, mirroring trends in the southern Netherlands. This architecture signaled an openness to broader European cultural currents, even as the region wrestled with internal and external strife.

For **music and literature**, the 16th century laid a foundation for future growth. Local balladeers or traveling minstrels adapted songs to reflect the mood of conflict and hope, while a few literate figures tried writing chronicles or historical sketches that documented the fractious times. These works, though rarely printed in large runs, contributed to a nascent sense of Frisian historical consciousness, recalling earlier independence struggles even as new political realities emerged.

8. The Dawn of the 17th Century: Setting the Stage for Ongoing Turmoil

8.1 The Legacy of 16th-Century Transformations

By 1600, Frisia had weathered a century of **economic reorganization** under Habsburg dominion, limited though it may have been in practice. Agricultural consolidation, improved maritime trade frameworks, and partial integration into the Netherlands' administrative systems marked significant departures from the medieval era's decentralized localism. Culturally, the region absorbed influences from the Northern Renaissance and early Reformation debates, even as Catholic structures still dominated official religious life.

This uneasy blend of old and new, of partial external rule and lingering local traditions, set a precarious foundation. The Dutch Revolt's initial salvos ensured that the 17th century would bring more disruption, especially as Frisia's strategic location made it a valuable prize for competing powers. Politically, the 16th century ended with many open questions: Would Frisia fully join the rebellious provinces seeking independence from Spain? Could it preserve any vestige of its vaunted communal freedoms if it aligned with the emergent Dutch Republic? Or would Spanish or imperial forces reassert tighter control?

8.2 Transition Toward the "Golden Age" or Further Conflict?

As the wider Low Countries moved into the 17th century, parts of what would become the Dutch Republic prospered from global commerce. Frisia stood to benefit if it joined the revolt and integrated into Dutch commercial networks. Yet, that path involved entanglement in a protracted war with Spain—complete with siege warfare, religious confrontation, and shifting alliances. Alternatively, siding with Spain might preserve certain local privileges, but risked isolation if the rest of the Netherlands broke free. These dilemmas would frame Frisian decision-making in the coming decades, as political, economic, and religious turmoil converged.

CHAPTER 16: POLITICAL RESTRUCTURING AND RELIGIOUS TURMOIL

1. Introduction: Frisia in the Maelstrom of Change

By the late 16th century, Frisia's integration into the Habsburg Netherlands had already introduced new administrative frameworks and economic linkages, yet local autonomy and the memory of "Frisian freedom" still resonated. The **Dutch Revolt** (1568–1648) against Spanish-Habsburg rule now provided a defining test: Would Frisia align with the nascent Dutch Republic, or remain under the Catholic monarch Philip II and his successors? Religious strife, especially between rising Protestant movements and entrenched Catholic authorities, intersected with these political choices, bringing another wave of upheaval to the region.

This chapter explores **political restructuring** in Frisia and the **religious turmoil** that accompanied it from roughly the 1560s through the mid-17th century. We will follow the region's shifting allegiances in the Eighty Years' War, the internal divisions over faith, and the eventual incorporation of Frisia into the emergent United Provinces of the Netherlands. By the century's end, Frisia's medieval structures had transformed decisively, though local traditions left an indelible stamp on how the province engaged with Dutch republican governance.

2. Prelude to the Dutch Revolt: 1560s Tensions

2.1 Spanish-Habsburg Policies Under Philip II

When **Philip II** of Spain inherited the Netherlands from his father, Charles V, he inherited a region of diverse principalities and free cities, many chafing under centralizing reforms. In Frisia, Philip II's local governors expanded taxes, enforced strict anti-heresy edicts, and maintained Spanish garrisons in key ports. These measures aimed to stamp out Protestantism and secure consistent revenue, especially as Spain's global commitments grew. Yet they alienated many Frisians who saw them as heavy-handed intrusions on local custom.

Complaints from Frisian nobles and city magistrates echoed those from Holland, Zeeland, and other provinces. They resented the disregard for historic charters and the persecution of suspected Calvinists, Lutherans, or Anabaptists. In rural areas, fear of Spanish soldiers—often foreigners from distant Catholic enclaves—intensified anti-Habsburg sentiment. By the 1560s, tensions had reached a boiling point, though open rebellion was not yet universal. Some loyalist chieftains or Catholic burghers still supported Philip's regime, hoping it preserved order.

2.2 Emergence of Protestant Pockets

While much of Frisia remained nominally Catholic through the mid-16th century, **Protestant "pockets"** expanded, especially in port towns with strong trade ties to northern Germany or England. Lutheran ideas had trickled in earlier, but by the 1560s, **Calvinist influences** from the southern Netherlands and France grew more prominent. Underground congregations formed, meeting in barns or private homes. Ministers risked arrest for preaching Reformed doctrine. Some local leaders, inspired by Calvinist teachings, quietly aided these groups, seeing them as a vehicle for opposing Spanish oppression.

The shifting religious balance also destabilized local alliances. A chieftain historically allied with Catholic leaders might convert to Protestantism, forging new ties with rebels in Holland. Town councils that once tolerated mild Catholic oversight could find themselves drawn to radical preachers who promised moral renewal and liberation from Spanish burdens. This phenomenon was not uniform—some districts remained stubbornly Catholic, others were divided internally. But the cumulative effect was to erode any monolithic loyalty to the Habsburg crown, leaving Frisia increasingly open to rebellion.

2.3 Early Incidents of Resistance

In the late 1560s, small **incidents** foreshadowed broader revolt:

- **Iconoclastic Riots** (Beeldenstorm): Though more widespread in Flanders and Brabant, a few Frisian churches experienced attacks on statues or paintings by zealous Protestants. These outbursts shocked conservative Catholics and spurred Spanish authorities to crack down.

- **Band of Sea Beggars**: On the Frisian coast, some rebel privateers—aligned with William of Orange—raided shipping or small garrisons. While not a massive threat yet, these "Sea Beggars" tested the loyalty of coastal towns forced to choose between harboring them or denouncing them to Spanish officials.
- **Noble Petitions**: Frisian nobles, often overshadowed by powerful urban elites or overshadowed by Habsburg appointees, made common cause with their counterparts in other provinces by sending petitions to the Spanish regent. They demanded respect for local privileges and an end to religious persecution. Philip II's regime responded harshly, branding them troublemakers or heretics.

These scattered events set the stage for deeper revolt as the 1570s arrived, when the Dutch Revolt properly ignited across the northern provinces.

---

3. The Early Dutch Revolt in Frisia (1570s–1580s)

3.1 The Tide of Rebellion Spreads North

In 1572, rebel forces captured key towns in Holland and Zeeland, declaring open war against Spanish rule. **William of Orange**, recognized as the revolt's political and military leader, appealed to the northern provinces, including Frisia, for support. Encouraged by rebel successes, certain Frisian towns expelled Spanish garrisons or declared loyalty to the Prince of Orange. Others hesitated, worried about Spanish reprisals or internal divisions. Nonetheless, the momentum of rebellion grew, aided by a new wave of Protestant fervor.

Spanish reprisals were swift. Armies or loyalist chieftains retook towns, punishing rebel collaborators. Fears of Spanish "Blood Councils" (harsh tribunals) spurred more communities to cast their lot with the rebels rather than risk brutal subjugation. The war escalated into a patchwork of sieges and counter-sieges across Frisia. The region's watery terrain allowed local defenders to flood fields, hamper Spanish cavalry, and rely on small rebel fleets to move supplies. Yet these same conditions made it hard for either side to achieve rapid breakthroughs, prolonging the conflict.

3.2 Shifts in Religious Policy

As the rebel cause expanded, it began establishing **Reformed church structures** in areas under its control. Calvinist pastors replaced Catholic priests in prominent urban churches, iconoclasm sometimes flared anew, and Catholic worship was restricted if not outright banned. Many ordinary folk found these sudden changes jarring. A rural parish might have been devoutly Catholic for generations, only to see a new Reformed preacher installed by rebel authorities. Some conformed reluctantly; others fled to Catholic enclaves or towns still loyal to Spain.

For their part, Spanish-loyal authorities strove to **enforce Catholic orthodoxy** in districts they controlled, often using intimidation or imprisonment. This polarized the population further. Families were torn as siblings or cousins chose opposite sides, shaped by religious conviction or pragmatic alliances. The war's confusion allowed extremist elements—whether Protestant fanatics or Catholic zealots—to commit atrocities. Chroniclers lamented that the once-insular feuds of Frisia were now overshadowed by a continent-wide struggle of faith and sovereignty.

3.3 Emergence of Stadtholder Leadership in Frisia

Amid the shifting battle lines, rebel leaders recognized the need for local governance. They appointed **stadtholders**—representatives of William of Orange or the rebel States General—to oversee provinces. In Frisia, individuals like **George of Lalaing (Count of Rennenberg)** or others took the stadtholder's role, though their allegiance sometimes wavered if they faced Spanish overtures. Over time, a stable pro-Orange group of Frisian nobles and urban magistrates consolidated around stadtholder leadership, forging administrative continuity.

By the 1580s, it was clearer that the **northern provinces** (Holland, Zeeland, Frisia, Groningen, Overijssel, and others) would form the core of a "United Provinces," embracing Protestantism and rejecting Spanish monarchy. Yet the process was messy. Spanish armies periodically retook pockets of Frisia, forcing families to choose loyalty anew. The economic toll grew severe—harbors closed, farmland was ravaged. Nevertheless, the rebel side gradually tightened its grip, backed by Dutch naval power and alliances with England or Protestant German princes.

4. Consolidation of the Dutch Republic and Frisia's Role

4.1 The Union of Utrecht (1579) and Formal Alliances

In 1579, several northern provinces signed the **Union of Utrecht**, a foundational treaty for the Dutch Republic. Frisia, though divided by local conflicts, ultimately joined, pledging to coordinate defense and governance with the other united provinces. The Union enshrined principles of mutual aid against Spain and outlined shared sovereignty under the States General. For Frisia, this arrangement promised relief from Spanish oppression and a voice in the emergent republican structure. Yet it also required conformity with the overarching Calvinist orientation that shaped the new state.

Not all Frisians welcomed the shift. Some districts remained Catholic or harbored loyalties to the Habsburg empire. Tensions within Frisia lingered, especially if a local chieftain or town had pinned hopes on Spanish favor. Nonetheless, the **Union of Utrecht** was a watershed moment, symbolizing the broad alignment of Frisian rebels with the other northern provinces. Over the next decades, the Dutch Republic functioned as a de facto independent polity, even though formal recognition by Europe's powers would only come gradually.

4.2 The Reduction of Groningen and Eastern Frisia

Frisia's boundaries were fluid. The **city of Groningen** and its surrounding Ommelanden region often wavered between Spanish and rebel loyalties. By the 1590s, the Prince of Orange's forces "reduced" (i.e., brought under control) Groningen, securing the eastern flank of the Republic. This development also integrated the eastern portion of Frisia more firmly into Dutch structures. Meanwhile, East Frisia (under the Cirksena family) was tangentially involved, sometimes cooperating with the Dutch, sometimes maintaining neutrality or dealing with the Holy Roman Emperor. The evolving tapestry of alliances revealed how the old medieval fractiousness was gradually superseded by modern state boundaries.

For central Frisia, the **States of Friesland** (provincial assembly) emerged as the local legislative body, working with the stadtholder. This assembly balanced aristocratic and urban representation, though it leaned strongly Protestant after the Spanish defeats. Over time, the States of Friesland gained experience in taxation, legal reform, and diplomatic relations with other Dutch provinces, forging a cohesive identity within the Republic.

4.3 Economic Consequences of War

Decades of warfare inevitably exacted an **economic toll**. Farmsteads near battle zones were destroyed or heavily taxed to feed armies. Harbors suffered blockades or raids. Yet from the 1590s onward, the rebel provinces capitalized on expanding global trade, funneling goods through Amsterdam, Enkhuizen, and other ports. Frisia, though less central than Holland or Zeeland, still participated—its agricultural produce and livestock contributed to feeding urban centers, and some Frisian merchants tapped into Baltic or North Sea commerce aligned with the Dutch navy's protection.

Overall, the shift from Spanish to Dutch Republican control brought certain benefits: fewer random exactions by foreign troops, more stable trade policies, and the chance to unify behind a single currency or legal system. On the flip side, local Catholic enclaves faced restrictions or property confiscations if they refused to adopt Calvinist rule. Social tensions simmered, as communities once united by Catholic devotions were forced to adapt or go underground with their faith. By the early 17th century, Frisia had thus emerged as a province of the Dutch Republic, albeit with lingering wounds from decades of religious and political strife.

---

5. Religious Turmoil and the Establishment of Calvinism

5.1 Official Calvinist Church in Frisia

As the Dutch Republic solidified, **Calvinism** became the officially endorsed faith in most provinces, including Frisia. Provincial synods oversaw church governance, appointing Reformed pastors and regulating doctrine. Church consistory boards gained influence in local society, enforcing moral discipline, regulating marriage, and sometimes policing tavern behaviors. The synergy between civic authorities and Reformed clergy gave the new church a strong institutional backbone.

For many ordinary Frisians, this transition was jarring. While some embraced Reformed teachings enthusiastically—valuing sermons in the vernacular and the simplified worship style—others clung to Catholic traditions or remained less doctrinally driven. The provincial authorities generally tolerated no open Catholic parishes; Catholicism retreated into private chapels or hidden worship gatherings. Meanwhile, minority Protestant sects (Lutherans, Mennonites, etc.) found cautious acceptance in certain districts, though strict Calvinists occasionally harassed or expelled them. Religious uniformity was the ideal, but not always the reality in a pluralistic region.

5.2 Iconoclasm and Church Transformations

During the height of the revolt, **iconoclastic outbreaks** had removed statues, paintings, and decorations from many Frisian churches. In the early 17th century, local congregations completed the transformation of worship spaces. Altars were replaced by pulpits at the center, focusing on preaching rather than sacramental rites. Walls were whitewashed, removing elaborate medieval murals. Stone images of saints or biblical scenes were sometimes smashed or sold off. Church interiors took on a stark aesthetic that symbolized the Reformed emphasis on scripture and word.

Although this "cleansing" was not uniform—some rural areas kept partial vestiges of medieval art—the general trajectory was a radical shift from Catholic visual culture to a more austere environment. Parish communities that once took pride in flamboyant feasts or saint's days now organized simpler gatherings around Sunday sermons and communal prayers. Not all accepted these changes willingly. Older villagers might recall a time when the church was full of color and incense; some lamented the loss. But the official line, backed by the States of Friesland, pressed forward with Calvinist norms.

5.3 Religious Minorities: Catholics and Other Protestants

Despite the official Reformed Church, pockets of **Catholic believers** persisted. Some retreated to private chapels in noble households or disguised barns (the so-called "schuilkerken"), served by clandestine priests. The authorities often turned a blind eye if these worshipers remained discreet and paid taxes, though occasional crackdowns targeted outspoken Catholic leaders. Meanwhile, **Lutheran** or **Anabaptist** (Mennonite) congregations also existed, reflecting the maritime connections to northern Germany, where these denominations thrived. The Dutch

Republic's pragmatic tolerance usually let them function as long as they did not challenge Calvinist hegemony or create public scandal.

Over time, Frisia's religious landscape stabilized into a broad Calvinist mainstream with scattered enclaves of Catholics, Lutherans, and Anabaptists. This pluralism, though restricted by official policy, signaled a departure from the medieval uniformity. Religious identity became intertwined with political loyalty to the Republic or to the memory of Spanish Catholic rule, shaping familial and communal ties for generations.

6. Political Restructuring Under the Dutch Republic

6.1 The States of Friesland and the Stadtholder

The newly minted **Dutch Republic** organized each province with its own "States" assembly, comprising representatives of towns and nobles. In Friesland, the **States of Friesland** balanced power among urban delegates (from Leeuwarden, Franeker, etc.) and rural nobility. This body set taxes, oversaw local defense, and cooperated with the States General in The Hague on foreign policy. A **stadtholder**, often a member of the House of Orange-Nassau, acted as the provincial executive and military commander.

Though part of a federal republic, Frisia retained certain historical privileges—echoes of "Frisian freedom." For instance, the States of Friesland insisted on controlling local water boards and land laws. They negotiated with the States General to avoid undue interference in dike management. Meanwhile, the stadtholder's power rose or fell depending on broader Dutch politics. At times, strong stadtholders used military prestige to influence Frisian policy heavily; at other times, an anti-Orangist faction in the States gained ascendancy. This interplay made Frisian politics lively and often contentious throughout the 17th century.

6.2 Administrative and Judicial Reforms

Under the Republic, **administrative reforms** slowly replaced ad hoc medieval offices. The States of Friesland appointed bailiffs, tax collectors, and local magistrates in consultation with city councils. A more standardized judicial hierarchy emerged—lower courts in towns, higher appeal courts for the province, and ultimate recourse to the Supreme Court of Holland, Zeeland, and Friesland in The Hague (though the name varied over time). This rationalization aimed to foster legal clarity, encouraging commerce and social order.

Still, customary law did not vanish. Many local disputes were settled in communal assemblies or water boards, especially those concerning farmland or dike responsibilities. In practice, local notables who had once been petty chieftains adapted to the new roles of "grietman" (local judge or mayor) or "dijkgraaf" (water board official). The continuity of personnel helped ease the transition from medieval autonomy to early modern bureaucracy. Over the decades, a new class of educated lawyers emerged, bringing uniform procedures and Latin-based legal codes to a region once governed by oral tradition.

6.3 Military Obligations and Fortifications

As part of the Dutch Republic's war effort against Spain, Frisia bore **military obligations**. Though not as central as Holland or Zeeland in naval power, Frisian funds and manpower supported the Republic's armies. New fortifications arose in strategic border towns like Dokkum or near the German frontier, reflecting ongoing threats from Spanish or Imperial forces. Town councils had to budget for garrisons, artillery, and upkeep of walls. Some local men enlisted in the States Army, experiencing discipline and tactics aligned with the nascent "Dutch military revolution."

These military demands sometimes clashed with local pride in minimal external control. Yet the shared struggle against Spain fostered a sense of belonging to the broader rebel cause. By the war's later stages (post-1609 Twelve Years' Truce and beyond), Frisian regiments formed part of the cohesive Dutch military system. The region's old fractious feuds were overshadowed by the necessity of communal defense under the Republic's banner.

7. Economic and Social Developments in the 17th Century Context

7.1 Recovery and Growth Post-Dutch Revolt

The final decades of the **Eighty Years' War** saw Frisia relatively spared from the worst fighting compared to the southern provinces. After the 1580s, Spanish offensives mostly targeted Flanders, Brabant, and parts of eastern Dutch lands. This relative calm let Frisia focus on **economic recovery**. Agricultural output rose as reclaimed polders expanded. Towns participated in Baltic and North Sea trade, feeding the blossoming commercial networks of the Dutch Golden Age. Urban guilds specialized in textiles, brewing, or ship carpentry, albeit on a smaller scale than Amsterdam or Rotterdam.

Meanwhile, religious upheaval settled into a stable pattern of a dominant Calvinist church with tolerated minorities. The new social environment prized industriousness, moral discipline, and communal order—values that matched well with the broader Dutch ethos of the 17th century. Though not as wealthy as the maritime powerhouses of Holland, Frisia found its niche, balancing rural productivity and modest but steady trade.

7.2 Social Stratification and Urbanization

As the war receded, **social stratification** became more visible. A merchant-patrician class and Reformed church leadership enjoyed higher status in towns, forging alliances with landed gentry in the countryside. Former chieftain families that adapted to the Republic's structures often retained local influence. In contrast, Catholic noble lines or families that had clung to Spanish loyalties found themselves marginalized or forced into discreet living.

Urbanization proceeded slowly but steadily, with Leeuwarden emerging as the provincial capital, hosting the States of Friesland. Smaller towns grew around new trade opportunities or specialized crafts. Still, a majority of Frisians remained in rural villages, governed by water boards and local courts. Literacy expanded further, especially among the middle ranks—artisans, minor officials, and farmers with moderate holdings. Over the century, printing presses in Leeuwarden and other towns produced religious tracts, almanacs, and local histories, reinforcing an evolving sense of a shared Frisian identity within the Dutch Republic.

7.3 Cultural Flourishing Within the Republic

Despite the overshadowing dominance of Holland's cultural centers, Frisia partook in the **Dutch Golden Age** to a lesser extent. Wealthy provincial elites sponsored artists or supported local miniaturists. Architecture in towns gained the classic Dutch Renaissance or Mannerist style—stepped gables, ornamental facades. The Reformed Church shaped musical traditions, emphasizing psalm-singing with organ accompaniment, though grand Catholic or medieval church music had waned.

A few **local authors** penned chronicles or moral treatises in Dutch or early modern Frisian. By the mid-17th century, historians like **Occo Scarlensis** (a semi-legendary name used to illustrate a local chronicler) tried to compile accounts of Frisian involvement in the Dutch Revolt or earlier centuries, mixing factual detail with romantic myth. Such texts, while not widely distributed, fueled a modest literary awakening that paved the way for more robust cultural production in later eras.

---

8. Concluding Reflections on 16th–17th Century Transformations

8.1 The Eclipse of Medieval Independence

Comparing Frisia at the dawn of the 16th century to its status by the mid-17th century reveals a sweeping transformation. The old mosaic of semi-autonomous districts under nominal Burgundian or Habsburg oversight gave way to membership in the **Dutch Republic**. The medieval "Frisian freedom" ideal still echoed in local customs and assemblies, but real power now lay with provincial States integrated into a federal republican system. Religious uniformity under Calvinism replaced Catholic unity, although pockets of dissent persisted.

Yet it would be simplistic to say that all medieval autonomy vanished. Water boards remained in local hands, communal traditions shaped day-to-day governance, and a sense of distinct Frisian identity survived, even within the wider Dutch polity. The synergy of local resilience and external structures defined early modern Frisia—no longer fully independent, but not entirely subservient either.

8.2 Religious Resolution and Ongoing Pluralism

By 1650, the **Protestant Reformed Church** dominated public religious life, while Catholics and other minorities worshipped discreetly. Though strict Calvinist orthodoxy was official, the Dutch Republic's relative tolerance allowed quiet survival of differing beliefs. In that sense, Frisia mirrored the broader Union: outwardly Reformed, inwardly diverse. Tensions still arose—periodic crackdowns on "heretical" or "papist" gatherings occurred—but widespread religious bloodshed eased after the revolt's peak. The region settled into a guarded pluralism that, while not wholly inclusive, was more flexible than many contemporary European states.

8.3 The Lasting Impact of the Revolt and Restructuring

The **Dutch Revolt** and subsequent war lasting into 1648's Peace of Westphalia proved the crucible that restructured Frisia's political and religious foundations. Monarchical feudal overlordship by Spain or the Habsburgs faded, replaced by a republican form of governance that valued representation—albeit restricted to elites—and recognized local privileges, in principle. The synergy between agrarian traditions, maritime commerce, and alignment with the Dutch Golden Age economy spurred moderate prosperity. Meanwhile, cultural expressions, from architecture to printed literature, embraced the energy of a broader European Renaissance, shaped by Reformed convictions and local pride.

Thus, by the late 17th century, **Frisia stood firmly within the Dutch Republic**, its medieval phase definitively over. A new era of provincial governance, combined with religious settlement, anchored the region in early modern Europe's shifting landscape. The path that began in the 16th-century turmoil had led to a stable, if imperfect, equilibrium—one that would endure into subsequent centuries, forming the basis for future developments in Frisian law, society, and identity.

CHAPTER 17: THE SEVENTEENTH CENTURY

1. Introduction: Frisia in the Dutch Golden Age

By the dawn of the **17th century**, Frisia had been incorporated into the emerging **Dutch Republic** (or Republic of the Seven United Provinces), alongside Holland, Zeeland, Utrecht, Overijssel, and Groningen. The war against Spain continued, though the northern provinces gained considerable autonomy following major successes in the late 16th century. This era, often heralded as the "Dutch Golden Age," featured expanding global trade, cultural achievements, and new forms of state administration. While the province of Holland claimed the spotlight for commercial might and cultural influence, Frisia also found opportunities in maritime endeavors and local innovation.

The 17th century in Frisia was a time of **social shifts**, influenced by growing market connections, agricultural changes, and the pressures of an ongoing, though fluctuating, Eighty Years' War that would officially end in 1648 with the Peace of Münster (part of the Peace of Westphalia). Even thereafter, the province's place within the Dutch Republic continued to evolve. This chapter surveys these transformations: from the intensification of maritime pursuits—fishing, whaling, and trade—to the subtle but significant developments in Frisian social structures, religious life, and cultural identity. We will see how local assemblies adapted to republican governance, how farmers and merchants weathered economic ups and downs, and how an enduring sense of Frisian distinctiveness coexisted with the overarching Dutch framework.

2. The Broader Context: The Dutch Republic in the 17th Century

2.1 Post-Union of Utrecht Consolidation

The **Union of Utrecht (1579)** set the foundation for the Dutch Republic by uniting the northern provinces. Over the ensuing decades, the Republic solidified its institutions—States General, Provincial States, and stadtholders drawn from the House of Orange-Nassau. For Frisia, representation occurred through the **States of Friesland**, comprising representatives from towns and rural districts, along with the stadtholder who served as the province's executive and military leader. This arrangement provided a balance between local autonomy and centralized direction in wartime.

Though the revolt against Spain was ongoing, by the early 17th century it had settled into phases of truce (notably the Twelve Years' Truce, 1609–1621) and renewed conflict. Meanwhile, commerce boomed in the Republic's core maritime provinces, fueled by overseas trade in spices, textiles, grain, and other commodities. Frisia was less central to this "Golden Age" economy than Holland or Zeeland, yet it benefited indirectly from a rising tide of Dutch maritime and financial prosperity. Local entrepreneurs found ways to supply or augment the shipping networks, forging new opportunities in coastal shipping, fishing, and specialized crafts.

2.2 Impact of Global Commerce on Frisia

Europe's **Age of Exploration** had launched wide-reaching global trade routes. The Dutch East India Company (VOC) and the Dutch West India Company (WIC) led the Republic's expansion into Asia and the Americas. While the largest ships and capital typically came from Amsterdam or other major ports, smaller Frisian ports provided auxiliary shipping services: building vessels suitable for shallow coasts, offering skilled sailors, and engaging in the "feeder trade" that connected local produce to main export routes. Moreover, some Frisian sailors and merchants ventured far, finding employment on VOC or WIC ships and returning with stories, minor capital, or exotic goods.

Simultaneously, the **Baltic grain trade** remained crucial. Dutch ships imported large volumes of rye and wheat from the Baltic region to feed growing urban centers. Frisian coasters also plied these routes. Although overshadowed by the bigger ports of the Zuiderzee or the expanding metropolis of Amsterdam, Frisian merchants retained a foothold in these commercial lanes. Alongside commerce, a portion of Frisian maritime activity encompassed fishing (herring, cod, and flatfish) and, increasingly, whaling, as the Dutch exploited Arctic seas around Spitsbergen and beyond.

2.3 Ongoing Conflict and Naval Defense

Though the major theaters of the Eighty Years' War often lay outside Frisia, the province was not immune to **military pressures**. Naval skirmishes between Dutch and Spanish fleets could spill into the Wadden Sea or the Zuiderzee. Coastal towns worried about privateers—some still loyal to Spain, others mere pirates exploiting the conflict. In response, local militias and small squadrons of armed vessels patrolled Frisian shores. The stadtholder in Frisia coordinated with the States of Friesland and the States General in The Hague to finance these defenses.

By the mid-17th century, the official conclusion of the war (1648) reduced direct Spanish threats, but new challenges emerged, such as rivalry with England and tensions within Europe's shifting alliances. The resulting Anglo-Dutch Wars (starting in the 1650s) also affected Frisian shipping, as English fleets targeted Dutch maritime commerce. Once more, local shipowners needed to adapt, either arming their vessels or seeking naval convoys from the Republic's formidable navy. This environment of near-constant maritime vigilance helped shape 17th-century Frisia's focus on seafaring and defense readiness.

---

3. Intensification of Maritime Activity

3.1 Herring and Cod Fisheries

Fishing had been a longstanding pillar of Frisian coastal life, but the **17th century** saw it become more systematically organized. The **herring fishery**, famously associated with the Dutch Republic at large, found some participants in Frisia. Though the largest herring fleets hailed from Holland's ports, Frisian skippers and crews joined or supported these fleets. They contributed smaller "buizen" (herring vessels) or provided supplies like salted fish or barrels. Cod fishing also expanded, with Frisian fishermen targeting northern waters. Over time, certain coastal villages specialized in gear-making, net-mending, or producing the best wooden barrels for fish packing.

Profits varied with seasonal catches and war disruptions. When fish stocks were good and markets strong, villages thrived; if storms or conflict interrupted shipping, finances suffered. Local investors—often members of the rising burgher class—pooled capital to outfit fishing expeditions, sharing risks and rewards. Religious regulations (like the Calvinist discouragement of lavish feasts) had minimal direct effect on the fishing economy; the impetus lay in broader market forces and the reliability of shipping routes.

3.2 Whaling and Arctic Ventures

One notable expansion in the Dutch maritime sphere was **Arctic whaling**. Around the early 17th century, Dutch ships began frequenting Spitsbergen (Svalbard) and Greenland seas to hunt bowhead whales. Frisia participated to a modest extent. Frisian merchants and shipowners joined whaling "chambers" established by local investors, either independently or in partnership with bigger ports. These chambers financed whaling vessels, employing crews who braved harsh northern waters to harvest whale oil and baleen. Whale oil served as an essential commodity for lamps, soap, and industrial uses, while baleen (whalebone) found markets in fashion and manufacture.

Though overshadowed by major whaling hubs like Amsterdam's Noordsche Compagnie, a portion of the workforce came from Frisian fishing communities, seeking higher pay than routine coastal fishing. The tough conditions and risk of ice entrapment demanded skill and resilience—traits many Frisians possessed from generations of coastal living. Profits could be substantial if a ship returned laden with whale products, fueling local capital accumulation in certain towns. Over time, these gains underwrote investments in farmland, shipping, or urban building projects, weaving whaling earnings into Frisia's broader economic tapestry.

3.3 Coastal Shipping and Inter-Provincial Trade

Beyond long-distance fisheries, **coastal shipping** remained crucial. Frisia's shallow-draft vessels carried peat, salt, grain, and dairy produce to larger Dutch or German ports. Towns like Harlingen or Dokkum served as nodes linking rural hinterlands to the maritime network. Farmers who produced butter, cheese, or livestock found expanded markets in the growing cities of Holland and abroad.

Meanwhile, peat extracted from Frisian bogs provided fuel for many urban households in the Republic, transported by barges or small ships.

To facilitate this commerce, local authorities improved harbors, erected warehouses, and dredged silted waterways. Water boards, famous for managing dikes and drainage, sometimes oversaw navigable canals as well. The synergy between controlling floodwaters and enhancing shipping channels underscored how crucial water management remained to Frisian prosperity. In addition, certain small industries—textiles, ceramics, or rope-making—catered to maritime demand, employing craftspeople in and around port towns. While overshadowed by the manufacturing might of Holland or Brabant, these local crafts gave stable work to parts of the Frisian population.

---

4. Social Structures and Community Life

4.1 Rural Hierarchies: Gentry, Farmers, and Laborers

Despite the shift from medieval feudalism to a republican framework, **social hierarchies** persisted in Frisian rural areas. A minor nobility or gentry (some descended from old chieftain lines) retained large estates, often consolidated through strategic marriages or inheritance. They formed a local elite, frequently serving as grietmannen (municipal judges or mayors) or water board officials. Below them, a prosperous stratum of **medium-scale farmers** emerged, benefiting from the 16th-century land consolidation. These farmers cultivated larger plots, invested in improved drainage or livestock breeding, and wielded modest political influence through local assemblies.

At the lower tiers were **tenant farmers** with smaller plots and **landless laborers** who worked on bigger farms seasonally. They had limited means to amass capital or property, dependent on wages that fluctuated with harvest success. Many laborers also engaged in part-time fishing or peat digging, diversifying income. The environment demanded communal cooperation—everyone participated in dike repairs or drainage projects—yet inequalities shaped everyday life, from diet and housing to marriage prospects. The Calvinist ethic, which valued thrift and diligence, often aligned with the social aspirations of upwardly mobile farmers or artisans. However, those stuck in poverty found few safety nets beyond local parish charity or meager poor relief funds.

4.2 Urban Growth and Guild Dynamics

Frisian towns, though smaller than Holland's urban centers, still **expanded** modestly in the 17th century. Leeuwarden, as the provincial capital, housed the States of Friesland and a growing administration, attracting lawyers, notaries, and merchants. Harlingen and Franeker also gained from trade or educational institutions. **Guilds** played a significant role in these urban economies—organizing bakers, brewers, carpenters, and other crafts. Membership rules ensured quality standards but could restrict newcomers from practicing trades freely, thus reinforcing the established burgher class.

The synergy of guild power and local government was evident in councils (vroedschappen) that included guild representatives alongside patrician families. Guild heads negotiated taxes, market regulations, and occasional expansions of city fortifications. Religious lines blurred within guilds: while the official stance favored Reformed Protestants, Catholics or Lutherans sometimes participated if they kept a low profile. Over time, guild dynamism helped shape a stable urban middle class, forging ties with rural suppliers and maritime traders. For social identity, guild membership offered respectability, shaping a craftsman's place in the layered hierarchy of 17th-century Frisian towns.

4.3 Communal Identities and Festivals

Communal **festivals** remained integral to Frisian life, though many Catholic feast days had been replaced or stripped of overt religious pageantry under Calvinism. Instead, city charters might sponsor secular fairs coinciding with major trade events, drawing crowds from the countryside. Market squares filled with stalls offering farm produce, cloth, pottery, and wares from afar. Street performers or traveling musicians provided entertainment, albeit with Reformed leaders cautioning against "ungodly revelry." In rural villages, older festivities tied to sowing, harvesting, or water management achievements quietly continued, shaped more by local tradition than official church sanction.

Additionally, clan or family gatherings—weddings, baptisms, funerals—still bound communities together, bridging gaps between gentry and commoners. Though class distinctions persisted, neighbors often cooperated for survival against floods or bad harvests. This shared vulnerability to the environment sustained a sense of communal identity. At the same time, the cultural shift away from medieval Catholic rites reshaped symbolic bonds, anchoring them less in lavish saints' festivals and more in local or family-based customs. Over the century, these new forms of collective identity solidified the weaving of old Frisian communal ties with the emergent Dutch Reformed ethos.

5. Religious Landscape and Intellectual Currents

5.1 Calvinist Orthodoxy and Provincial Synods

After the Dutch Revolt established the **Reformed Church** as the public church of the Republic, provincial synods guided local congregations. In Frisia, these synods convened regularly, discussing pastoral appointments, doctrinal discipline, and moral conduct among parishioners. Ministers trained at Dutch Reformed institutions—like the universities in Leiden or Franeker—spread a consistent Calvinist theology. Sermons stressed predestination, scriptural authority, and communal moral standards. Church consistory boards disciplined those accused of adultery, drunkenness, or other "offenses," though actual enforcement varied from town to town.

Franeker University (founded in 1585) became a hub for **Reformed scholarship**, attracting theologians and students across the region. Though smaller than Leiden or Utrecht, it served as an intellectual nucleus for Frisian ministers and lay scholars. Debates over finer points of Calvinist doctrine, such as the Arminian controversy, filtered into Frisian congregations. Some local pastors adopted moderate stances, while more rigid Calvinists insisted on strict orthodoxy. Such debates occasionally erupted into local conflicts, though they rarely escalated to widespread violence as in earlier times of religious turmoil.

5.2 Catholic and Other Minorities

Despite official Reformed dominance, a **Catholic minority** persisted discreetly. Rural hamlets or noble estates might host clandestine Masses in private chapels. The authorities often tolerated these gatherings so long as they remained inconspicuous, consistent with the Dutch Republic's broader policy of pragmatic tolerance. Similarly, Lutherans maintained small congregations in towns with historical German ties, while Mennonites or other Anabaptist groups quietly thrived in pockets where pacifist beliefs or local acceptance shielded them from persecution. Over time, these minority communities contributed to a subdued religious pluralism.

Still, Catholics faced social limitations. They could not hold major public offices, and they risked suspicion in times of war with Catholic powers. Jesuit missionaries sometimes ventured into Frisia to offer spiritual support, risking arrest if discovered. Meanwhile, Mennonites faced scrutiny from Reformed synods or local officials suspicious of their refusal of military service. Yet, in line with the Republic's de facto tolerance, as long as such groups did not openly contest the Reformed Church's public status, they generally avoided severe crackdowns. This arrangement nurtured a quiet tapestry of faith communities beneath the official Calvinist veneer.

5.3 Intellectual and Cultural Debates

Beyond strict theological matters, **intellectual currents** shaped Frisian cultural life. Franeker University, though modest, hosted scholars in classical languages, law, and natural philosophy. The interplay of Renaissance humanism and Reformed theology produced an environment valuing scholarly debate. Lectures in moral philosophy or scriptural exegesis formed clergy well-versed in both tradition and reason. Some instructors gained reputations beyond Frisia, occasionally attracting students from Germany or Scandinavia.

In the broader Dutch context, the 17th century witnessed a flourishing of **scientific inquiry** (as exemplified by figures like Hugo Grotius or Christiaan Huygens in other provinces). Frisia partook in smaller ways—local savants studied astronomy, mathematics, or medicine, sometimes drawing on knowledge from maritime exploration. Meanwhile, laypeople consumed pamphlets and almanacs that combined biblical references, folk wisdom, and rudimentary science. Although not a leading center of the Dutch intellectual "Golden Age," Frisia found a niche, producing a handful of notable scholars and embracing an ethos that blended practical maritime knowledge with Reformed-hued literacy.

6. Environmental Pressures and Water Management

6.1 Ongoing Storm Surges and Flood Control

Frisia's **coastal vulnerability** never relented. The 17th century saw multiple severe storms, each threatening dike systems. Local water boards continued their vital role, organizing communal labor to repair or raise dikes. The intensification of farmland usage demanded more robust defenses, since inundation could ruin entire harvests. Town expansions also called for improved drainage canals and protective ramparts.

Advanced engineering knowledge—partially shared across the Republic—helped refine dike construction. Surveyors used better surveying instruments; carpenters or stonemasons introduced new bracing methods for dike revetments. In particularly exposed zones along the Wadden Sea or near the Zuiderzee (later the IJsselmeer), the States of Friesland might allocate funds for large-scale dike projects. Yet, storms such as those that occasionally battered the coast around 1625 or the devastating floods in the 1650s revealed that total security remained elusive. Each flood reminded Frisians that water management was an ongoing communal imperative, forging solidarity that transcended class and religious divides.

6.2 Policing Land Reclamation

At the same time, entrepreneurial **land reclamation** continued. Wealthy merchants or gentry financed polders, draining marshy tracts to create new farmland. The local authorities had to balance these projects with the broader interest of not destabilizing existing dike lines. If one polder's drainage was poorly done, it could weaken adjacent areas or hamper drainage channels. Water boards often required strict compliance with technical standards, collecting fees to maintain shared infrastructure. Disputes erupted if a reclamation scheme threatened neighbors' drainage or if local laborers felt exploited by low wages on large-scale polder works.

Still, many communities welcomed new farmland if it boosted the local economy. Families moved onto these reclaimed plots, forming new hamlets behind the newly raised dikes. Over time, these expansions slightly alleviated population pressures in older villages. The synergy of advanced maritime commerce, improved engineering, and communal water boards thus shaped a distinctive Dutch-Frisian approach to land stewardship. By the late 17th century, a patchwork of older terpen and new polders, combined with layered dike systems, formed Frisia's evolving landscape.

6.3 Adaptive Farming Methods

As farmland expanded and markets grew, **Frisian agriculture** adopted more specialized methods. Livestock breeding gained sophistication—selecting robust cattle that yielded higher milk production or thrived in damp conditions. Butter and cheese production became central to many farms, feeding the Republic's urban consumers. Some areas planted rye, oats, or barley, rotating fields to maintain soil fertility. Peat extraction continued, though at a slower pace in certain districts to avoid land subsidence that risked flooding.

This agrarian intensification required capital investment: better plows, barns, and drainage channels. Wealthier farmers could afford these, enhancing yields and further consolidating land. Meanwhile, smaller farmers or tenant laborers faced stiffer competition, sometimes losing out or taking wage work on bigger estates. Such class tensions occasionally surfaced in local assemblies, where the well-to-do favored more ambitious reclamation or taxation policies that burdened poorer folk. However, the broad prosperity of the Dutch Golden Age generally improved living conditions—at least for those who avoided severe misfortunes from war or storm.

---

7. Political Evolutions Toward the End of the Century

7.1 Stadtholder Disputes and the Frisian Perspective

Within the Republic, the **House of Orange-Nassau** provided stadtholders who combined military leadership and political influence. Yet, from time to time, "Orangist" supporters clashed with "Republican" (or "States") factions, particularly in the mid-17th century after the death of stadtholder Frederick Henry (1647) and later the death of William II (1650). These power struggles shaped every province, including Frisia. Some Frisian regents favored strong stadtholder leadership for defense and unity; others wanted to curtail the Orange family's power, ensuring provincial autonomy. The shifting alliances produced political tensions, occasionally intense, but rarely descending into the factional violence of earlier centuries.

By 1650, Frisia, along with other provinces, entered the **First Stadtholderless Period** (1650–1672), when the office of stadtholder was vacant in several key provinces, though in Frisia itself, distinct arrangements sometimes kept a local branch of the Nassau family in place as stadtholder. These complexities underscore how local tradition still mattered: while Holland could go without a stadtholder, Frisian elites sometimes insisted on having one from a related Nassau line, preserving continuity with older forms of leadership. This interplay of local preference and broader republican structures exemplified Frisia's nuanced stance within the union.

7.2 Wars with England and France

The mid to late 17th century saw the **Anglo-Dutch Wars** (1652–1674) and the Franco-Dutch War (1672–1678) among other conflicts. Though major naval engagements occurred closer to the southern North Sea, Frisian shipping inevitably felt the impact. English blockades or privateers could target Frisian vessels, while any land invasions from the east threatened the province's border with the Holy Roman Empire. The "Disaster Year" of 1672, when French armies overran large parts of the Dutch Republic, sowed panic in many provinces. Frisia largely escaped direct occupation, but it mobilized militias and fortifications to repel potential encroachment.

During these crises, the storied figure **William III of Orange** (stadtholder from 1672) rose to unify the Republic's defense. Many Frisian leaders rallied behind him, seeing strong central leadership as necessary for survival. William III's eventual ascension to the English throne (in 1688, as co-monarch with Mary II) allied the Republic with England, altering the geopolitical landscape. Yet local friction in Frisia persisted whenever the stadtholder's centralizing ambitions clashed with the States of Friesland's desire to safeguard provincial privileges. By century's end, while the Republic's external wars shaped broad policy, internal autonomy debates never fully vanished.

7.3 Late-Century Social Trends

As the 17th century drew to a close, **demographic growth** in Dutch cities slowed, partly from the toll of wars and changes in trade routes. In Frisia, the population stabilized. Some towns saw moderate expansions or new building sprees financed by whaling or commerce profits. Religious lines hardened—Calvinist orthodoxy was well entrenched, though fractious theological disputes (Arminian vs. Contra-Remonstrant) occasionally cropped up, echoing earlier controversies. Catholic and Mennonite communities remained low-profile, accepted as part of the local fabric.

Culturally, **printing** gained momentum: local presses produced more pamphlets, sermons, and almanacs in Dutch or Frisian. A few amateur poets or chroniclers glorified Frisian historical legends, building on the older notion of "Frisian freedom" to craft a romantic narrative within the Dutch context. This budding sense of cultural pride foreshadowed the 18th- and 19th-century revival of Frisian language interests. Meanwhile, everyday life for most rural inhabitants continued to revolve around the rhythms of farm work, water management, and periodic trade fairs.

---

8. Conclusion of Chapter Seventeen

The **17th century** stands as a formative era for Frisia under the overarching structure of the Dutch Republic. While overshadowed by Holland's commercial might, Frisia made its mark via **maritime activity**—fishing, whaling, coastal shipping—and a robust local economy tied to agriculture and careful water management. Social transformations unfolded as old chieftain lineages integrated into the new provincial and republican governance systems, while Calvinist orthodoxy molded religious life. Minorities—Catholics, Lutherans, Mennonites—coexisted discreetly within a framework of practical tolerance.

Though war and naval conflict occasionally disrupted trade, Frisia generally enjoyed more stability than in previous centuries of factional violence or Spanish occupation. The province's integration into the Dutch polity was never total assimilation; local assemblies and water boards preserved time-honored traditions of communal decision-making. By century's end, a distinct yet more thoroughly "Dutch" Frisia had emerged, with new opportunities and challenges on the horizon. **Chapter Eighteen** will address the **18th century**, where evolving European power dynamics, Enlightenment ideas, and internal reforms tested Frisia's capacity to adapt in an age of state centralization and shifting global currents.

CHAPTER 18: THE EIGHTEENTH CENTURY

1. Introduction: Frisia and the Waning Dutch Golden Age

As the **18th century** dawned, the Dutch Republic was still a major European power, though signs of decline compared to its 17th-century zenith were becoming apparent. Competition from emerging maritime nations—like Britain and France—eroded Dutch trade dominance. Military burdens and economic changes tested the Republic's decentralized structure. In Frisia, these broader shifts manifested in trade slowdowns, political stasis, and an ongoing tension between local assemblies and stadtholder authority. Meanwhile, new intellectual currents, often labeled "Enlightenment" ideas, began to circulate among elites, prompting calls for administrative reforms.

This chapter explores the **18th century** in Frisia, examining how the province navigated shifting European geopolitics, war fatigue, and economic challenges. We will see attempts at **reforms**, some spurred by Enlightenment ideals of rational governance, others by pragmatic necessity—like improving dike maintenance amid storms. Socially, the century witnessed incremental changes in class relations, religious tolerance, and the role of the Frisian language. By the century's end, preludes to the Batavian Revolution (in the 1790s) would foreshadow a more dramatic restructuring, but the seeds of modern transformations were already planted in these earlier decades.

2. European Context: Great Power Rivalries and Dutch Decline

2.1 The War of the Spanish Succession and Subsequent Conflicts

In the early 18th century, the **War of the Spanish Succession (1701–1714)** engulfed much of Europe. The Dutch Republic allied with Britain and Austria against France and Spain to prevent the Bourbon dynasty from controlling Spain and its empire. Though the Republic emerged on the winning side, the prolonged war drained finances and confirmed that the Netherlands was no longer the unchallenged maritime titan it had been a century before. For Frisia, higher taxes to fund the Republic's armies weighed heavily on farmers and merchants alike.

Later conflicts, such as the **War of the Austrian Succession (1740–1748)** and the **Seven Years' War (1756–1763)**, had more limited direct impact on Dutch soil but still disrupted trade routes and required military preparedness. Each conflict chipped away at the Republic's treasury, weakening the once-flourishing economy. Meanwhile, Britain emerged as a formidable naval rival, overshadowing Dutch shipping in global markets. These shifting power dynamics cast a long shadow over Frisian commerce, as shipping volumes declined and profit margins shrank relative to the previous century.

2.2 Stagnation in the Dutch Economy

Though pockets of prosperity persisted, the **Dutch Golden Age** momentum was largely spent by the 18th century. Bankruptcies rose among smaller merchant houses, and the once-dominant East India and West India Companies struggled with corruption, mismanagement, and stiffer competition. For Frisia, the ramifications included fewer maritime ventures, a dip in Arctic whaling profitability, and a narrower range of export markets for local butter, cheese, and agricultural goods. Some Frisian ports saw reduced ship traffic, prompting local councils to debate investing in harbor improvements or pivoting to alternative economic strategies.

This overarching stagnation also fueled discontent. A growing chorus of critics in the Republic argued that the decentralized system—where provincial States, stadholders, and regent families in each city vied for power—had become complacent and self-serving. In Frisia, elites sometimes quarreled over how best to revive commerce or rationalize governance, but the impetus for deep reform met resistance from entrenched interests who preferred the status quo. Over time, these tensions set the stage for more radical changes near the century's end.

2.3 Continuing Anglo-Dutch Rivalries

While the 17th century had seen three major Anglo-Dutch Wars, rivalries with Britain persisted in the 18th century, albeit in different forms. Britain's ascendant colonial empire eroded Dutch shares in global trade. Diplomatic alliances shifted—sometimes the Republic and Britain joined forces against France, other times they were at odds. Frisian merchants, reliant on stable shipping lanes, found themselves whipsawed by these changing relationships. Moreover, Britain's superior navy overshadowed the Dutch fleet, reducing the impetus for large-scale Dutch maritime expansion. In short, the 18th century's geopolitical environment undermined the confident maritime posture that had once characterized the Netherlands, with ripple effects for Frisia's ports and seafaring population.

---

3. Provincial Politics and Administration in 18th-Century Frisia

3.1 The Stadtholderate and Orangist Influence

Frisia continued to have a **stadtholder**, typically from the House of Orange-Nassau, though the exact arrangement evolved. After the "Second Stadtholderless Period" (1702–1747) in some provinces, the entire Republic reinstated the position, culminating in **William IV** and later **William V**. In Frisia, support for the Orange family often ran strong among rural communities who saw the stadtholder as a unifying figure, especially in times of war. However, wealthy regent families in towns sometimes viewed the stadtholder's centralizing ambitions with suspicion, preferring local autonomy and the power of the States of Friesland to remain paramount.

This tension manifested in **provincial disputes** over taxation, militia organization, or appointments to judicial and civic offices. The stadtholder, seeking broader authority, might push for uniform policies across the Republic, while the States of Friesland guarded the older principle of provincial sovereignty. On the ground, these disagreements rarely erupted into open conflict but contributed to a sense of drift: no sweeping reforms took hold, even as commerce weakened and dissatisfaction simmered in certain strata of society.

3.2 Regent Oligarchies and Calls for Reform

Alongside the stadtholder's presence, power in Frisian towns lay with **regent families**—a small circle of burghers who held seats in city councils and controlled key magistracies. They often perpetuated their influence through tight-knit marriage alliances, effectively creating an oligarchy. Middle-class artisans and smaller merchants resented this concentration of power, noting that council seats were rarely opened to newcomers. In rural areas, parallel dynamics existed where a handful of gentry or wealthy farmers dominated local assemblies, overshadowing smaller landholders and tenant laborers.

By the mid-18th century, murmurs of discontent rose. Influenced by Enlightenment thought circulating from France, England, and the Dutch intellectual circles, some voices demanded more **transparency**, less nepotism, and fairer representation in local governance. These proto-"patriot" sentiments anticipated the more forceful Patriot Movement of the 1780s, but in the earlier decades they manifested as mild pamphlet campaigns or quiet lobbying within the States of Friesland. Nonetheless, friction mounted as younger educated elites—some trained in law at Franeker University or in Holland—questioned the complacency of established regent families.

3.3 The Role of Water Boards and Communal Structures

Even as regent oligarchies controlled much of civic and provincial administration, **water boards** remained relatively democratic in structure, requiring broad participation from landowners to manage dikes and drainage. Each polder or district elected "hoofdingelanden" (head landowners) or officials, balanced by oversight from the States of Friesland for major waterworks. This system, deeply rooted in Frisian tradition, functioned with surprising efficiency well into the 18th century, preserving a measure of communal spirit.

Conflicts sometimes arose if wealthy investors tried to monopolize reclaimed land or if water boards demanded heavy labor or taxes for dike upgrades. Yet, on the whole, water management retained an aura of communal necessity that transcended political faction. In an era where many aspects of governance were criticized as corrupt or elitist, water boards stood out as practical institutions anchored in the collective fight against flooding. Their continuing success provided a stabilizing factor in Frisian society.

---

4. Economic Realities: Agriculture, Trade, and Industry

4.1 Agricultural Patterns and Estate Consolidation

Throughout the 18th century, **agriculture** remained the backbone of Frisia's economy. Dairy farming, in particular, sustained many rural communities. Improved cattle breeding techniques, plus better management of meadows, boosted output of butter and cheese. Market demand from Holland's cities and abroad still existed, though competition increased as other regions modernized. Large estate owners—some noble, some wealthy burghers—consolidated farmland, employing tenant farmers under lease contracts. These estates shaped a quasi-feudal dynamic in rural areas, though formal feudalism had long been abolished.

Smaller landholders managed to persist, but they found it challenging to expand in the face of estate growth. Some local assemblies occasionally tried to limit large-scale land grabs or pressured estate owners to uphold fair rental terms. However, the rising costs of war taxes and the lure of stable incomes from renting out farmland meant that estate consolidation continued at a moderate pace. Social tensions simmered but did not explode, as the stability of the Dutch Republic (compared to war-torn states in central Europe) still offered relative security for farmers at all levels.

4.2 Declining Maritime Vigour

Compared to the 17th century, **Frisian maritime pursuits** saw a slow decline in the 18th century. Whaling in Arctic seas became less profitable due to reduced whale stocks near traditional hunting grounds and stiff competition from other nations. Cod and herring fisheries persisted but faced narrower margins. Coastal trade remained important—carrying local produce to Dutch or German ports—but no major expansions materialized. Shipyards in Frisian towns built small to medium vessels, yet they struggled to compete with the advanced yards of Amsterdam or Rotterdam.

At the same time, the **Dutch East India Company (VOC)** still operated but was in slow decline, plagued by corruption and external rivalry. Few Frisian investors held large shares in the VOC or WIC by this period, diminishing the chances for local shipping to piggyback on colonial trade. Some younger Frisian men sought maritime careers in Holland's bigger ports or joined foreign navies, draining local maritime talent. Harbors like Harlingen managed to stay active, though overshadowed by the massive trade flows of the Randstad. This partial stagnation left many Frisians reliant on stable agricultural exports rather than the high-risk, high-reward maritime commerce of earlier days.

4.3 Modest Industrial Ventures

The Dutch Republic's early industrialization in the 18th century was modest by later standards. Frisia saw **small-scale industries**—brickworks, ropewalks, salt-refining works, and breweries—catering to local or regional markets. Some farmland owners diversified into peat extraction for sale as fuel, though depletion concerns rose. In towns, guild-regulated crafts continued, though the traditional guild system, increasingly viewed as restrictive, faced criticism from reform-minded intellectuals. Indeed, Enlightenment thinkers pointed out that guild monopolies hindered innovation and prevented new entrepreneurs from entering trades.

Despite such criticisms, no radical overhaul of guilds occurred in Frisia during this century. Economically, the emphasis remained on proven, steady activities rather than bold industrial leaps. The pragmatic worldview of local elites, combined with a stable but conservative political structure, prevented large-scale shifts in manufacturing. Overall, 18th-century Frisia's economy was stable but unremarkable—profiting from agriculture, modest shipping, and localized crafts, yet lagging behind the dynamic mercantile expansions of earlier times or of other European regions heading toward industrial revolutions.

5. Social and Cultural Dimensions

5.1 Social Stratification and the Poor

By the mid-18th century, **class distinctions** in Frisia had become fairly rigid. A small elite of old noble families and wealthy burghers held provincial or municipal offices, controlling policy through networks of patronage. The middle stratum comprised farmers of moderate holdings, guild craftsmen, and shopkeepers in towns. Below them lay a substantial group of tenant farmers, day laborers, and the urban poor. Traditional charity extended by church deacons or guild funds provided limited relief, but it was inconsistent. Critics of the regent oligarchies argued that poverty alleviation was neglected or overshadowed by the self-interest of the ruling class.

Rural poverty sometimes led landless laborers to migrate to towns, seeking wages in minor industries or service jobs. Others joined seasonal labor migrations, traveling to harvest fields in Germany or shipping out for short-term maritime work. While not typically leading to mass unrest, these conditions laid the foundation for potential grievances that later Patriot reformers and revolutionary movements would exploit at the century's end.

5.2 Religion and Enlightenment Thought

The **Reformed Church** maintained its established position, often entwined with local governance. Ministers preached from pulpits about moral living, discipline, and loyalty to the Dutch Republic. Catholic enclaves and other Protestant minorities continued under a regime of cautious tolerance, with no major flare-ups akin to the earlier Reformation conflicts. Yet, by the 18th century, a new wave of religious introspection emerged, partly influenced by **Pietism** from Germany or the broader Enlightenment's rational critiques of dogma.

Some Frisian elites, educated at Franeker University or abroad, embraced **Enlightenment ideals**—valuing reason, empirical observation, and the notion that government should serve the public welfare. A few among the regent class read Montesquieu, Voltaire, or Dutch Enlightenment thinkers like the radical Coccejans. While none advocated overthrowing the Reformed Church, they pressed for a more inclusive society, reduced guild privileges, and modernized legal frameworks. Meanwhile, devout Calvinists worried that "enlightened" attitudes undercut religious orthodoxy. This quiet tension between progressive Enlightenment influences and conservative Reformed orthodoxy typified many Frisian intellectual circles.

5.3 Language and Cultural Expressions

The **Frisian language**, though increasingly overshadowed by Dutch in official usage, remained vibrant in rural communities. Village folk and farmers conversed in local Frisian dialects, passing down oral traditions, proverbs, and songs. A handful of minor authors produced poems or moral tracts in Frisian, sometimes blending in Dutch forms. Yet for upwardly mobile families or city dwellers, Dutch was the key to accessing provincial administration, merchant networks, and higher education. As a result, Frisian retained strong emotional resonance but lacked formal institutional support outside a few cultural societies that sporadically championed its heritage.

Folk customs endured, including seasonal communal gatherings for harvest celebrations or dike-building milestones. Music and dance events survived, albeit toned down by Calvinist modesty. In towns, the better-off classes indulged in refined "salon" culture, hosting musical recitals or intellectual discussions. The lively synergy that had once existed between Catholic feast days and popular festivals no longer shaped public culture, so celebrations took more secular or familial forms. Overall, 18th-century Frisia blended older communal traditions with the subdued etiquette of a changing, partially aristocratic, Reformed society.

---

6. Water Management and Environmental Episodes

6.1 Storm Floods and Dike Reinforcements

Continuing the centuries-old pattern, **major storms** periodically tested Frisian dikes. Notable floods in the early 18th century (such as those in 1717, the "Christmas Flood," which heavily affected the North Sea coast) devastated farmland, drowned livestock, and caused fatalities. Water boards sprang into action, soliciting emergency funds from the States of Friesland, wealthy estate owners, and occasionally from philanthropic city burghers. Repairs included broadening crest heights, reinforcing dike slopes with clay and wicker frameworks, and constructing additional sluices to manage storm surges.

Each flood also provoked debate over cost-sharing. Farmers far from the breach resented tax hikes for repairs in another district, pointing out local boards usually financed local dikes. In response, the States sometimes mandated broader cost distribution, arguing that catastrophic floods anywhere threatened market stability for all. The net result was incremental improvements in dike engineering, a testament to the region's centuries-old water management ethos. Despite these efforts, the unpredictable North Sea ensured that vigilance never waned, forging communal solidarity even in a socially stratified society.

6.2 Land Reclamation Projects

Various 18th-century land reclamation initiatives advanced, especially where shallow coastal waters or peat bogs offered prospects for new farmland. Joint-stock "compagnieën" formed among landowners or regents, pooling resources to build ring dikes, install drainage pumps, and systematically drain large polders. Technology improved—wooden windmills were refined for more efficient water lifting, while iron components occasionally appeared. Although these reclamations sometimes met ecological challenges (subsidence, brackish soil), many succeeded in creating fertile fields, which were then leased out at profitable rates.

Local laborers benefited from wages in dike building, but large-scale reclamations typically reinforced the concentration of land in the hands of well-capitalized investors. Tensions surfaced if tenant farmers felt rent was too high or if environmental side effects impacted neighboring farmland. Still, the fundamental impetus—to expand arable land, feed a stable population, and generate revenues—kept reclamation popular. By century's end, swaths of the Frisian coastline looked different from prior centuries, sporting geometrically arranged polders behind robust dikes.

6.3 Canals and Transport Upgrades

The 18th century also saw moderate expansion of **canal networks** to facilitate transport within Frisia and to major trade hubs. Though overshadowed by Holland's dense canal systems, Frisia recognized the economic benefit of linking farmland more efficiently to towns. The States of Friesland approved budgets for dredging silted waterways or adding locks that allowed vessels to navigate height differences. These canal improvements offered safer, faster routes for shipping cheese, butter, and other farm goods, bypassing certain shallow or hazardous coastal routes.

City councils also recognized that robust internal transport aided local guilds and shops, ensuring a steady flow of raw materials and customers. Meanwhile, canal tolls provided a revenue stream for both local boards and the provincial treasury. Despite these positives, the scale of canal-building in Frisia remained modest; the region's lower population density and lesser commercial volume limited grand canal projects. Nevertheless, incremental improvements in inland navigation gradually lowered transport costs, keeping Frisian agriculture competitive in the Dutch market.

---

7. Steps Toward Reform: Enlightened Regents and Patriot Ideas

7.1 Intellectual Clubs and Societies

Influenced by the **Enlightenment** blossoming in Europe, some Frisian elites formed "**Societies of Learning**" or "**Reading Clubs**." They debated philosophical works of Locke, Montesquieu, or Dutch reformist thinkers. These gatherings often took place in private homes or university circles, overshadowed by the Reformed Church's wariness toward radical doctrine but tolerated as long as they remained civil. Discussions ranged from mild calls for administrative efficiency to more daring criticisms of regent nepotism or aristocratic privileges.

A few philanthropic undertakings emerged from these societies, such as improved schooling for poor children or modest attempts at agricultural innovation. While not revolutionary, these projects signaled a shift among some regents from complacent oligarchy to paternalistic improvement. They tried to cast themselves as "enlightened guardians" of the common good, albeit within the constraints of the old system. Some local pastors joined these societies, balancing theological orthodoxy with a desire to foster moral and intellectual uplift in rural parishes.

7.2 Internal Critiques of Oligarchy

Critics of the **oligarchic regent system** grew louder as the 18th century progressed. Middle-class guild members or smaller merchants complained that city councils were closed circles. Younger noble families, locked out of the top tier of offices, voiced frustration at the nepotistic selection of burgomasters and magistrates. Pamphlets circulated accusing the regent families of "hereditary corruption." In some Frisian towns, small protests or petitions demanded freer elections or rotation in office.

Yet the regent class, allied with powerful stadtholder or princely interests, typically suppressed or ignored these calls. They argued that stability required "experienced families" in governance. This standoff mirrored developments in other Dutch provinces, culminating in the broader **Patriot Movement** of the 1780s, which advocated for more democratic city councils and a reduction in stadtholder power. In Frisia, the seeds of that movement were planted in the 1760s and 1770s by local pamphleteers who admired Enlightenment critiques of absolute monarchy and oligarchy, seeking a reformed republic guided by reason and genuine civic participation.

7.3 Religious Tolerance as a Reform Topic

In tandem with political reform discourses, some Enlightenment-influenced regents or intellectuals advocated for **expanded religious tolerance**. They argued that official favoritism of the Reformed Church hindered social harmony and that Catholics, Lutherans, or Mennonites should enjoy fuller civic rights. Traditional Reformed clergy opposed such liberalization, warning it might erode moral order and provoke divine displeasure. The authorities mostly maintained the status quo: non-Reformed faiths remained tolerated privately but barred from significant public offices.

Nevertheless, the mere presence of these debates foreshadowed an era of potential transformation. A handful of towns eased restrictions on Catholic chapel construction or allowed Lutherans to hold processions with minimal fuss. These steps, while modest, chipped at confessional barriers. As political tensions mounted in the latter half of the century, some Patriot thinkers would connect religious pluralism to broader ideals of citizen equality, forging an ideological link that would shape events at the century's close.

8. Late 18th-Century Upheaval and Transition

8.1 Economic and Political Pressures Converge

By the 1780s, the **Dutch Republic** faced mounting economic stagnation, burdens of repeated wars, and internal dissatisfaction with the stadtholderate. The Patriot Movement, calling for civic militias and more democratic municipal government, gained momentum in provinces like Holland and Utrecht. In Frisia, echoes of Patriot grievances surfaced in pamphlets criticizing high taxes, nepotism, and stadtholder interference. Patriot groups formed local "Free Corps" militias, training in public squares under Enlightenment-influenced slogans. They demanded municipal reforms and an end to regent oligarchy.

Stadtholder **William V** resisted these movements, supported by conservative regents and many rural folk who feared unrest. Tensions escalated, culminating in sporadic clashes between Patriot Free Corps and Orangist militias. In Frisia, these incidents were less dramatic than in Holland, but towns like Leeuwarden saw Patriot demonstrations calling for new elections to city councils. The looming threat of Prussian intervention to restore the stadtholder loomed over the entire Republic, fueling anxieties that any local revolution might be crushed by foreign arms.

8.2 Prussian Intervention and Orangist Restoration

In 1787, **Prussia** invaded the Dutch Republic to support William V after Patriot forces insulted his wife, Wilhelmina of Prussia. Patriot strongholds collapsed rapidly under the superior Prussian army. In Frisia, Patriot councils disbanded or fled, while Orangists regained firm control. The provincial States reaffirmed loyalty to the stadtholder, and Patriot sympathizers were purged from local offices. This event ended the immediate wave of Patriot reforms, restoring the old oligarchic system. Many reformers went into exile, curtailing any attempt at deeper democratic or Enlightenment-inspired changes.

Still, the seeds of discontent were not extinguished. The structural issues—stagnant economy, regent power, and limited representation—remained. Those seeds would germinate again in the 1790s, when revolutionary fervor from France would upend the entire Dutch political landscape, eventually leading to the **Batavian Republic** (1795) and subsequent transformations. Thus, as the 18th century neared its end, Frisia stood at a crossroads: forcibly returned to the old order, yet harboring an undercurrent of reformist aspirations that would soon resurface.

8.3 Conclusion: The Stage Set for Revolutionary Change

By **1790**, the Dutch Republic, including Frisia, was locked in a conservative "restoration," stifling Patriot calls for openness and democracy. The region's economy trudged along, overshadowed by British and French competition. Social tensions over class inequality, regent privileges, and confessional restrictions lingered. Culturally, Enlightenment ideas circulated among a small educated elite, while the majority maintained older communal or Reformed traditions.

As the new decade dawned, **France** itself was in revolution (1789–1799). The shockwaves would soon spread across Europe, culminating in French armies that invaded the Netherlands in 1795. That moment would end the stadtholderate, herald the Batavian Republic, and drastically reorder the provinces. Frisia, for centuries shaped by local assemblies and water boards, would be thrust into a more centralized regime with modernizing impulses. Chapter Nineteen will address how **the 19th century** brought nationalism, language revival, and further struggles over Frisian identity—though still before the modern era. For now, we close the 18th century with Frisia perched on the brink of revolutionary upheaval, its old structures battered by external pressures and internal calls for reform.

CHAPTER 19: THE NINETEENTH CENTURY

1. Introduction: Frisia on the Eve of Modern Transformations

By the start of the **19th century**, Frisia was poised on the threshold of great change. The tumultuous close to the 18th century had seen the **Patriot Movement** suppressed and the old Dutch Republic nominally restored. However, winds of revolution blowing from France soon reshaped the entire political landscape of the Netherlands, including Frisia. Over the next decades, Napoleonic rule, the subsequent formation of the Kingdom of the Netherlands, and Europe-wide movements of nationalism, liberal reform, and linguistic revival all left their mark on Frisian society.

This chapter explores how these 19th-century upheavals molded Frisia's politics, economy, and cultural identity. We will examine Frisia's experiences under French occupation, the initial decades of the new Dutch kingdom, and the mid- to late-century developments that gave rise to **nationalist sentiments** and **Frisian language revival**. By century's end, many Frisians saw themselves as both Dutch citizens and members of a distinct Frisian community with its own historical traditions and linguistic heritage. This dual sense of belonging illustrates the complex interplay of local and national identities during a transformative era.

2. The Napoleonic Era and Its Aftermath

2.1 French Invasion and the Batavian Republic

In 1795, **French revolutionary armies** swept into the Netherlands, toppling the stadtholder regime of William V. Patriot exiles returned in their wake, establishing the **Batavian Republic (1795–1806)** with strong French backing. Frisia, like other provinces, found its governance structures overhauled. The old provincial States were temporarily dissolved or reorganized into new administrative departments, sometimes discarding centuries of tradition in a push for uniform, centralized rule. In these early years, local patriots celebrated the chance to implement the reforms once stifled in the 1780s, such as broader civic participation and the dismantling of regent oligarchies.

However, actual autonomy was severely limited. The Batavian Republic remained under French influence, forced to adopt revolutionary policies and provide resources for French military ventures. For ordinary Frisians, the shift brought heavier taxes, mandatory army conscriptions, and ideological rhetoric from Paris that many rural folk found alien. Nonetheless, some positive changes occurred: local men of modest standing gained access to newly formed municipal councils, and medieval constraints on guilds or religious minorities loosened under general principles of "Liberté, Égalité, Fraternité." These measures improved legal equality on paper, though in practice they were unevenly enforced.

2.2 Kingdom of Holland and Napoleonic Annexation

The **Batavian Republic** evolved into the **Kingdom of Holland (1806–1810)** under Napoleon's brother, Louis Bonaparte, who tried to balance French dictates with Dutch sensibilities. In Frisia, this meant further administrative reorganization: the province was divided into districts run by prefects reporting to the central monarchy in The Hague. Louis displayed a surprising sympathy for Dutch traditions, attempting to learn the Dutch language and mitigate French burdens, but the overall direction of policies still emanated from Napoleon's grand strategy. Heavy conscription demands for the Grande Armée extended to Frisian young men, a source of widespread resentment.

By 1810, Napoleon deemed the Kingdom of Holland insufficiently compliant and **annexed** it into the French Empire outright. All Dutch provinces, including Frisia, became part of France. French law codes (the Napoleonic Code) were introduced, uniform taxation enforced, and French was briefly mandated in official documents—though local administrators often translated them into Dutch for daily use. In rural areas, this direct French domination felt like a foreign occupation. People complained bitterly about conscription, confiscated resources, and the erosion of historical rights, even if some modernization measures (e.g., standardized weights and measures) had long-term benefits. The end of Napoleonic rule thus became a fervent hope for many Frisians.

2.3 The Fall of Napoleon and the United Kingdom of the Netherlands

Napoleon's defeat in 1813–1814 brought **liberation** from French control. A wave of patriotic euphoria followed as Dutch leaders, including the returning Prince of Orange (William I), proclaimed a new monarchy. In 1815, the **United Kingdom of the Netherlands** was formed, joining the northern provinces with the southern regions (modern-day Belgium). Frisia found itself once again a province in a restored Dutch state, though now under a constitutional monarchy instead of the old republic. Many local elites who had survived the French era jostled for office in the new monarchy, while peasants and townsfolk welcomed an end to confiscatory French taxes.

The monarchy of **King William I** sought rapid modernization—building roads, canals, and encouraging industrial growth. In Frisia, this entailed improvement of certain water routes (e.g., the canal from Leeuwarden to the Zuiderzee) and attempts to unify local administration. However, when southern provinces revolted in 1830, forming Belgium, the new kingdom's energies were diverted, leaving some of William's centralizing projects incomplete. Nevertheless, the monarchy's push for standardization—whether in law, taxes, or language—would be felt acutely in Frisia, where centuries-old traditions had endured. Tensions emerged between local pride and the king's drive for a uniform Dutch identity, foreshadowing later cultural debates.

---

3. Political Life in 19th-Century Frisia

3.1 The Constitutional Framework and Provincial Representation

In the early 19th century, King William I introduced a constitutional monarchy with a States General in The Hague. Each province, including Frisia, sent representatives to a national parliament. However, suffrage was extremely restricted, limited to wealthy property owners or notables. Frisia's local governance was reorganized into a **Provincial Council**, presided over by the King's appointed Commissioner (Commissaris van de Koning), effectively the old stadtholder role in a new guise. The council handled provincial matters—road building, waterworks funding, local taxation—under the watchful eye of national authorities.

For a region proud of its communal traditions, this top-down structure provoked mixed reactions. On one hand, the monarchy provided stability and investment in infrastructure. On the other, the old sense of Frisian distinctiveness felt stifled by centralized oversight. Over time, moderate liberals in Frisia joined liberal movements across the Netherlands, pushing for broader parliamentary powers and expanded suffrage. Landmark changes, such as the **constitutional reforms of 1848** under King William II and the liberal statesman Johan Rudolph Thorbecke, partially democratized the system—still limited, but enough to allow a fraction of the Frisian bourgeoisie and progressive rural gentry a voice. These reforms laid the groundwork for more robust local representation and a new wave of civic engagement.

3.2 Aristocratic and Regent Families in Transition

Even after the Napoleonic interlude, certain **aristocratic families** or old regent lines retained local influence in Frisia. They adapted to monarchy by obtaining titles recognized by King William I or forging alliances with the new court. Some families leveraged their wealth and genealogical prestige to secure seats in the upper chambers of the Dutch parliament. Others served as mayors or commissioners in the province, perpetuating centuries-old traditions of local leadership. Meanwhile, younger scions often studied in universities—Franeker had closed in 1811 under Napoleon, but Leiden or Groningen remained accessible—absorbing liberal or conservative ideas and returning to shape policy.

Yet the **19th-century liberal ascendancy** began chipping away at old oligarchic privileges. The law codes derived from Napoleonic reforms established uniform civil rights, diminishing feudal remnants that might have lingered in rural property relations. Over decades, an emerging professional class of lawyers, teachers, and civil servants challenged the aristocratic monopoly on administration, citing the post-1848 constitutions. Some noble families updated their image, presenting themselves as enlightened patrons of local charities or agricultural societies, thereby maintaining a measure of respect amid shifting times. Overall, while not vanishing, the aristocracy had to adapt to a society that prized merit, education, and broader civic participation.

3.3 Influence of Liberal and Conservative Currents

By the mid-19th century, Dutch politics polarized around liberal vs. conservative lines, with **Thorbecke's liberal reforms** championing parliamentary sovereignty and civil freedoms, while conservatives defended royal prerogative and social hierarchy. In Frisia, these ideological currents intertwined with local concerns—water management, farmland prosperity, religious sensibilities. Liberals in towns championed freer trade policies to spur commerce, an expanded electorate to reflect changing demographics, and rational administration that might help modernize rural areas. Conservatives, often rural notables or devout Reformed leaders, cautioned against rapid change that could destabilize community life.

Thus, the **Provincial Council** became a stage for debates over property taxes, road-building priorities, or school funding. Each municipality's delegates aligned with broader national factions but also reacted to local pressures—like how best to finance a new canal or whether new factory owners should receive tax breaks. By century's end, liberal ideas gradually gained ground, though always tempered by a strain of Frisian caution about altering communal traditions too fast. This measured approach led to incremental improvements in infrastructure and governance, while safeguarding older forms of local participation, especially in water boards.

4. Economic and Social Developments in the 19th Century

4.1 Agricultural Modernization and Rural Class Relations

Agriculture remained Frisia's dominant economic sector, but the **19th century** witnessed important shifts. Innovations in crop rotation, selective breeding of cows, and the introduction of new machinery—e.g., mechanized threshers—boosted productivity. The government promoted model farms and agricultural societies to spread best practices. Land reclamation slowed somewhat compared to earlier centuries, but the existing polders were refined with better drainage ditches and pumping stations (including the spread of steam-driven pumps after mid-century).

The **social fabric** of rural areas also evolved. Large estate owners or well-off farmers (the "boerenaad") enjoyed rising incomes, reinvesting in larger barns, improved dairies, and schools for their children. Smaller tenant farmers often struggled with rent burdens, though the monarchy's policies sometimes tried to shield them from exploitative leases. Agricultural laborers, at the bottom rung, still faced precarious livelihoods. Yet the relative stability of the Dutch state, combined with philanthropic or religious charity, prevented mass rural unrest. Gradual population growth led to labor surpluses, prompting some Frisians to migrate westward in search of factory jobs, especially after the Netherlands belatedly entered the industrial age.

4.2 Maritime Continuities and Decline

While no longer a major player in global shipping, **Frisian maritime activity** persisted in coastal trade, fishing, and barge transport. Harlingen, among other ports, served as a regional hub, shipping out butter, cheese, and livestock to Amsterdam or exporting to Germany. Steam navigation gradually replaced sail on some routes in the latter half of the century, though the transition was slow in smaller Frisian harbors. The advent of iron-hulled ships in major Dutch shipyards overshadowed the modest wooden shipbuilding traditions in Frisia, leading to the closure or consolidation of smaller local yards.

Fishing communities adapted to new techniques, including using improved nets, but faced pressure from British or German competition in the North Sea. Some Frisian sailors found careers in the Netherlands' oceanic merchant marine, leaving local coasters behind. Others pivoted to the Wadden Sea tourist trade later in the century, especially as small-scale tourism to island beaches began among wealthier Dutch families. Overall, maritime livelihoods did not vanish but continued on a smaller scale, overshadowed by the dynamic changes in Amsterdam, Rotterdam, and overseas colonial routes.

4.3 Early Industrial Enterprises

The **Netherlands' late industrialization** had uneven effects on Frisia. A few sugar refineries or brick factories emerged near major water routes, employing tens or hundreds of workers with steam-powered machinery. Leeuwarden saw minor expansions in textiles or metal workshops. But large-scale industrial complexes, akin to those in the Ruhr or parts of Belgium, never took deep root in Frisia due to limited local coal resources and smaller markets.

Nonetheless, these small factories impacted social relations. They drew rural laborers seeking higher wages than agriculture could offer, forming a nascent industrial workforce. Some entrepreneurs—often younger members of regent families—invested in these ventures, merging old capital with new technologies. Worker demands for better conditions or wages occasionally surfaced, though labor unions were in their infancy. Consequently, while Frisia never became an industrial hotspot, these small steps signaled an incipient modernization that dovetailed with broader 19th-century European trends.

5. Nationalism, Language Revival, and Cultural Expressions

5.1 The Rise of Dutch Nationalism

Following Belgian independence in 1830, the **Kingdom of the Netherlands** became more cohesive, forging a Dutch national identity that celebrated shared history, Protestant monarchy (later with broader religious inclusion), and a standardized Dutch language. For many in Frisia, this **Dutch nationalism** resonated somewhat. Military service in the national army introduced Frisians to recruits from other provinces, fostering a sense of common Dutch citizenship. Newspapers circulated national debates, forging links between Frisian towns and the political center in The Hague or Amsterdam.

At the same time, local pride in Frisian history—its centuries of communal self-governance, storied "Frisian freedom," and distinctive maritime traditions—remained robust. A tension emerged between assimilation into a Dutch national narrative and preserving local distinctiveness. Younger elites educated in Dutch universities sometimes championed a romanticized vision of Frisia's medieval grandeur, spurred by the nationalist mood sweeping Europe. This "regional patriotism" paralleled the broader wave of European regional revivals that sought to reconcile local folklore with a new sense of belonging to a nation-state.

5.2 Frisian Language Movements

Out of this interplay came the **Frisian language revival**. Though used daily in many villages, Frisian lacked official status—schools and government used Dutch almost exclusively. Around the mid-19th century, intellectuals formed societies like the **"Selskip foar Frysk Tael en Skriftekennisse"** (Society for the Frisian Language and

Literature) to promote standardized spelling, publish Frisian poetry, and gather folk tales. Inspired by German Romanticism and Dutch cultural nationalism, these enthusiasts argued that Frisian was not just a rural dialect but a sister language to Dutch, deserving literary cultivation.

They organized local events celebrating Frisian songs, proverbs, and historical epics. Periodicals published in Frisian gained modest readership among teachers, pastors, and landowners. Some scholars wrote linguistic treatises, comparing Frisian with Old English or German. The monarchy's government did not strongly oppose these activities as long as they did not incite political separatism. Indeed, many Frisian language advocates considered themselves loyal Dutch citizens who merely cherished their local heritage.

5.3 Literary, Historical, and Artistic Expressions

As part of the cultural flowering, a small **Frisian literary scene** emerged. Authors produced poems and short prose celebrating pastoral landscapes, seafaring traditions, or medieval legends of Redbad and other heroes. Though overshadowed by mainstream Dutch literature, these works reflected a pride that transcended mere nostalgia, presenting Frisia as a living culture within the kingdom. Local historians dug into archives, writing romantic accounts of medieval freedoms or the uniqueness of Frisian law, thus feeding the sense of an enduring identity.

Music societies, or "**Fryske Koor**" groups, performed choral pieces with Frisian lyrics, blending folksong idioms with the romantic style popular in mid-19th-century Europe. Painters from the region occasionally depicted watery landscapes, terp farmhouses, or old-fashioned rural gatherings. While not widely recognized outside provincial circles, these artistic endeavors enriched a local cultural domain. By century's end, a modest network of cultural associations fostered a new generation of Frisian teachers, pastors, and minor civil servants who valued bilingualism—Dutch for official affairs, Frisian for communal ties.

6. Religious Evolution in the 19th Century

6.1 Protestant Pluralism and Catholic Emancipation

The **Reformed Church** remained the largest denomination, but the 19th century brought greater religious pluralism. **Lutherans**, **Mennonites**, and other Protestant groups maintained their presence, while **Catholics** slowly reemerged from clandestine chapels to build more visible churches following legislation that relaxed restrictions under the new monarchy. In 1853, the reestablishment of the Catholic episcopal hierarchy in the Netherlands (the so-called "Catholic emancipation") stirred controversy in strongly Protestant regions, including parts of Frisia. Yet the monarchy's policy of tolerance endured, ensuring no return to the old confessional strife.

Within the Reformed community itself, theological rifts emerged. The mid-19th century saw a **Secession** (Afscheiding) movement in 1834, as orthodox congregants broke from the mainstream Reformed Church to form more conservative denominations. In Frisia, several parishes joined the Secession, reflecting discontent with perceived liberal theology in official circles. These breakaway churches built small chapels, emphasizing strict Calvinist doctrine. The monarchy allowed such groups to exist, though local frictions occurred when entire villages split between the established Dutch Reformed Church and the newly formed congregations. Gradually, a broader mosaic of Protestant denominations shaped local religious life, with each forging its own schools and social networks.

6.2 Social Welfare and Clerical Initiatives

A notable aspect of 19th-century religious life was the **clergy's involvement** in social welfare. Reformed pastors, Catholic priests, and Mennonite preachers all confronted poverty and illiteracy in rural parishes. Many championed improved schooling, founding or supporting denominational schools that imparted both basic literacy and religious instruction. They also organized benevolent societies to distribute alms or sponsor "diaconal farms," where unemployed laborers could work. This philanthropic approach aimed to forestall radical social unrest. In an era before robust state welfare, these faith-based initiatives were crucial, albeit sometimes paternalistic.

Additionally, clergy in certain parishes took up the Frisian language revival cause. They integrated Frisian hymns or translations of Scripture into worship—an attempt to connect with local hearts more intimately. Not all church authorities approved; some saw these local languages as a hindrance to national unity. Yet the impetus for a more personal faith expression paralleled the general romantic interest in local culture. By century's end, a patchwork of religious communities—some leaning progressive, others conservative—existed, each with its own blend of spiritual mission, social action, and local engagement.

6.3 Pilgrimages and New Devotions

While large-scale medieval-style pilgrimages had faded long before, smaller local pilgrimages or processions persisted in Catholic enclaves. Some chapels dedicated to Mary or local saints quietly attracted devotees. Meanwhile, Reformed communities developed new forms of devotion—regular catechism classes, youth gatherings, Bible study societies—that mirrored the broader 19th-century evangelical or revivalist ethos across Protestant Europe. In Mennonite circles, lay-led study groups stressed ethical living and community solidarity, forging close-knit relationships that bridged rural-urban divides.

These religious expressions coexisted with an expanding sense of Dutch identity, shaped by monarchical ceremonies, national holidays (like the king's birthday), and official commemorations of the 1813 liberation from France. For devout Frisians, reconciling local piety, denominational loyalty, and membership in the kingdom formed part of daily life. The potent mix of religious devotion and emerging national pride set the cultural mood, overshadowed by neither radical secularism nor uniform theocracy but living in a tension that allowed incremental adaptation over time.

---

7. End-of-Century Social Shifts and Emerging Movements

7.1 Industrial Catch-Up and Worker Organizations

In the latter decades of the 19th century, the Netherlands slowly embraced **industrialization** at a larger scale, spurred by new technologies like steam power, railroad expansion, and (eventually) electricity. Frisia, though still predominantly agrarian, felt these changes through improved **rail connections** to other provinces.

Railways built in the 1860s–1880s linked Leeuwarden, Harlingen, and other towns to the national network, reducing travel times and broadening markets for local produce.

As factories sprang up in larger Dutch cities, some Frisians migrated for industrial jobs. Within Frisia, small-scale expansions in food processing or brickmaking employed more workers. **Worker organizations** or early labor unions formed. Often spurred by socialist or Christian-social thought from beyond the province, these groups advocated for safer working conditions and fair wages. While the monarchy and liberal politicians tried to contain radical ideologies, moderate labor associations gradually took root. By 1900, seeds of a broader working-class consciousness were planted, though agricultural laborers and small-town artisans remained the majority.

7.2 Cultural Nationalism and Frisian Intellectual Societies

Building on mid-century efforts, **Frisian cultural nationalism** gained momentum after 1875. Societies focusing on Frisian language, history, and folklore expanded membership. These groups published journals featuring newly composed poems, essays on Old Frisian law, or genealogical research tying modern families to medieval lineages. Schoolteachers integrated Frisian readings into extracurricular programs, though Dutch remained the mandated medium of instruction.

A fervent romanticization of the region's medieval "freedoms" or ancient ties to Anglo-Saxon heritage shaped local intellectual circles. They organized public lectures or historical festivals in period costumes, celebrating Redbad or other legendary figures. While the monarchy tacitly tolerated these displays of regional patriotism, some conservative officials worried that too much emphasis on distinct identity might undermine national unity. In reality, most Frisian nationalists saw themselves as loyal Dutchmen preserving a cultural inheritance. This synergy of local pride within a broader Dutch monarchy encapsulated late 19th-century Frisian identity: fervent but rarely separatist.

7.3 Toward Broader Political Reforms

The last decades of the 19th century saw a push in the Netherlands for **wider suffrage**, culminating in partial expansions of the electorate in 1887 and, more substantially, after 1894. In Frisia, liberal and progressive spokesmen pressed for reforms to enfranchise more farmers, artisans, and small merchants. Conservative landowners or religious parties, on the other hand, feared political upheaval or socialist infiltration. The friction played out in local elections, with heated debates over whether universal male suffrage would lead to radical changes or hamper local traditions.

Nevertheless, unstoppable trends favored democratization. As newspapers proliferated in towns and villages, public awareness of national issues soared. Voters demanded accountability in spending, especially for water infrastructure or poor relief. Clergy and teachers, better educated, championed social improvements like compulsory primary education (legislated in 1900). While these developments nudged the region toward modern governance, the turn of the century still found Frisia a mostly agrarian society with lingering hierarchies. Full democratization, women's suffrage, and advanced welfare policies lay in the future, beyond our historical scope.

8. Conclusion of Chapter Nineteen

Throughout the **19th century**, Frisia navigated a series of seismic transformations, from the **Napoleonic era** that toppled old republican structures, through the establishment of the Kingdom of the Netherlands, to the mid- and late-century waves of **nationalism, industrial stirrings, and cultural revival**. Political life transitioned from aristocratic or regent dominance to a constitutional monarchy with limited but expanding participation. Economically, the province maintained its agricultural backbone and modest maritime pursuits, gradually integrating new technologies like railways and small factories. Socially, a more complex class structure emerged, shaped by land consolidation, partial industrialization, and liberal political currents.

In parallel, a **Frisian cultural resurgence** gained traction, fueled by romantic nationalism and the desire to preserve local language, folklore, and historical memory. By century's end, Frisia's identity was multi-layered—anchored in the Dutch state yet proud of its linguistic and historical distinctiveness. This dual alignment set the stage for the final decades of pre-modern history, in which debates over political reform, social welfare, and cultural autonomy continued to unfold. **Chapter Twenty** will offer **reflections on this historical legacy** through the late 19th century, concluding our extensive narrative of Frisian developments before the modern era fully dawned.

CHAPTER 20: REFLECTIONS ON HISTORICAL LEGACY

1. Introduction: Looking Back on Frisia's Long Trajectory

Having traced Frisia's history from prehistoric times through the 19th century, we arrive at a moment of **reflection**. By the late 19th century, Frisia existed within the modernizing **Kingdom of the Netherlands**, shaped by centuries of political evolution, maritime enterprise, communal water management, and cultural resilience. This final chapter revisits key themes—freedom, local governance, language, and economic adaptation—showing how they converged to form a distinctive Frisian identity on the cusp of the modern era.

We will summarize how major epochs contributed to Frisia's sense of self: prehistoric adaptation to coastal marshes, the Roman era's early contacts, medieval independence under shifting powers, the fractious but communal Middle Ages, the Dutch Revolt's forging of a Reformed provincial identity, and the subsequent centuries of monarchy and nascent industrial changes. Our reflections underscore the interplay of continuity and transformation. By the late 19th century, older communal traditions coexisted with national frameworks, medieval echoes merged with Enlightenment reforms, and the Frisian language thrived quietly beneath official Dutch usage. These legacies set the stage for the 20th century's even more dramatic transformations, lying beyond our historical scope here.

2. The Heritage of Communal Freedom and Water Management

2.1 Ancient Roots of Local Autonomy

From the earliest dwelling mounds (terpen) in prehistoric times, **Frisians** had adapted to a watery environment, building communal structures to manage floods. This necessity fostered traditions of cooperation, visible in the medieval water boards and assemblies. The medieval period's famed "Frisian freedom" concept—mythically traced to Charlemagne or justified by local law codes—reflected a real historical tendency toward self-governance, even if external powers (Carolingians, counts of Holland, bishops of Utrecht) contested it. Over centuries, Frisian communities clung to local customs, forging an identity that prized **independence** in decision-making.

By the late 19th century, those communal impulses still resonated. Dike boards remained emblematic of collective stewardship, bridging social strata. Even after centralized monarchic oversight was established, these boards functioned with a measure of democratic input—landowners electing representatives to manage water affairs. Thus, a lineage from ancient self-rule to modern local administration shaped Frisian civic culture. Observers from other provinces sometimes admired the communal spirit in water management, seeing it as a living vestige of medieval autonomy adapted to 19th-century conditions.

2.2 Evolving Institutions in Modern Context

No longer free from feudal obligations or outside rule, 19th-century Frisians still experienced a measure of local autonomy via municipal councils, the Provincial Council, and the water boards. In debates over canal construction, agricultural modernization, or poor relief, the imprint of communal traditions was visible. Elite families or regent oligarchies might overshadow direct popular participation, but the sense that "we manage our own dikes, we know our lands best" endured. This mindset sometimes clashed with national ministries seeking to standardize procedures, yet compromises emerged—Frisians accepted certain Dutch reforms while preserving local prerogatives in water engineering or farmland organization.

These institutions, while transformed from medieval roots, provided a continuity bridging multiple eras. They enabled the province to handle environmental threats and integrate new technologies. Hence, in the late 19th century, many Frisians saw themselves as guardians of a communal legacy that had served them well, validating local input even in an increasingly centralized kingdom. That interplay of local tradition and national law would remain a hallmark of Frisian governance well into the modern era.

---

3. Maritime and Agricultural Legacies

3.1 Declining but Persistent Maritime Culture

Though overshadowed by the 17th-century Dutch Golden Age, **Frisia's maritime identity** remained a potent cultural symbol. Fishing villages, small coastal trades, and the memory of whaling adventures or older sea battles all contributed to local folklore. Families that once prided themselves on seafaring prowess now adapted to smaller markets, operating coasters or fishing smacks. Ports like Harlingen or Lemmer carried on, though with fewer global ambitions, mainly serving national or Baltic routes.

Nineteenth-century developments—like steam-powered vessels—further changed the maritime landscape. Frisians found themselves balancing tradition and modernization: some embraced new shipping technologies, others lamented the decline of sail-based commerce or the demise of smaller shipyards. By the late 19th century, maritime pursuits were no longer the central economic driver they once were, but they retained a romantic hold on cultural memory, fueling local maritime festivals or stories that reminded communities of their ancestors' seafaring legacies.

3.2 Strengthening Agricultural Prosperity

At the same time, **agriculture** flourished overall, thanks to improved methods, stable markets, and state-building efforts that protected domestic production. Frisian dairy products—especially cheeses and butter—found strong demand in Dutch cities. The farmland expansions of previous centuries now paid dividends, as polders yielded robust harvests and supported large herds. Estates and progressive farmers experimented with selective breeding (the "Friesian" breed of cattle gained renown), advanced drainage, and the introduction of certain mechanical implements. Surplus produce sold well within the Netherlands and occasionally for export, fueling incremental rural wealth growth.

Still, this success was uneven. Tenant farmers' fortunes depended on estate owners' policies, and laborers often saw only marginal improvements in wages. Mechanization threatened some manual jobs, although changes proceeded slowly compared to industrial hotspots in other European regions. By the final decades of the 19th century, signs of a more commercial farming sector, with specialized dairy processing and cooperative ventures, emerged. These cooperatives, sometimes formed by local notables, would become a key feature of early 20th-century agrarian organization, though that lies beyond our scope.

4. Cultural Renaissance: Language, Literature, and Identity

4.1 Nineteenth-Century Frisian Intellectual Circles

As described in the previous chapter, the **Frisian language revival** gained momentum mid-century, led by societies and journals that strove to standardize orthography and encourage literary production. By the late 19th century, several local historians, poets, and schoolteachers had achieved moderate recognition for their Frisian-language works. They formed **intellectual circles** in towns like Leeuwarden, meeting in reading rooms or coffeehouses to discuss folk traditions, translations of foreign literature, and comparisons of Frisian with other Germanic tongues. Some corresponded with philologists in Germany or Britain, feeding into academic interest in Old Frisian legal texts.

This cultural renaissance overlapped with Dutch nationalism, which championed a unified language for administration. Tensions occasionally flared when well-intentioned patriots from other provinces dismissed Frisian as a mere dialect. In response, Frisian intellectuals insisted on its distinct linguistic status, citing historical documents and linguistic research. They forged a dual identity: loyal members of the Dutch Kingdom, yet committed to preserving an ancient cultural heritage. This stance was rarely separatist; rather, it sought official respect and a place for Frisian in local schools or printed media.

4.2 Folklore Collection and Romantic Historiography

A wave of **folklore collection** accompanied the language revival. Field researchers—often amateurs, sometimes local pastors or teachers—collected proverbs, riddles, fairy tales, and legends from rural villagers. The materials were published in Frisian journals or used in newly composed "romantic" histories that emphasized the heroic qualities of earlier Frisian eras. This phenomenon paralleled European Romantic nationalism, wherein scholars collected vernacular culture to validate modern claims of a unique peoplehood. In Frisia, legendary tales about Redbad or later medieval freedom fighters found fresh retellings that blended fact and embellishment, shaping popular conceptions of the region's past.

Similarly, certain historians wrote multi-volume works on Frisian law codes, the Vetkoper-Schieringer feud, or the region's medieval alliances. While modern academic rigor was still emerging, these efforts stoked local pride and set a foundation for 20th-century academic studies. By 1900, an entire generation had grown up with easy access to "Frysk" cultural material, fostering a sense that Frisian heritage was not relegated to the past but actively cherished. This literary and historiographical activity would, in later times, bolster movements for greater Frisian linguistic rights and cultural autonomy.

4.3 Music, Arts, and Civic Festivals

Late 19th-century **musical societies** proliferated, some focusing on choral singing in Frisian or the performance of regionally inspired compositions. Towns organized singing competitions or "Kulturfeste" reminiscent of Germanic traditions, highlighting local band music. The monarchy's presence was acknowledged through national celebrations—King's Day festivities or commemorations of the monarchy's founding—yet local flavor abounded in the form of Frisian costumes, dances, or comedic sketches referencing rural life. Meanwhile, a handful of painters depicted Wadden Sea landscapes, terp villages, or bucolic farmland scenes in a romantic style, though few achieved fame outside regional circles.

These cultural expressions reinforced a pride in place that matched the broader European vogue for rediscovering local identities within nation-states. Middle-class families, employing these events as forms of social cohesion, found a constructive outlet for civic energy. Religious leaders—Protestant or Catholic—often endorsed them as morally uplifting alternatives to the perceived moral hazards of urban amusements. In effect, the synergy of local language societies, music clubs, and ephemeral festivals wove a cultural tapestry that balanced Dutch national frameworks with the uniqueness of Frisian communal life.

5. Social Tensions and Incremental Reforms

5.1 Poverty, Worker Rights, and Emerging Social Movements

Despite a generally stable 19th-century society, pockets of poverty persisted in both rural and urban contexts. Agricultural surpluses did not always trickle down to laborers. In towns, small factories or craft workshops might pay subsistence wages. Influenced by liberal and socialist ideas drifting in from Germany or other Dutch cities, some workers formed **friendly societies** or early unions. They demanded basic protections—an end to child labor, a shortened workday, or minimal wages. Landowners and factory owners often resisted, fearing disruptions to profitability.

Though these proto-labor movements remained modest in scale, they signaled a new social consciousness. Certain pastors or teachers supported these calls for moral reasons, aligning them with Christian duty or Enlightenment notions of human dignity. By the 1880s, a few cooperative experiments sprang up, such as dairy cooperatives where farmers and laborers shared profits. These mild forms of collectivism seldom threatened property rights but did suggest the potential for broader social reforms in the 20th century. The monarchy tolerated such developments, so long as they did not advocate outright revolution.

5.2 Gradual Electoral and Administrative Reforms

After liberal constitutional amendments in 1848, the Netherlands inched toward **expanding suffrage** for men, culminating in reforms in the 1880s–1890s. Frisia's electorate thus grew beyond the narrow circle of aristocrats and wealthy burghers. Middle-class merchants, teachers, and farmers gained the vote, injecting fresh perspectives into local councils. The friction between conservative landholders and liberal or radical voices became more pronounced. Issues like local tax distribution, school funding, or how to integrate Frisian language into public events stirred new debates in the Provincial Council.

Additionally, national laws mandated more consistent record-keeping, birth registrations, and other bureaucratic measures, building on the Napoleonic Code's legacy. The monarchy's government took a bigger role in overseeing poor relief or schooling, though municipalities retained day-to-day control. In practice, local councils still had wide latitude, especially in water management or cultural affairs, preserving a sense of continuity with older communal traditions. By century's end, the tension between old paternalistic structures and newly empowered citizens created an evolving local democracy, incomplete but forward-moving in spirit.

5.3 Religious and Moral Concerns

Religious convictions continued shaping moral codes. **Sunday observance** was strictly enforced in many Reformed communities. Taverns faced restrictions on hours or behaviors. Schools typically included daily prayers or Scripture lessons, though a new generation of liberal educators championed secular approaches. Temperance societies emerged, paralleling movements across Europe that criticized alcohol abuse as detrimental to family life and economic efficiency. Though not as widespread as in some countries, these moral reform groups found moderate traction in Frisian towns.

The monarchy's neutrality among denominations, combined with the legacy of Dutch tolerance, allowed confessional pluralism to remain stable. Catholics built or renovated churches openly, Lutherans and Mennonites maintained their congregations, and no single church commanded the entire public sphere. Still, the Reformed Church's historical privileges lingered—prominent representation in official ceremonies, association with monarchy, and strong rural support. Only in the early 20th century would deeper secularization and the "pillarization" of Dutch society expand alternative denominational pillars more robustly.

---

6. Late 19th-Century Outlook: Continuity and Change

6.1 Comparisons with Other Provinces

Relative to Holland's rapid urban growth or the southern provinces' industrial pockets, **Frisia** remained a predominantly **rural** region with a modestly sized capital, Leeuwarden, and a scattering of smaller towns. Observers from the Randstad sometimes viewed Frisia as conservative or behind the times. Yet Frisians prized their countryside, dairying success, and communal ethos, seeing them as virtues that protected against the social upheavals plaguing rapidly industrializing areas. The tensions between modernization and tradition that roiled other Dutch provinces were present but tempered by Frisia's slower pace of economic change.

Indeed, outsiders occasionally romanticized Frisia's farmland and folk culture, linking it to a simpler, "authentic" Dutch rural identity. Writers or painters from the Randstad might visit to capture the big skies, flat fields, and old farmsteads. Some claimed Frisia preserved a moral clarity lost in more cosmopolitan cities. This external fascination melded with local pride, reinforcing an image of Frisia as both distinct and integral to the kingdom—a farmland realm steeped in archaic freedoms yet loyal to the House of Orange.

6.2 Anticipating 20th-Century Developments

Many transformations that would define the 20th century—universal suffrage, advanced industrialization, mass education, or expanded social welfare—had only begun to glimmer in the late 19th century. Still, the seeds were sown: literacy rates were climbing, new technologies (railroads, steam shipping) were threading Frisia closer to national networks, and liberal reforms were slowly broadening democratic participation. Additionally, the Frisian cultural revival was setting the stage for future language activism, eventually leading to 20th-century demands for bilingual education or official recognition of Frisian as a co-official language.

Meanwhile, growing interest in agricultural cooperatives and the scientific study of farmland signaled that the region was preparing for more sophisticated approaches to dairying and land management. These cooperatives would become crucial in the 20th century's agricultural modernization drive, binding small farmers together to compete in larger markets. Summarily, while the late 19th century did not see revolutionary leaps, it laid a foundation for the expansions and reforms that followed, bridging the old communal ethos with incremental modernization.

6.3 The Legacy of Historical Trajectories

In reflecting on Frisia's entire historical arc up to this point, one sees repeated motifs:

- **Environmental adaptation**: From prehistoric mounds to 19th-century dike boards, controlling water remained a unifying factor.
- **Communal freedom**: Medieval concepts of local self-rule found renewed expression in water boards and partial autonomy within the Dutch monarchy.
- **Cultural resilience**: Despite external powers—Carolingians, Burgundians, Habsburgs, Napoleonic France, the Dutch kingdom—Frisians continued cherishing their language, folklore, and sense of a distinct heritage.
- **Integration into broader states**: By the 19th century, Frisia firmly belonged to the Netherlands, balancing national frameworks with local identity.

These legacies coalesced in the late 19th century as a province both changed by modernization and anchored in tradition, neither "frozen in medieval custom" nor "fully assimilated into a uniform Dutch mold." The result was a region comfortable with belonging to the Dutch nation while maintaining pride in its Frisian historical journey.

---

7. Conclusion

7.1 From Prehistory to the Late 19th Century

Over the course of these twenty chapters, we have traced **Frisia's evolution** across millennia:

1. **Prehistoric Settlement**: People adapting to coastal marshes, building terpen for flood safety.
2. **Roman Contacts and Early Identities**: Tribes labeled Frisii by outside observers, forging local distinctiveness.
3. **Medieval Independence and Fragmented Power**: The "Frisian freedom," water boards, and cyclical feuds shaping communal governance.
4. **Viking Threats, Christian Missions, and Integration**: The maritime resilience tested by Viking raids, followed by acceptance of Christianity and partial submission to Carolingian/Frankish or other external controls.
5. **Rise of Vetkoper–Schieringer Factions**: Internal rivalries that ironically opened the door for Burgundian, then Habsburg, domination.

6. **Dutch Revolt and the Republic**: The forging of a Reformed provincial identity under the Dutch Republic, with maritime activity pivotal in the Golden Age.
7. **18th-Century Challenges**: Stagnation, oligarchic rule, Patriot stirrings, and suppressed reforms.
8. **Napoleonic Upheaval**: French occupation, subsequent monarchy formation, thorough reorganization of local administration.
9. **19th-Century Nationalism and Cultural Revival**: Balancing integration into the Dutch state with reawakened Frisian language pride and communal traditions.

Through each phase, the tension between local autonomy and external pressures, plus the impetus to adapt to an often-harsh coastal environment, defined Frisian history. While no single power or policy fully subdued the region's distinct ethos, each era left layers of influence, culminating in a 19th-century province that was Dutch in governance yet Frisian in spirit.

7.2 Enduring Themes: Freedom, Identity, and Adaptation

Three overarching themes stand out in this retrospective:

- **Freedom**: From medieval articulations of "Frisian freedom" to modern local governance under monarchy, the drive for communal autonomy persisted. Water boards and local assemblies symbolized a collective decision-making tradition rarely eradicated, even by powerful overlords.
- **Identity**: A sense of being Frisian—linguistically, culturally, historically—flourished despite centuries of foreign rule or national integration. The 19th-century revival of language and folklore stands as testament to the deep roots of this identity, which survived Napoleonic annexation, Dutch state-building, and modernization.
- **Adaptation**: Every epoch forced new adaptations, whether grappling with Vikings, forging alliances under Burgundian rule, adopting Reformed Protestantism, or yielding to Napoleonic codes. Each adaptation revealed resilience and a pragmatic ability to integrate fresh influences while retaining communal cohesion.

7.3 A Prelude to Further Developments

Our narrative closes in the **late 19th century**, by which time Frisia, as part of the Dutch Kingdom, had stabilized under constitutional monarchy and begun experiencing the early stirrings of industrial and social changes that would intensify in the 20th century. Looking ahead—beyond our scope—one would see expansions of democratic rights, deeper linguistic activism leading to official Frisian recognition in certain domains, and eventual transformations under the broader complexities of two world wars and European integration. Nonetheless, the seeds of those modern breakthroughs all lie in the rich, multi-layered historical tapestry we have examined.

In summarizing **Frisia's complete history** up to the late 19th century, we see a people shaped by water, forging traditions of communal governance that weathered feudal overlords, factional feuds, and external empires. By integrating maritime enterprise, farmland prosperity, and strong local culture, Frisians navigated each epoch's demands, emerging with a self-awareness that combined pride in local heritage with acceptance of wider frameworks—first medieval and feudal, then republican and monarchical, and ultimately national. This dynamic interplay between tradition and adaptation stands as the defining legacy of Frisia's story, one that persisted into the modern age, though that age lies beyond the scope of our present chronicle.

www.ingramcontent.com/pod-product-compliance
Lightning Source LLC
LaVergne TN
LVHW012038070526
838202LV00056B/5536